Race and the Decline of Class
in American Politics

Race and the Decline of Class in American Politics

Robert Huckfeldt
and
Carol Weitzel Kohfeld

University of Illinois Press
Urbana and Chicago

This book is printed on acid-free paper.

Library of Congress Cataloging-in-Publication Data

Huckfeldt, R. Robert.
    Race and the decline of class in American politics / Robert Huckfeldt and Carol
Weitzel Kohfeld.
        p.   cm.
        Bibliography: p.
        Includes index.
        ISBN 0-252-01600-9 (alk. paper)
        1. Democratic Party (U.S.) 2. Voting—United States. 3. Race discrimination—
Political aspects—United States. 4. Racism—Political aspects—United States.
5. Social classes—Political aspects—United States. 6. United States—Race relations. 7. Afro-Americans—Politics and government. 8. United States—Politics and
government—1945-   I. Kohfeld, C.W. II. Title.
JK2316.H83 1989
324'.0973—dc19   88-26109
                                                                      CIP

For Christopher, Karen,
Kurt, Peter, Rachel,
and Sharon

Contents

Preface

The thesis of this book is that the politics of race often proves to be incompatible with the politics of class in American political life. More precisely, race frequently serves as a wedge that disrupts lower-class coalitions, thereby driving out class in our political arrangements. Working-class and lower-middle-class whites are frequently unwilling to participate in a coalition that depends upon the votes of blacks in order to win elections, and thus the natural constituency of a lower-class coalition is frequently ruptured along racial lines. Our focus generally rests upon the post–World War II period in American politics, but the problematic interdependence of race and class extends back in time at least to the late nineteenth century and forward to the headlines of today.

As we complete this manuscript in the summer of 1988, the Democratic party is once again experiencing the internal contradictions posed by the logic of its own appeal. These contradictions took on heightened drama in the winter and spring of 1988 because they were embodied so vividly in the presidential candidacy of Jesse Jackson. At the same time that Democrats could rightfully congratulate themselves on a party that was able to sustain a serious candidacy by a black, most would also admit that his chances of being elected president, or even securing the Democratic nomination, were remote. Jackson's candidacy, moreover, illustrates the strains of race and class that define the political dilemma of the Democratic party.

The most vivid and lasting impression of the 1988 primaries may turn out to be the level of racial polarization that existed within the Democratic party. In spite of Jackson's efforts to construct a Rainbow Coalition, and regardless of media accounts that stressed the broadening of his appeal, he was unable to claim a basis of support within the white Democratic electorate that even remotely approached a majority. Thus, the Democratic electorate was badly fractured along racial lines, with nearly unanimous Jackson support among black Democrats and an overwhelming majority of white Democrats supporting a variety of white candidates.

Political commentators were curiously reluctant to focus upon the racial divide. They stressed the high level of white support for Jackson among whites, evidently based on an implicit assumption that he would fail to receive *any* white support. Yet, when attempts were made to explain why he did not receive a *higher* level of white support, the explanation generally avoided race. Commentators seriously argued that whites were reluctant to support Jackson primarily because of his lack of experience in foreign affairs! These convoluted efforts to avoid race in the explanation of Jackson's difficulties among whites produced some curious racial overtones. If whites judged Jackson to be lacking in foreign policy expertise, why did blacks support him? Were blacks unable to make judgments regarding foreign policy? If blacks supported Jackson *because* he is black, it is difficult to argue that race was unrelated to the reason that whites generally *failed* to support him.

Some whites did, of course, support Jackson's candidacy. A crucial question, then, both for the Democratic party and for the nation, is which whites? Jackson constructed a class based appeal that reached out to the poor and the dispossessed, and journalists spent great amounts of time interviewing unemployed white workers who supported his candidacy. But was this truly the locus of his support among whites? No, it was not, at least not according to the polling data available from the states that had primary elections. In some states Jackson realized levels of support among higher-income whites that exceeded his level of support among lower-income whites; in other states his levels of white support were roughly equivalent across income levels. He was not able to succeed, however, in putting together a coalition of blacks and lower-income whites—he was not able to attract great numbers of lower-class whites to his candidacy. This is not intended to minimize the success of the 1988 Jackson candidacy. Much more so than in the 1984 campaign, he was able to broaden his base of support beyond the black electorate, but it would be a serious error to believe that he succeeded in uniting the interests of race and class within the Democratic party.

As a result, the Democratic party was badly divided along racial lines as it approached its national convention in Atlanta. The resulting unity feast at the convention was a tribute to the political expertise of both Michael Dukakis and Jesse Jackson. The interests of neither Jackson nor Dukakis would have been well served by a racially fractured party. It remains to be seen how long such unity will be maintained, and the degree to which voters—especially white voters—will ratify the show of unity by voting Democratic.

The seemingly natural coalition for Jackson's populist appeal would have been lower-income blacks and whites. Instead, his coalition frequently centered among blacks and liberal, mostly middle-class whites. And thus political conflict structured along racial lines once again proved incompatible with political conflict structured along class lines. The 1988 presidential primary campaign was not the first time that this incompatibility afflicted the Democratic party. Indeed, the 1988 campaign served as the continuation of a long tradition in our national political life—a tradition in which race has persistently submerged class as a structural feature of American political life. This book is concerned with the tensions and contradictions that are inherent within a political party, and within a political system, where class and race serve as competing bases of political organization.

Acknowledgments

A number of friends and colleagues have sustained and supported us in this project. Early on, John Sprague told us that the problem was too big for an article, that it really required a book. We are grateful to him for his advice as well as his patience—each of us is involved in separate projects with him that have paid the price of diverted attentions. Through it all John has been a willing reader and listener, as well as an important source of encouragement, suggestions, and insight. Quite a few colleagues have responded to all or parts of the manuscript, as well as graciously responding to our musings on the subject: Ted Carmines, Dennis Judd, Jerry Wright, Lucius Barker, C. R. D. Halisi, Michael MacKuen, Courtney Brown, Bernie Grofman, Jennifer Hochschild, Paul Abramson, Bob Boynton, Mary Weiler, Tina Brickell, Leslie Leip, and the anonymous reviewers. We are also grateful for the enthusiastic support of Larry Malley, associate director of the University of Illinois Press. He has made this project more pleasant than it would otherwise have been and has helped us bring it to a rapid conclusion. All authors should be so lucky. Finally, this research was supported, in part, by National Science Foundation grants SES-8706940 and SES-8415572 to Indiana University, and by grant SES-8722726 to the University of Missouri, in St. Louis.

A number of people, including some of those just mentioned, have expressed reservations about various aspects of our argument. We expect that other readers might be troubled as well, and we certainly do not intend to offer any last word on race and politics in America. Quite the opposite, our hope is to encourage others to discuss these issues in more detail. Only through a continued, open discussion of the role that race plays in American politics can a greater political sophistication be achieved among both blacks and whites—a sophistication that will, in turn, make it more difficult for politicians to exploit the divisive issue of race within our nation's political life.

1 The Problem

Race in the south, as in the nation, has always overwhelmed class.

Carl N. Degler (1972:102)

Race continues to be the most important line of conflict in American electoral politics. In the 1984 presidential election, nine out of ten black voters supported the Democratic candidate, while only one out of every three white voters cast a Democratic vote. Levels of racial polarization were even higher in the South: only one out of four southern white voters supported the Democratic candidate, and only one out of six white Mississippi voters voted Democratic. These figures indicate a level of polarization between racial groups unequaled by any other social boundaries. At a time when the political differences separating the poor and affluent, the well educated and semiliterate, the working and middle classes sometimes seem on the verge of extinction, the politics of race has emerged as the most meaningful boundary in American politics during the last third of the twentieth century.

This is not intended to minimize or dismiss the politics of class. Beginning at least with the analysis of C. Vann Woodward (1966) it has become abundantly clear that the politics of race serves both to disguise and to disrupt the politics of class. Racial politics serves as a disguise for class politics because, above all, the unifying impetus behind the politics of race is the disadvantaged status of blacks in society. The political unity of American blacks extends beyond issues of class, status, and social disadvantage, but these issues provide the core around which black political consciousness revolves. Thus the politics of race is fundamentally anchored in the politics of class.

The politics of race disrupts class politics because, as long as the majority of blacks belong to a disadvantaged class, the social and political isolation of blacks benefits advantaged groups in American politics. It serves this end by fracturing the political vehicle of lower-class interests: party competition structured along class lines. Woodward (1966), Key (1949), and Schatt-schneider (1960) have taught us that racial conflict between partners in a lower-class coalition leads to the demise of class-based politics. Stated differently, class-based politics is uniquely vulnerable to the unraveling consequences of race—it is frequently unstable as a result of the disruptive effects of racial competition.

The politics of race has never been far below the surface in the history of the Republic: the three-fifths compromise in the Constitution, the early nineteenth-century activity of radical abolitionists, the nullification crisis, the great compromises, the carnage of the Civil War, the battle over Southern Reconstruction and Redemption, the installation of Jim Crow, the effort to dismantle the legal framework of a racially segregated society, white and black race riots in American cities, and the continuing struggle over race within the Democratic party. The irony is that the dynamics and salience of race are so frequently ignored in the treatment of contemporary American politics. It is as if we believe that the matter of race was fundamentally resolved with the passage of landmark civil rights legislation in the 1960s. While that legislation served to transform the structure of American politics, it would take a very naive civics student to believe that politics in America has become color blind.

Our thesis is simply stated: the decline of class as an organizing principle in contemporary American electoral politics is directly related to the concurrent ascent of race. In this book we discuss the rise of race and the decline of class and build an argument that ties the two together. The prominence of race in American politics is not so much the consequence of virulent racism at the level of individuals, even though such racism often exists. Rather it is the frequent result of electoral competition that is structured in terms of both race and class. In that competition, race is likely to drive out class and emerge as the most significant factor in electoral politics.

The Decline of Class and The Rise of Race

Disregard for race is especially apparent in the commonly of-fered explanations for the decline of class in American politics. The level of class politics has been declining during the postwar period in the United States, just as it has been declining in other Western democracies. This decline is illustrated for the United States in Figure 1.1, along with the concurrent rise in the politics of race. As these data show, class differences were very large in 1948, and they were relatively pronounced in 1944, 1952, 1964, and 1976. They were very nearly extinguished in 1972, however, and they have been extremely low in the past two presidential elections. The long-

Figure 1.1. Race and class in American presidential elections, 1944–84.

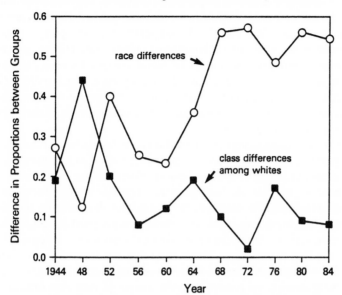

Note: The race difference is the proportion of blacks voting Democratic minus the proportion of whites voting Democratic. The class difference is the proportion of working-class whites voting Democratic minus the proportion of middle-class whites voting Democratic.

Source: National Opinion Research Center and Center for Political Studies survey data (Abramson, Aldrich, and Rohde 1986).

term trend seems clear: an electorate whose preferences are increasingly unstructured by class membership at the same time that their preferences are increasingly structured by race.

Explanations for the decline in class politics generally group the United States together with European democracies in a search for a common explanation, the most popular being some variant of the postindustrial society thesis (Lipset 1981; Inglehart 1977). According to this argument, the politics of economically and technically advanced Western nations has been transformed by economic changes emerging since World War II. Two features of these changes are especially germane to the demise of class-based politics.

First, the growth of the industrial working class has stagnated, resulting in a decline of organized labor. The working class has ceased to grow as a proportion of the work force, or even in terms of its absolute size; therefore, political coalitions are hard-pressed to construct a winning coalition with an explicit appeal to the working class (but see Przeworski and Sprague 1986). Moreover, a large portion of the decline in the American working class has been in its industrial sector, which is also its unionized sector. These are the workers who have traditionally supplied the Democratic party with the core of its support, and a class-based coalition is severely damaged by their relative diminution.

Second, in the aftermath of World War II an extraordinary overall increase has occurred in the general level of affluence for the inhabitants of advanced Western nations. This rising level of prosperity has supplanted the material-ist impetus that drove politics forward during the rise of the modern Democratic party in the United States and throughout the history of social democracy in Europe. For both the middle class and the working class, other concerns have displaced the focus upon fundamental bread-and-butter issues in the political system. Quality of life issues have replaced quantity of life issues. Concerns over minimum wage laws, workplace safety, social secu-rity, and unemployment compensation have frequently given way to a lengthy agenda of nonmaterial issue concerns: energy, the environment, pro-life versus pro-choice, and so on. Workers who own two cars, a boat, and a house in the suburbs have the freedom to become concerned over issues that are ancillary to the social welfare–labor agenda that secured this new affluence.

This postindustrialism thesis has, at first examination, an appealing fit to reality. The working class realized steady gains in its standard of living in the postwar period. The traditionally defined working class is no longer grow-ing, and labor unions in the United States are certainly on the retreat. But do these factors adequately explain the demise of class politics in the American context? At what point does the explanation come up short?

We argue that the postindustrialism explanation falls seriously short in accounting for the demise of class in the American context. In particular, abundant evidence is available to suggest that the rising tide of American prosperity has seriously receded, leaving a significant portion of the popula-tion beyond the embrace of postindustrial affluence. While the United States made impressive prosperity gains in the period immediately following World War II, more recent evidence is not so comforting. A persistent decline in American productivity growth since 1973 has caused serious concern among economists and fostered analyses of factors such as labor quality, investment in capital and innovation, and labor composition shifts between sectors as possible explanations (Baily 1986). For example, Thurow (1987) argues that lowered productivity is a result of the downgrading of jobs from manufactur-ing to the service sector. We do not have to choose between these alternative explanations to note that productivity is down, that policy analysts and responsible policy makers are seriously concerned, and that the affluence hypothesis is no longer operative. Increasing affluence has not been the recent pattern in the United States, and thus the postindustrialism thesis warrants further attention in a later chapter.

For present purposes it is only important to note that the warm glow of postindustrial affluence fails to shine not only on vast portions of the

American working class but on significant portions of the lower middle class as well. Indeed, it has left significant elements exposed to the cold draft of unemployment, underemployment, and a declining standard of living. Thus we argue that the decline of class in American politics must be seen within the context of the rising political significance of race.

Democrats Since Roosevelt: The Rise of Race

Franklin D. Roosevelt was many things to many people, but few would argue that he was a champion of the needs and interests of black Americans, except as those interests coincided with the interests of disadvantaged Americans generally. The New Deal coalition, and the legislative successes of the Roosevelt presidency, depended fundamentally upon support from the solidly Democratic congressional delegations of the southern states (Ladd and Hadley 1978). Thus, the New Deal could not afford to offend the racial sensibilities of white southerners.

This is not to say that the Roosevelt administration was indifferent to the plight of blacks. Eleanor Roosevelt, Harry Hopkins, and Frances Perkins were administration figures who made serious attempts at addressing the difficulties faced by black citizens. Indeed, all New Deal agencies were governed by a nondiscrimination clause, but the enforcement of the clause varied across programs and agencies. The political realities of decentralized local control over many New Deal programs meant that the provision was often unenforced (Holmes 1972).

Regardless of New Deal attitudes concerning civil rights, blacks did not play a crucial role in the Roosevelt coalition. Two circumstances elevated their strategic status after Roosevelt's death. First, northern liberal Democrats like Paul Douglas and Hubert Humphrey championed their cause. Second, and more important, the migration of southern blacks into northern cities, which began intensively in the 1920s and abated during the Depression, was renewed in earnest during the 1940s. Many blacks who had been disenfranchised in the South became concentrated in northern cities at the same time they obtained the vote. As a result, the political status of blacks was dramatically altered and the parameters of American politics were significantly changed.

During this period organized labor often played a critical role in introducing immigrant blacks to the Democratic party. As they moved out of the South and into northern cities, many blacks looked for jobs in the factories and industries of their new homes. Indeed, much of the impetus for the migration lay in hopes of a better economic future. Once black migrants were employed in the factories, or once their relatives and friends were employed, they became an important part of the CIO and, ultimately, organized labor in general. Thus they adopted the political preference and supported the political organization that coincided with their status as members of the urban working class.

The stage was set for the black minority's gradual acquisition of political influence within the Democratic party structure. Yet their place within organized labor and within the Democratic party was never fully secure. They were frequently resented by whites who viewed them with suspicion and hostility. Ultimately, however, an uneasy process of mutual accommodation took place, where the black minority came to be recognized by many white political leaders as a crucial political resource. This process began under Roosevelt and continued through the presidencies of Harry S Truman and Lyndon B. Johnson to the present. The process produced a solid core of support for politicians in the Hubert Humphrey tradition, and it led to a situation in which northern white liberals like Humphrey could argue that it was good practical politics to be liberal toward blacks.

Against this backdrop, it is no small irony that the two presidents in this century who have done the most for black interests, Truman and Johnson, were neither northerners nor widely acclaimed liberals. Truman desegregated the armed forces and supported the adoption of a civil rights plank at the 1948 Democratic National Convention. In the process his chances for reelection were dealt a severe blow by the convention walkout of Strom Thurmond and the Dixiecrats. The 1948 election foreshadowed the tension within the Democratic coalition, which was not resolved until 1964. In the ensuing three elections—1952, 1956, and 1960—Adlai E. Stevenson and John F. Kennedy attempted to solidify the bond between northern blacks and the Democratic party; but they also attempted to avoid offending white southern Democrats. It was not until the presidency of Lyndon Johnson that this balancing act was abandoned and the tension resolved in favor of black interests.

The Democratic Transformation:
Stevenson and Johnson

In order to understand the transformation of the Democratic party in relation to civil rights during the 1950s and 1960s, it is useful to focus upon the two figures who were perhaps most influential in shaping the party during this period: Adlai Stevenson and Lyndon Johnson. Neither man began the 1950s as a crusading national advocate for black freedoms. This is perhaps most surprising in the case of Stevenson, who has historically been identified so strongly with the liberal, intellectual elements within the Democratic party. In contrast, Johnson was a son of the South: he was a populist-progressive who came to political maturity during the New Deal and became a favorite of Franklin Roosevelt but whose progressivism did not extend to matters of race. The important point is that the late forties and early fifties did not offer political circumstances congenial to the embrace of black aspirations, even by liberal-minded politicians.

During his 1952 presidential election campaign, Stevenson made two major speeches that spoke directly to his political, if not personal, caution regarding the South and blacks. The first, on August 28, 1952, at the New York State Democratic Convention, addressed equal rights. Perhaps the most striking feature of the speech, given its theme, was the infrequent mention of blacks. Stevenson also made an extreme effort to be conciliatory to the southern wing of the party:

> In saying this [discrimination against minorities] is not a sectional problem, I do not mean to say that there is no particular problem in the South. Of course there is a problem in the South. In many respects, the problem is more serious there than elsewhere. But, just as it is chastening to realize our own failures and shortcomings in the North, so it is both just and hopeful to recognize and admit the great progress in the South. . . .
> . . . I think—indeed, I know—that there are leaders in the South who are just as anxious as we are to move ahead. But we must frankly recognize their local difficulties. We must recognize, too, that further government interference with free men, free markets, free ideas, is distasteful to many people of good will who dislike racial discrimination as much as we do. (Stevenson 1953: 26–27)

Stevenson went on to support an equal employment opportunity program embodied in a proposed congressional bill that would only involve federal coercion as a last resort. The bill would require that a federal commission undertake a nationwide education program, "to proceed by persuasion as far as possible, and in cases of complaints of violation, to proceed by very careful deliberation and full and fair hearings" (1953:28). In short, in his central speech on equal rights in 1952, Stevenson bent over backward not to offend the South.

In a speech delivered later during the campaign in Richmond, Virginia, Stevenson extolled the political genius of the South. After speaking at length of the post–Civil War suffering while the South was under the rule of a venal Republican party, Stevenson said: "Among the most valuable heritages of the Old South is its political genius, which in many respects was far ahead of its time. Even today some of the finest products of Southern governmental thought are only beginning to win the general acceptance which they have so long deserved. . . . A classic example, it seems to me, is the Constitution of the Confederacy. . ." (1953:153).

Stevenson then made an interesting appeal in his effort to reconstruct the New Deal coalition.

> One thing that I have learned is that minority tensions are always strongest under conditions of hardship. During the long years of Republican neglect and

exploitation, many Southerners — white and Negro — have suffered even hunger, the most degrading of man's adversities. All the South, in one degree or another, was afflicted with a pathetic lack of medical services, poor housing, poor schooling, and a hundred other ills flowing from the same source of poverty.

The once low economic status of the South was productive of another — and even more melancholy — phenomenon. Many of the lamentable differences between Southern whites and Negroes, ascribed by insensitive observers to race prejudice, have risen for other reasons. Here economically depressed whites and economically depressed Negroes often had to fight over already gnawed bones. (1953:154)

Once again, Stevenson made a heroic effort to avoid offending the southern wing of the party. In a testimony to his political courage, he addressed the issue of race before his Richmond audience, but he did so in terms of biracially shared class concerns. Clearly, the hope of the candidate was to maintain a party coalition attractive to both blacks and white southerners by virtue of its color-blind devotion to the disadvantaged. This strategy, of course, leaves out any consideration of federally enforced guidelines upon the treatment of minorities *per se*.

The Democrats evidently felt they had learned a lesson in 1948, when Harry Truman pursued the issue of race more vigorously than had any other president since Lincoln. As a result of his effort, a large segment of the party's southern wing bolted, and the incumbent president nearly lost the election. Democrats were not accustomed to losing presidential elections, and they took actions designed to maintain their electoral hegemony.

Democratic party ambivalence on civil rights did not end with Adlai Stevenson. John Kennedy also attempted to balance his appeal to both blacks and the white South. Much has been made of the phone call from Kennedy to Coretta Scott King during the latter stages of the 1960 campaign. Martin Luther King, Jr., was being held in a southern jail, and Kennedy offered his support. Dramatic as it was, that act must be seen in the larger context of the times. With some success Kennedy assured the white southern leadership that he would not be disruptive on civil rights. The first years of his administration created significant frustration among the black leadership, who had expected much more progress on civil rights. Indeed, the civil rights measure sent by the president to the Congress in 1963 was generally acknowledged to be too weak. As a result of this fact, and because of increased racial tensions nationwide, the Kennedy administration sent up a more aggressive bill, but even this piece of legislation was weaker than the bill ultimately reported out by the House Judiciary Committee (Congressional Quarterly Service 1967: 4). In short, President Kennedy did not move as fast as the Congress in pursuing civil rights legislation, but vigorous presidential leadership on civil rights was forthcoming, in the unlikely person of Lyndon Johnson.

In 1948 Johnson ran for election to the U.S. Senate. During his years in the House he had been firmly identified as a New Deal Southerner and an emulator of Roosevelt. According to Harry McPherson, a Johnson assistant: "Lyndon loved to say that when he came up here [to Washington] in the thirties as a congressional secretary and later as a congressman, that all his friends were Bolsheviks. And I don't know that that was an overstatement" (Miller 1980: 71). But things had changed by 1948, and Johnson aimed for a statewide victory in a conservative state. In the speech announcing his candidacy, he said: "The civil rights program is a farce and a sham—an effort to set up a police state in the guise of liberty. I am opposed to that program. I have voted AGAINST the so-called poll tax repeal bill; the poll tax should be repealed by those states which enacted them. I have voted AGAINST the so-called antilynching bill; the state can, and DOES, enforce the law against murder. I have voted AGAINST the FEPC [Fair Employment Practices Commission]; if a man can tell you whom you must hire, he can tell you whom you can't hire" (Miller 1980: 118).

With his racially conservative credentials thus in tact, Johnson proceeded to a career in the United States Senate and a subsequent transformation on matters of race. During his career as Senate majority leader, Johnson served a broker role between liberal Democrats, Republicans, and southern Democrats in passing important civil rights legislation. Liberals might criticize him for failing to adopt suitably aggressive legislation, and southern Democrats might consider him a traitor to the cause, but in the end Johnson was central to the passage of civil rights legislation in the 1950s. Clearly he was already aiming toward the presidency and realized he would have to break free of his narrow, southern, parochial position toward civil rights. Just as he needed to focus upon a wider Texas constituency in 1948, so in the 1950s he needed to focus upon a wider national constituency, and this fact helps to explain the final transformation of Lyndon Johnson.

It is important to remember that Vietnam was not the only crisis awaiting Lyndon Johnson when he became president; he also faced a fundamental threat to the viability of the Democratic coalition that arose because the tenuous balance between black and southern white elements in the Democratic party had become impossible to maintain. As a result, both groups were showing decreased levels of support for the Democratic party.

Johnson addressed the crisis directly and unambiguously. First, he reconceived poverty in America in a manner that allowed him to construct a domestic program whose primary beneficiaries were urban blacks. The advent of poverty as a policy issue in the 1960s was not framed solely or even predominantly in terms of black poverty. *The Other America* (Harrington 1962), for example, focused upon white rural poverty as much as it did upon black urban poverty, and early poverty proposals put forward by the Kennedy administration focused upon rural Appalachian whites. Johnson took advantage of the opportunity to turn this issue into a vehicle that would cement the bond between blacks and the Democratic party (Donovan 1973: chapter 1; Judd 1984: chapter 10).

A second strategy adopted by Johnson was more significant in its long-term implications: the first southern president since the Civil War became a champion of civil rights when he embraced the Civil Rights Act of 1964. This action was especially important in a politically strategic sense because Barry Goldwater, the Republican presidential nominee, voted against the Act, thereby redefining the position of the Republican party with respect to civil rights. Until this time the Republicans had a relatively respectable record on matters of race and civil rights. Everett Dirksen, the Republican Senate minority leader, was himself a full participant in the adoption of civil rights legislation in the 1950s. This is not to say that the Republican party was a champion of black interests—Republican failures in this regard are abundant and well documented (Peltason 1971: 46–55). In the context of the times, however, and in the context of a solid white Democratic South, the Republican party was at least the equal of the Democratic party in its support for black rights.

The events of 1964 marked a clear divergence from the Republican party's previous record on civil rights. Now the party of Lincoln had chosen as its leader a man who was firmly on record in opposition to any extension of federal efforts to secure equal rights for blacks. Perhaps Ladd (1982:8) is correct regarding the short-term folly of this position, calling it an act of "supreme stupidity." Yet in the long-term it firmly established the Republican party in an advantageous position when the white electorate became less enthusiastic in its pursuit of equal rights for blacks.

This final transformation of Johnson was complete in 1964. In that year, as a new president, he vigorously pursued a far-reaching civil rights bill. And as if to make up for all the compromises he made in passing civil rights legislation in the 1950s, he refused to make any concessions in 1964. The result was significant new legislation that ultimately led to a restructuring of American politics, and to a transformation of both the Democratic and Republican parties.

Carmines, Renten, and Stimson (1984) show how crucial the events of 1964 were in restructuring the issue of race in American electoral politics. Before 1964 the electorate saw little difference between the two parties in terms of race. After 1964, however, the electorate developed a clear perception of the Democratic party as more favorable to black interests. Just as important, this perception was closely related to reality. Not only did the 1964 presidential candidates take divergent positions on civil rights, but House Democrats also became more liberal on civil rights issues than House Republicans. Senate Democrats had become almost as liberal as Senate Republicans after the 1958 elections, but they become even more liberal in

1964. In short, the events of 1964 served to restructure permanently the relationship between the parties on issues of race (Davison 1985).

Johnson's support of the 1964 Civil Rights Act was important for a second reason as well: it permanently widened the breach between the national Democratic party and white southern Democrats. Indeed, five Deep South states cast their electoral votes for Goldwater, and these five states had the lowest voter registration rates among blacks. By contrast, unprecedented levels of turnout and Democratic voting by blacks in another five southern states were either decisive or very close to being decisive in providing Johnson with those state's electoral votes (Congressional Quarterly Service 1967: 72). Without black support Johnson would have probably lost the election in several of these states and come very close to losing in the others.

It is in this context that the 1965 Voting Rights Act must be seen. How could the Democratic party recover its position in the South? The answer was dramatic but simple: send federal marshals into southern counties to register blacks who were being kept off the rolls. The newly enfranchised blacks would, in turn, offset Democratic losses among whites and maintain Democratic hegemony in the South. The boldness of this action cannot be ignored. In 1963 Matthews and Prothro argued that black participation was a problem that defied easy solution: ". . . reformers should not expect miracles in their efforts, through political and legal means, to increase the size and effectiveness of the Negro vote in the South. The Negro registration rate is low, in rather large part, because of the social and economic characteristics of southerners—both Negro and white" (1963: 43).

Yet a miracle is exactly what occurred. There is hardly any other way to describe the resulting increase in black voter registration (see Table 1.1), or its profound consequences for the political and social structure of the South. The peaceful demonstrators who suffered under the fire hoses and police dogs of Birmingham police chief Bull Connor in 1963 would probably view it as a miracle that Birmingham now has a black mayor. Governmental coercion and force accomplished what the collective hearts and minds of white southerners could not: incorporate black men and women into the political structure of the South.

This bold action was possible not only because Johnson's own narrowly defined self-interest had changed, but more importantly because the interests of the Democratic party had changed as well. The strong Democratic ties to blacks, forged during the New Deal, had been seriously weakened by the events of the 1950s. Both Kennedy and Stevenson had tread softly on matters of race while a Republican administration and Republican congressional leadership were cooperating in the passage of civil rights legislation. As a result, the party of Lincoln took on renewed attraction for many blacks. Roughly 40 percent of voting blacks chose Eisenhower in 1956, and about one-third voted for Nixon in 1960. Figure 1.2 gives the mean level of

Table 1.1. Proportion of blacks registered to vote in southern states, 1960–70

	1960	1964	1970
Alabama[a]	.137	.230	.640
Arkansas	.377	.544	.716
Florida	.390	.637	.670
Georgia[a]	NA	.440	.636
Louisiana[a]	.309	.320	.618
Mississippi[a]	.061	.067	.675
North Carolina	.382	.468	.548
South Carolina[a]	NA	.388	.573
Tennessee	.641[b]	.694	.765
Texas	.337[c]	.577	.847
Virginia	.230	.457	.607

[a]These states' electoral votes went to Barry Goldwater in 1964.
[b]Based upon data from 63 counties.
[c]Based upon data from 213 counties.
Source: Congressional Quarterly Service (1967, 1970).

Figure 1.2. Mean proportion of the vote for Democratic presidential candidates in the black precincts of twenty-four southern cities, 1952–72.

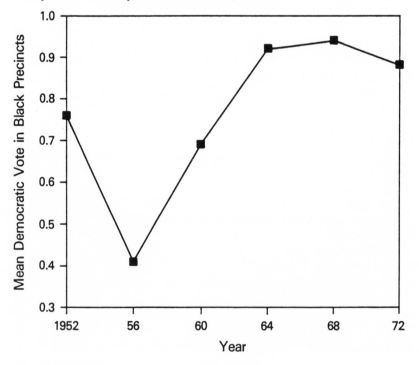

Source: Southern cities data, Bartley and Graham (1978).

Democratic voting in presidential elections for black precincts in twenty-four southern cities from 1952 through 1972. These data show quite vividly that the events of the 1950s led to attenuated ties between black voters and the Democratic party—ties that were revitalized by the events of 1964.

At the same time that black voters were losing faith in the Democrats, blacks as a group were taking on heightened strategic importance in national politics. The black migration to the North, which began after World War I, was renewed after the depression years. Black movement into northern cities during the postwar period, coupled with white emigration to the suburbs, produced significant black voting blocks in many northern areas. In 1950 blacks accounted for 5.3 percent of the population in St. Louis, 14.1 percent in Chicago, 16.4 percent in Detroit, and 16.3 percent in Cleveland. By 1970 blacks accounted for 41.3 percent of the population in St. Louis, 34.4 percent in Chicago, 44.0 percent in Detroit, and 39.0 percent in Cleveland (Judd 1984: 240). This trend has continued: a number of major cities, such as Detroit, now have black majorities, and several more cities, such as St. Louis, are on the verge of having black majorities.

In order to win a presidential election, the Democratic party ordinarily needs to win in Ohio and Illiniois. In order to win in Ohio and Illinois Democrats must win decisively in Chicago and Cleveland. In order to win decisively in Chicago and Cleveland they need to secure solid and unwavering support from the black population. The same calculation occurs for other states as well, and thus the strategic importance of the black population to the Democratic party is assured. In short, the concentration of black Americans in northern cities and their increased voice in national politics made it increasingly difficult for the Democratic party to continue straddling the race issue. A new set of structural conditions produced a new strategic reality, forcing the leadership of the party to address race and the continuing contradiction between black and southern white interests within the Democratic coalition.

None of this suggests that Johnson's dramatic appeals for equal rights for white children and black children were less than sincere. There is more than enough opportunity for criticizing a political figure such as Johnson, but even a book as critical as Caro's (1983) does not successfully call into question Johnson's fundamental political commitment to the disadvantaged. His roots as a populist ran deep: his father's political career, his sponsorship as a young congressman by Franklin Roosevelt, his early commitment to the New Deal. Rather, in the 1960s we saw an ambitious politician whose basic inclination coincided with his self-interest. According to Joseph Rauh, a long-time Democratic party activist, civil rights lawyer, and supporter of Hubert Humphrey: "Often you can honestly and truly and sincerely believe in something which is to your political best interest. Johnson really believed in this bill [the 1964 Civil Rights Act], and it's just impossible to say whether

Figure 1.3. Democratic mobilization among nonvoters in presidential elections, 1948–80, by race.

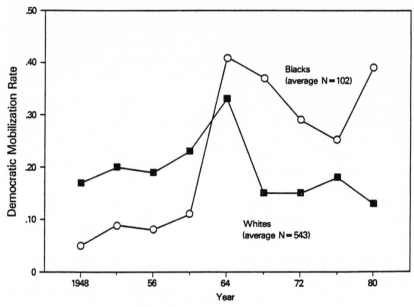

Source: National Election Studies, 1948–80.

he believed in it solely because of politics or whether he believed in it for the country. I want to give him the benefit there, that he believed in it for both reasons" (Miller 1980: 369).

The Democratic Party After 1964

The newly enfranchised blacks could not by themselves maintain Democratic dominance in the South because they comprised a minority in all the southern states. Thus, the strategy of assuring Democratic ascendancy in the South by efforts to enforce the political rights of blacks was inherently dangerous for the party. Indeed, the danger extended beyond the South to the rest of the nation as well. The crucial assumption was that the Democratic party could maintain some minimum level of white support, but even Lyndon Johnson underestimated the potential of race for unraveling the Democratic coalition and for undermining the support of whites. This fact was underscored on the night of the 1984 election, when Jesse Jackson told an interviewer on network television that Walter Mondale was losing the southern states due to his failure to capture even 30 percent of the white vote. According to Jackson, blacks did their part, but white Democrats let the party down.

The benefits and costs of the Democratic party's mid-sixties strategy are illustrated in Figure 1.3: 1964 clearly marks a disjuncture in the relationship between black Americans and the Democratic party. Between 1964 and 1980, the party succeeded in mobilizing, on average, roughly one-third of blacks who did not vote in the previous election, whereas from 1948 until 1960, they had only been able, on average, to mobilize roughly 8 percent of blacks who did not vote in the previous election. While 1964 marks a high point in the Democratic mobilization of nonvoting whites, these successes quickly diminished in subsequent elections.

Perhaps the most telling evidence regarding the failure of the Democratic party among the white electorate after 1964 is that the Republicans mobilized nonvoting whites at a higher rate than the Democrats in three of the four elections from 1968 through 1980. This is especially significant because the party of the disadvantaged, the working class, and the lower middle class would generally be expected to be the party of mobilization—the party that depends upon the recruitment of marginal members of the electorate. In short, the evidence suggests that the success of the Democratic party as the party of lower-class whites has been fundamentally compromised since 1964.

The aftermath of 1964 has been a Democratic party that is dependent upon racial harmony between historically antagonistic groups: blacks and lower-status whites. This new Democratic party had a difficult time securing 50 percent of organized labor's votes in the 1984 presidential election, even with a prolabor candidate like Walter Mondale and even when organized labor made an unprecedented effort to support that candidate. This new Democratic party is not the preference of party elites, even if it is their creation. Rather, it is the natural culmination of the need to secure heavy support among blacks, which in turn compromises the party's ability to secure the support of the lower-class whites. Thus the Democratic party has frequently become the party of blacks and liberal whites, two groups that do not constitute a winning coalition in American politics.

Racism in American Politics

Where does this leave us in terms of racism in American politics? Much of the debate is a matter of semantics. From one rhetorical perspective, American society is embedded in racism and the American political system revolves around and is constructed upon matters of racial dominance. We do not take issue with this perspective, so long as it is simultaneously recognized that, from another perspective, most individual Americans are not racists in the common usage of the term (for alternative definitions see Sears and McConahy 1973). America has travelled a long distance in forty short years, from a nation of individuals who did not share schools, beaches, playing fields, or drinking fountains between races, to a nation of individuals who may not be color-blind, but who are increasingly indifferent to matters of race in their own social relations.

The problem relates to a fundamental distinction between matters of race at the level of individuals and matters of race in the structure of politics. As Schelling (1978) has shown so convincingly, even moderate levels of racial antagonism at the individual level are fully capable of fostering extreme levels of racial polarization at the corporate level. We pay more attention to this issue in the chapters that follow, but for present purposes it is interesting to note that empirical social science may be addressing at last the normative imperative recognized so long ago: that morality at the individual level does not translate directly into corporate morality, just as corporate morality cannot always be directly traced to the actions of moral individuals (Niebuhr 1932).

The end result—racially polarized politics—is a direct consequence of the joint structure of race, class, and party competition in the American political environment. It is the motivation of politicians to win elections in such an environment, more than racial preferences and attitudes, which has created the current dilemma of the Democratic party. Thus, our objective is not simply an indictment of Americans as racists. Rather our goal is to analyze a political system that has produced a patently race-conscious result in national presidential elections—one in which blacks are homogeneously Democratic and in which a significant, oftentimes vast majority of white voters support the Republican candidate. Indeed, it has been nearly a quarter century since the majority of white voters supported the Democratic presidential candidate. Such an outcome is less the result of individual racists than it is the result of political conflict that has become increasingly dominated by race, and the watershed year for such an outcome was 1964.

2 Volatility in the Party Coalitions

Beginning with the 1948 Democratic National Convention and culminating in the 1964 presidential election, the Democratic party was transformed from a party that relied fundamentally upon the solidly Democratic white South to a party that relied fundamentally upon the solid, overwhelming support of blacks. Just as the 1948 election of Harry Truman was characterized by large-scale defections on the part of normally Democratic white southerners, so in the 1964 election of Lyndon Johnson these defections occurred again. The difference between these two elections was that by 1964 the critical period was over and the crisis resolved. White southerners were no longer solidly in the camp of the national Democratic coalition. Even Jimmy Carter, a southerner, won the 1976 presidential election with only a minority of white southern support. This is not to say that the Democratic party's presidential ticket can never again be competitive in the South, but the competitive calculus has been radically altered. Winning elections in the South has come to mean solid support from the black population, plus a significant level of minority support from the white community.

The resolution of this crisis within the Democratic party produced important consequences for the Republican party as well. In a two-party system both parties necessarily become conglomerations of interests and viewpoints that are at various points contradictory and competitive, and the Republican party is no exception. It has traditionally accepted into its ranks both civil libertarians and moral fundamentalists, economic "liberals" in the Adam Smith tradition and neopopulist economic interventionists. The main importance of the Democratic crisis for the Republican party was that, not unexpectedly, some elements within the Republican party scrambled to become the principal beneficiaries of the racial fissure within the Democratic coalition. This effort necessarily transformed the nature of Republicanism by shifting the balance of interests and viewpoints within the party. The 1964 presidential candidacy of Barry Goldwater, Richard Nixon's southern strategy, the passing of the Republican party as the party of civil rights, and the development of its conservative neopopulist appeal are the historical manifestations of this transformation.

Viewed in a somewhat different light, the decline of class voting among whites has not only meant that lower-class whites have become less willing to support the Democratic party, but it has also meant that they have become more willing to support the Republican party. Their support has come at a price: the restructuring of the Republican party's appeal. The upper-middle-class, socially progressive, but economically conservative wing of the party was the loser in this reorientation, while the lower-middle-class and working-class, morally and socially conservative wing of the party gained ascendancy.

For the most part Republicans have been able to maintain their image as the party of economic conservatism, but even this element of traditional Republican appeal frequently becomes obscured. Republican neopopulism involves conservatism on some issues, but it certainly does not square with traditionally defined conservative positions across the whole spectrum of public policy matters. As the nature of the Republican party has been transformed, so also has the nature of American conservatism (Sundquist 1983).

In summary, both party coalitions—the Republican and the Democratic—have been transformed in significant ways during the postwar period. In this chapter we examine a set of questions related to these transformations. To what extent have these transformations produced volatility within party coalitions? What is the source of the volatility? How has the volatility varied across parties, across races, across regions, and through time? How has the volatility been affected by the events of the mid-1960s?

Racial Conflict and Volatility in St. Louis: A Case Study

The transformed electoral environment of American politics is structured around racial conflict and has led to volatile, shifting alignments in electoral politics. The Democratic party depends upon a tenuous coalition of blacks and whites to win elections, and this coalition frequently comes undone. In the 1983 Chicago mayoral election, a huge majority of the white, normally Democratic electorate voted for Bernard Epton, an unknown Republican, when the Democratic party nominated Harold Washington, a black man, due to a split white primary vote. The Democrat narrowly won. In the 1984 North Carolina senatorial race, the Democratic candidate, James Hunt, a popular governor in a Democratic state, rushed to register as many blacks as possible, while Jesse Helms, the Republican incumbent, rushed to register as many whites as possible. The Republican narrowly won.

Other examples abound, but an especially dramatic illustration of the role played by race in Democratic party politics can be found in the recent political history of St. Louis, Missouri — one of the most racially segregated cities in America. St Louis is best understood as two separate cities, divided by Highway 40 into the black north and the white ethnic south. Not surprisingly, the politics of St. Louis is fundamentally organized by Highway 40 — its politics revolves around race. In particular, recent mayoral elections in 1981 and 1985 illustrate the polarizing effects of race and the extreme volatility of racially structured politics.

In the late 1970s, St. Louis mayor Jim Conway initiated a variety of redevelopment projects in both the central business district and in many residential neighborhoods. These projects were funded through the efforts of an aggressive grant writing department that successfully obtained major federal funding. Conway multiplied the benefits of these funds by attracting private investors, but he soon found that the distribution of redevelopment money within the city produced winners as well as losers. Not all neighborhoods felt they had received a fair share, which led to an erosion of Conway's support, particularly on the predominantly white south side. At the same time, St. Louis was facing severe inflation, increased costs for city services, a decline in the size of its middle-class population, and a shrinking city budget. The mayor moved to close Homer G. Phillips Hospital, widely perceived by blacks and whites as a black institution that both served and employed blacks in substantial numbers. Thus, on the eve of his 1981 re-election bid, Conway had managed to alienate a significant portion of the white population in south St. Louis and an even larger number of blacks in north St. Louis.

The data base for our analysis of the 1981 and 1985 St. Louis mayoral elections combines precinct election returns with census data that provide an estimate of the racial composition within precincts. Census information for 1980 has been allocated to St. Louis precincts using an algorithm developed by John Blodgett of the Urban Information Center at the University of Missouri–St. Louis. This estimation algorithm is necessary due to the suppression of data by the census in an effort to maintain the confidentiality of individuals within small geographic areas. Based on the Blodgett procedure, we were able to identify the racial composition of approximately 360 out of 400 precincts, with an average total population in each precinct of 1000. For the most part our analysis employs all-black and all-white precincts, thereby avoiding complications of ecological inference. Due to the logic of the allocation procedure, we designated precincts as all-white if they were allocated fewer than 25 blacks, and all-black if they were allocated fewer than 25 whites. This produced 88 all-black and 170 all-white precincts.

St. Louis has been a Democratic party stronghold since World War II, and for many municipal offices the Republican party does not even field candidates. Thus, the real election for mayor in St. Louis is typically the Democratic primary. In 1981 a young white Democrat from south St. Louis, Vince Schoemehl, challenged the white incumbent mayor Jim Conway for the Democratic nomination. With discontent in white southside neighborhoods, and with the recent uproar in the black community over the forced closing of Homer G. Phillips, the stage was set for a primary challenge. Like Boss Plunkett, Schoemehl "seen his opportunities and took 'em"—he proposed to reopen Homer G. Phillips. This overt appeal for the black vote, coupled with discontent in some of the south St. Louis neighborhoods, allowed him to win in both the white south and in the black north. Part A of Table 2.1 shows that Schoemehl ran ahead of Conway both in all-white precincts and in all-black precincts, but this fact masks the extreme racial structure that underlay the vote. While Schoemehl ran considerably ahead of Conway in all-white precincts, he enjoyed a remarkable 8 to 1 margin of victory in the all-black precincts.

Table 2.1. Average precinct vote in St. Louis, Missouri for all-black precincts, all-white precincts, and all-city precincts

	Average Vote		
	All-black precincts (N = 88)	All-white precincts (N = 170)	All precincts (N = 360)
A. 1981 Democratic Primary			
Vince Schoemehl (white, Democrat)	230	155	179
Jim Conway (white, Democrat)	27	117	80
Schoemehl-to-Conway ratio	8.52:1	1.32:1	2.24:1
B. 1981 General Election			
Vince Schoemehl (white, Democrat)	251	146	183
Jerry Wamser (white, Republican)	14	153	93
Schoemehl-to-Wamser ratio	17.93:1	.95:1	1.97:1
C. 1985 Democratic Primary			
Vince Schoemehl (white, Democrat)	92	203	153
Freeman Bosley (black, Democrat)	104	5	47
Schoemehl-to-Bosley ratio	.88:1	40.60:1	3.26:1

Source: St. Louis Election Commission; Urban Information Center, University of Missouri-St. Louis.

The Republicans attempted to take advantage of this racial division within the Democratic party and of the widely held perception of Schoemehl as a white Democratic candidate playing to black northside interests. Jerry Wamser, a white Republican, ran an aggressive campaign in the general election and did better among white voters than Schoemehl, but he had virtually no support among blacks. While the racial overtones were not enough to swing the election to the Republicans, it is clear that the election was structured in terms of race. Even though Schoemehl was a white Democrat running in a strongly Democratic city, Part B of Table 2.1 shows that he lost his advantage in all-white precincts, running slightly behind the Republican Wamser. His lead in the all-black precincts increased, however, to an 18 to 1 margin. The end result was a level of racial polarization in the general election that surpassed the already extreme level of polarization that had been present in the primary.

Once in office, Schoemehl was unable to reopen Homer G. Phillips, a fact which a significant portion of the black community did not forget. At the same time, however, he became a very popular mayor among whites, and even among many blacks, by enlisting neighborhood support from both north and south St. Louis for numerous self-help projects and by continuing to pursue a program of revitalization that produced both highly visible symbols and physically tangible results.

In the 1985 Democratic mayoral primary Schoemehl faced a well known black opponent named Freeman Bosley. On the surface this would seem to be a significant challenge, particularly in a city where roughly half of the population is black. In spite of the Homer G. Phillips issue, however, the mayor maintained considerable popularity within the black community, and Part C of Table 2.1 shows that Schoemehl ran only marginally behind Bosley in the all-black precincts. In this election it was the white voters' turn to engage in racial block voting, and the all-white precincts present a considerably different story. Voters in these precincts voted for Schoemehl over Bosley at a rate of more than 40 to 1.

What does St. Louis teach us regarding the nature of racial politics? First, it shows once again that racial politics produces extreme levels of polarization. In Mississippi for the 1984 presidential election, in North Carolina for the 1984 senatorial election, in Chicago for the 1983 mayoral election, so also in St. Louis for the 1981 and 1985 mayoral elections, racial politics had the potential to produce levels of polarization unequaled by any other divisions in American society. Second, the St. Louis experience emphasizes the incredible volatility that can be generated by the politics of race. Indeed, Schoemehl depended upon this volatility to win elections. In the 1981 general election, he overcame the lead of his Republican challenger among white voters with the homogeneous support he received among black voters. In the 1985 primary election, he overcame the lead of his Democratic challenger among black voters with the homogeneous support he received among white voters.

The St. Louis experience illustrates that racial conflict has the potential to turn politics upside down and inside out in relatively short order. In 1981 Schoemehl was the blacks' candidate for mayor, but by 1985 he had become the whites' candidate for mayor. Recent American electoral history teaches us, however, that obtaining the support of both blacks and whites in the same election is a more elusive goal because racial politics is competitive as well as being volatile.

Racial Conflict and Volatility in National Politics

The volatility of the Democratic coalition is not simply a matter of idiosyncratic events occurring in particular locales, even though racial conflict is best understood in terms of specific times, events, and locations. Rather, the stability of the Democratic party's national coalition has been fundamentally undermined by the ascent of race in American electoral politics. Actions on the part of the party leadership have had the unintended consequence of producing a party coalition compromised by its heavy reliance upon two fundamentally antagonistic groups: lower-class blacks and whites. While many members of both groups may consider themselves Democrats, and in particular cases may vote for the same Democratic candidate, they frequently cannot be accommodated within the same coalition.

Instability shows up most readily in the behavior of whites. The Republican party has frequently given black Americans only two choices: vote Democratic or stay home on election day. White Americans, by contrast, have increasingly availed themselves of the opportunity to vote Republican, but Republican voting is an episodic event for many whites, without any underlying permanent commitment to the party or its candidates. Thus, in securing the dependability of the black vote, the stable attachment of the white electorate to the Democratic party has been undermined. This shows up quite clearly in the trade-off between class and race as the central locus underlying electoral politics.

The politics of class has declined in American politics as the politics of race has become ascendant. While partisan differences between whites and blacks have grown more extreme in the postwar period, partisan differences between the white working class and the white middle class have been nearly extinguished. These are more than simultaneously occurring trends. Indeed, race serves as the wedge that fractures the lower class Democratic coalition and is thus responsible for increased levels of volatility in electoral politics.

The Democratic party has never been solely a working-class party, and as the industrial working class has continued to decline in size relative to the expanding middle class, it has become even more crucial for the Democrats to expand their base beyond the working class. Consequently, a core constituency of the Democratic party continues to be the working class in combination with the lower middle class, and it is difficult to conceive of a successful Democratic party that cannot secure the strong support of these groups. The important point for our analysis is that the political behavior of the working class has become virtually indistinguishable from the political behavior of the middle class. Thus, the ability of the Democratic party to expand its base beyond the working class becomes moot.

Rather than focusing upon trends in class voting and racial voting through time, it is instructive to examine the election-to-election changes in class voting as a function of the election-to-election changes in racial voting. The two time series displayed in Figure 1.1 can be reconsidered in a manner that focuses upon the inherent instability of a lower-class coalition dependent upon the votes of both blacks and whites. This is done in Figure 2.1, where each point in the scatterplot represents an election year, ordered by that year's change in both racial and class voting. It is clear that election-to-election changes in racial voting tend to correspond inversely with election-to-election changes in class voting. An increase in the level of racial voting corresponds with a decrease in the level of class voting among whites.

In summary, higher levels of partisan differentiation by race generally produce lower levels of partisan differentiation by class among whites. The relationship would be even stronger except for the landslide victory of Dwight Eisenhower in 1956, when his candidacy attracted both blacks and white workers. Clearly that election does not fit the predominant structure of elections in postwar America. The central message is that race undermines class as the defining characteristic of American electoral politics and that a continuing tension between the two is a permanent feature of postwar politics.

A number of factors make the rise of racially based politics and the decline of class-based politics a self-accelerating process. First, as Democrats lose the support of the lower-class whites they must rely more heavily upon votes from the black community, but as they become more reliant upon black votes the exodus of the lower-class whites is exacerbated. Second, whites not only respond to the behavior of blacks, they also respond to the behavior of other whites. Just as it required considerable determination and strength of character for a Mississippi white to vote Republican during the era of the solid Democratic South, so in 1984 it took an act of strong resolve to join the small minority among Mississippi white voters who supported Walter Mondale, the Democratic presidential candidate. We give more attention to these unraveling consequences of racial conflict in subsequent chapters, but the important point here is that even fairly low levels of initial hostility between races have the potential to snowball into significant levels of polarization along racial lines.

Figure 2.1. Election to election changes in class voting by election to election changes in racial voting, 1948–84.

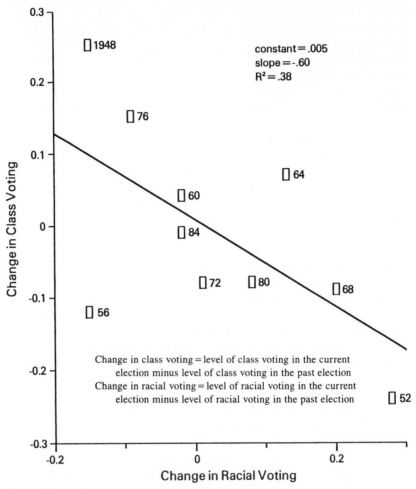

Source: Figure 1.1.

Volatility Within the Party Coalitions

Systematic evidence is available regarding the volatility of both national party coalitions. We employ survey data collected by the Center for Political Studies at the University of Michigan as part of their National Election Studies (NES) for two purposes. First, they can be used to determine reported support levels for the parties' presidential candidates within particular groups through time. Second, they can be used to calculate transition probabilities between three states—Democratic voter, Republican voter, and nonvoter—for sequenced pairs of elections. These transition rates are based upon the respondents' reported votes in the current and preceding elections. While people's recollections of their voting behavior four years earlier are not always reliable, the direction of the bias is undoubtedly conservative, overestimating consistency and stability. The NES data thus provide us with an opportunity to compare volatility among whites and blacks in the Democratic and Republican coalitions.

We treat electoral behavior in successive presidential elections as a Markov process (Bartos 1967). For each election we calculate a set of fixed probabilities, idiosyncratic to that election, providing the likelihood that Democratic voters, Republican voters, and nonvoters in the previous election vote Democratic, Republican, or do not vote in the current election. This procedure generates a three-by-three transition matrix with nine probabilities. Given these probabilities, fixed points can be calculated for the three equilibrium values implied by the electoral dynamic: the Democratic equilibrium, the Republican equilibrium, and the nonvoting equilibrium.

This is not to suggest that the first-order transition rates adequately capture the dynamic occurring across an entire thirty-two-year period of political history. Rather, the equilibrium is only used to characterize the dynamic occurring between a sequenced pair of elections. The equilibrium exhibits the partisan distribution implied, in the long run, by these short-run behavior changes. Although the fixed point is a long-run equilibrium, convergence in a discrete time Markov model is very rapid. Thus the equilibrium is not necessarily a substantively distant consequence of the recalled and reported vote. Once again, this equilibrium vector provides a purely descriptive measure of the dynamic between particular elections, and we do not commit ourselves to the notion that electoral politics is usefully conceived as a memory-free Markov process.

Given this interpretation of the fixed point, a comparison between the actual behavior and the equilibrium behavior provides a direct measure of electoral volatility for the group in question. Actual behavior divorced from the fixed-point equilibrium suggests volatile behavior—behavior that is politically adrift and at disequilibrium. Reported behavior close to the fixed point indicates a dynamic at equilibrium. Furthermore, the equilibrium projects the end result of the dynamic that came into play between elections. If the same dynamic was maintained, where would the party system be headed?

Change in Democratic Support Levels

The reported votes for the Democrats and the implied equilibrium for Democratic support are found in Figure 2.2 for the period from 1948

Figure 2.2. Reported Democratic vote and implied Democratic equilibrium for presidential elections from 1948–80, by race.

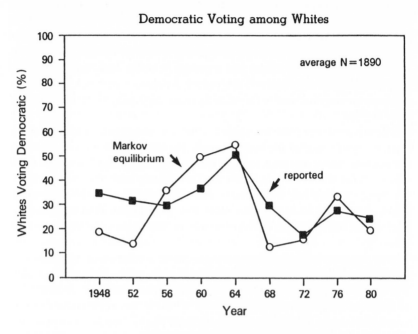

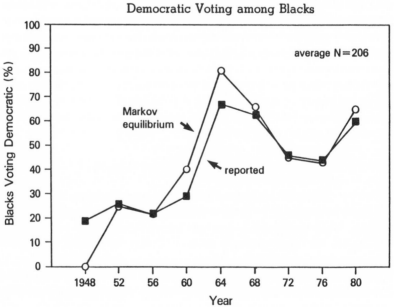

Source: National Election Studies, 1948–80.

through 1980. Both the reported votes and the equilibria are expressed as proportions of the relevant eligible black and white electorates. If we focus upon the discrepancies between actual and fixed-point Democratic support levels among whites and blacks throughout the period, we find evidence of the attenuated ties between white voters and the Democratic party. The white segment of the Democratic party is typically at disequilibrium, measured as the vertical distance between the reported behavior line and the implied equilibrium line. By contrast, the reported behavior of black Democratic voters comes much closer to their fixed points, especially after the watershed year of 1964.

The reported vote paths in Figure 2.2 force us once again to appreciate the critical significance of the 1964 election. For that one election in 1964, the Democratic party was able to increase its support among both blacks and whites. After that election support declined among both blacks and whites, but the decline among white voters was more ominous for the Democrats. Blacks continued to vote Democratic at a level higher than the pre-1964 period, but white support declined to a level that was less than the pre-1964 level.

The volatility of white Democratic support is reinforced by Table 2.2, which presents the retention rates for Democratic voters, Republican voters, and nonvoters by race. This rate is defined among white Democrats, for example, as the percentage of Democratic voters at the previous election who voted Democratic at the subsequent election. There is evidence of considerable volatility, across all three behaviors, for both blacks and whites. Retention rates are lowest, however, for Democratic support among whites. In the 1972 election the Democratic retention rate for white voters dropped below 50 percent: less than half of the white Democratic electorate in 1968 voted Democratic again in 1972. This result technically implies an oscillating (erratic) time path as the fixed point is pursued. Given these results, which are biased in the direction of stability, it is difficult to understand common wisdom which suggests that the American electorate is stable in terms of individual voting preferences.

Change in Republican Support Levels

A parallel analysis of Republican support can be carried out on the basis of Figure 2.3. Several features of this figure are particularly striking. While the reported white vote for the Democrats as a proportion of the eligible electorate generally declined during the period, the reported white vote for the Republicans did not increase correspondingly; indeed, the high plateau of Republican support in 1952 and 1956 was not quite equaled either during the Nixon years or by Ronald Reagan's first presidential election victory.

Table 2.2. Democratic, Republican, and nonvoter consistency: Percentage of respondents with a particular recalled vote who report the same current vote in presidential elections from 1948 to 1980, by race

current/recalled	race	Democratic consistency	Republican consistency	Nonvoting consistency
1948/1944	whites	65[a]	89	70
1948/1944	blacks	67	100	95
1952/1948	whites	61	90	53
1952/1948	blacks	69	83	90
1956/1952	whites	76	77	60
1956/1952	blacks	58	50	90
1960/1956	whites	79	67	56
1960/1956	blacks	78	52	85
1964/1960	whites	77	66	53
1964/1960	blacks	90	0	59
1968/1964	whites	55	84	61
1968/1964	blacks	79	0	61
1972/1968	whites	43	72	65
1972/1968	blacks	65	24	68
1976/1972	whites	64	57	70
1976/1972	blacks	66	18	73
1980/1976	whites	56	81	67
1980/1976	blacks	78	17	59
Average N for whites		635	620	543
Average N for blacks		86	12	102

[a]For example, 65 percent of the white respondents who reported a Democratic vote in 1944 also reported voting Democratic in 1948.
Source: National Election Studies, 1948-80.

In terms of volatility levels, we once again see significantly more erratic behavior among the white electorate. In particular, the equilibrium path for white Republicans is frequently divorced from the reported vote. Furthermore, not only is Republican support among whites at disequilibrium, but the equilibria tend to be quite erratic. The Republican equilibrium has been repeatedly redefined in response to the roller-coaster ride of political events shaping postwar electoral history. Using the equilibrium as an indication of

Figure 2.3. Reported Republican vote and implied Republican equilibrium for presidential elections from 1948–80, by race.

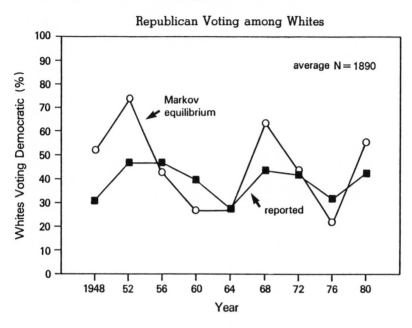

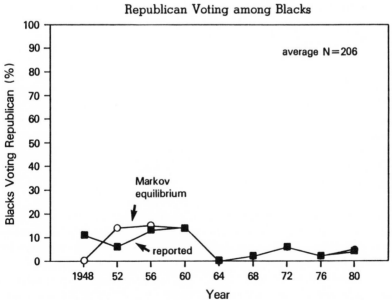

Source: National Election Studies, 1948–80.

Republican potential among whites, that potential crested in the first Eisenhower election and bottomed out in Gerald Ford's loss to Jimmy Carter following Watergate, with other important highs and lows along the way.

Black Republicanism, by contrast, shows a high level of consistency and stability. With the exception of 1948 and 1952, reported Republican support among blacks is almost entirely coincidental with equilibrium support levels. The overall level of support declines after 1964, but the stability of the pattern is maintained, both in terms of distance between reported and equilibrium support, and in terms of the range of variation in black Republican support through time. Given the history of race policy during the past twenty-five years, the decreased support for the Republican party among black voters is not surprising, nor is their increased support for the Democratic party (see Figure 2.2).

The stability of the small black Republican minority can be interpreted in two very different ways. Black voters who support the Republican party might be very special people indeed, with exceptional personal resources to resist the overwhelming partisan signal coming from the rest of the black community. Alternatively, it might well be the case that the black Republican minority resembles most other minorities: lacking in unity and cohesion, and socially overwhelmed by the political majority (Miller 1956; Huckfeldt and Sprague 1988). According to this second view, minorities are more likely to be sustained by a stochastic process—by small rates of attrition and conversion operating upon the larger mass of the majority. In short, the stability of the black Republican minority might be explained as a by-product of the inevitable, persistent, residual leakage from the overpowering majority.

We are not foolish enough to argue that the instability in the white Republican vote is typical of all white Republican supporters. Indeed, perhaps the most consistent level of support for a political party that has been isolated from national survey data comes from affluent, well educated, conservative, and highly partisan Republicans who furnished a remarkable example of partisan loyalty in the 1952 election. In a study of the 1964 election Converse, Clausen and Miller (1965) reviewed 1952 survey data in an attempt to evaluate the claim that vast numbers of conservative Republicans had been staying home on election day because prior Republican presidential candidates were of a hopelessly me-too stripe, offering an echo rather than a choice for potential Republican voters. As it turned out, these well educated, wealthy, conservative Republicans—those who tended to favor Robert Taft prior to the Republican National Convention—voted for Eisenhower at the highest rate isolated for any group in either party. The notion that disaffected conservative Republicans were staying away from the polls in great numbers was a myth and cannot explain the subsequent rise of the Republican party. Rather, the revitalized Republican party increased its support at the direct expense of the Democratic party, from the ranks of disgruntled Democrats.

The work of Converse, Clausen, and Miller (1965) is important for our argument because it points toward an alternative source of Republican volatility. The substantial volatility in the white Republican vote does not come from affluent, conservative Republicans. Rather, it comes from other groups that are occasional participants within the Republican coalition—groups of episodic Republican voters disaffected from the Democratic party but for whom the Republican party holds no permanent partisan appeal. Unlike blacks, who have been successfully mobilized and recruited by the Democratic party over post–World War II electoral history, the white population shows no trend toward consistently higher levels of Republican support. Democratic candidates have been rewarded with consistently high levels of support among blacks, but the Republicans have not achieved a similarly high level of consistent support within the white population.

Our argument is that volatility among the white population is the price the Democratic party pays for the consistent and durable attachment of black voters. Many potential white Democrats are uneasy with a party they perceive as being dominated by black interests and black voters; nor are they at ease with the Republican party. Some candidates in some years from both parties are able to overcome this uneasiness, but the potential volatility always lies just below the surface.

Changes in Turnout and Nonvoting

An inspection of nonvoting in Figure 2.4 shows a general decrease in turnout among the white majority during the post–World War II period. The black turnout pattern is substantially more complex. A dramatic increase in turnout took place from 1948 through 1964, followed by a more modest decline through 1976. Thus, while black participation has increased substantially since 1948, it has declined from its 1964 high point.

In contrast to earlier analyses, we see low levels of volatility in turnout. Among whites generally, and among blacks after 1964, reported turnout coincides very closely with the implied equilibrium levels. This is striking, particularly in view of the high rates of Democratic mobilization among black nonvoters (see Figure 1.3), and in view of the relatively low levels of consistent nonvoting (see Table 2.3). In spite of extensive efforts on the part of parties and candidates to mobilize nonvoters, we are left with an enduring portion of the American population that is disengaged from electoral politics and marginal to the political system. Entries and exits from this marginal population are substantial but well balanced, and thus a large pool of marginal citizens has become a permanent fact of life in late twentieth century American politics.

Figure 2.4. Reported nonvoting and implied nonvoting equilibrium for presidential elections from 1948–80, by race.

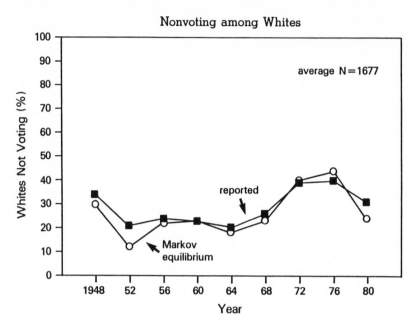

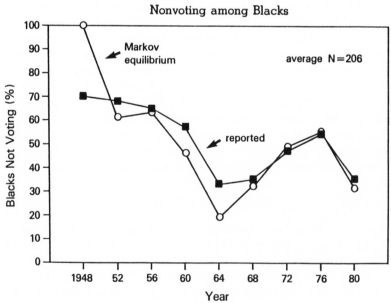

The overall increase in participation among blacks, coupled with their high levels of Democratic support, is central to the current intraparty politics of the Democratic party, and it has led to decreased support among lower-class whites. At the same time that many working-class and lower-middle-class whites are put off by a party that relies upon black voters, they also fail to be persuaded that the Republican party offers an alternative. Lower-class whites as a group are split in their voting preferences and thus are likely to encounter supporters of each party within their class grouping. As a result of these ambiguous political and social cues, lower-class whites are likely to vote for a particular candidate and for whatever they conceive to be in their own short run interests, if they vote at all. Two results flow from this behavior: partisanship is weakened or not learned at all, and participation levels deteriorate.

This line of reasoning perhaps reveals the source of the observed decline of voter participation during the past decade. The Reagan era is not reflective of a fundamental reorganization of electoral politics, but rather of an attractive and skilled campaigner who turns out to be an extraordinarily popular president. In short, the Reagan revolution lacks permanence; it is just one more idiosyncratic event in an increasingly long line of idiosyncratic events. Lacking strong partisan ties, the power of such events to produce dramatic electoral outcomes is magnified. Indeed, the overwhelming 1984 Reagan victory was characterized within the white population by rough uniformity of movement in all groups toward the Republican candidate. This pattern is typical of short-term, idiosyncratic partisan swings from one election to another. It occurred, however, in the context of a decline in participation. Hence, the victory does not represent a mobilization phenomenon, nor a massive partisan reorientation among voters, but rather confirms the interpretation of a continuing failure on the part of either party to offer a sufficiently compelling candidate to mobilize the marginal members of the white population in large numbers. In short, for very different reasons, neither party provides marginal members of the white electorate with an attractive alternative. Under such conditions, these marginal citizens have a lowered motivation to participate, and thus we see increased partisan volatility accompanied by declining participation.

Patterns in the South and Non-South

The patterns observed among the white electorate (Figures 2.2–2.4) are not dramatically altered when we compare the levels of Democratic support, Republican support, and nonvoting among whites in the South and non-South (see Figures 2.5–2.7). This is not to say that there are no differences because important differences do occur in patterns of behavior with respect to particular crucial elections. But there is a striking degree of

Figure 2.5. Reported Democratic voting and implied Democratic equilibrium for presidential elections from 1952–80, by region and race.

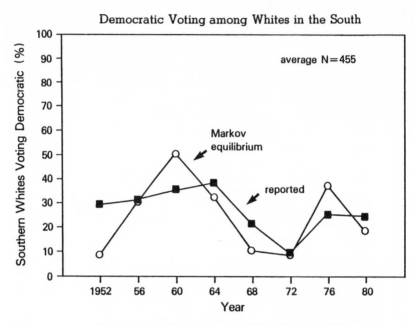

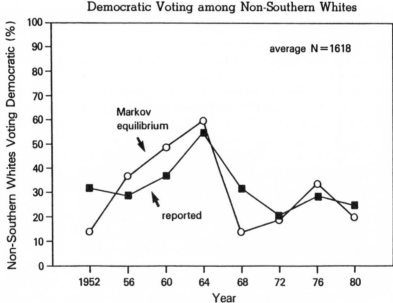

Figure 2.6. Reported Republican voting and implied Republican equilibrium for presidential elections from 1952–80, by region and race.

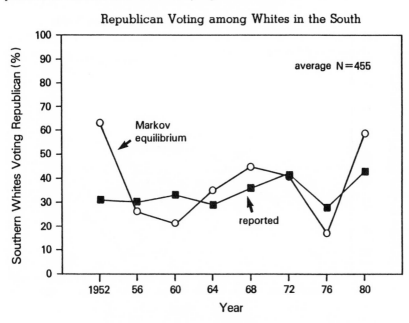

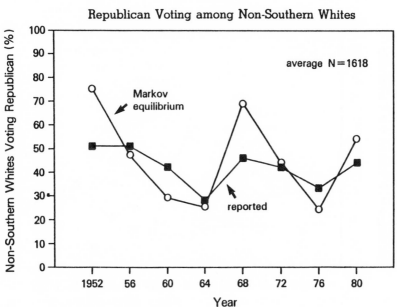

Source: National Election Studies, 1952–80.

Figure 2.7. Reported nonvoting and implied nonvoting equilibrium for presidential elections from 1952–80, by region and race.

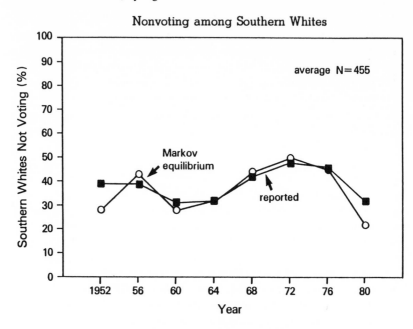

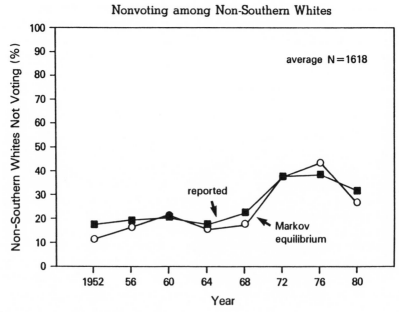

Source: National Election Studies, 1952–80.

similarity. For both southern and nonsouthern whites we see the attenuated ties between reported party support and equilibrium party support. And for both southern and nonsouthern whites we see a high level of consistency between reported nonvoting and equilibrium nonvoting.

The general contours of the reported vote patterns are also very similar. Perhaps the biggest difference between southerners and nonsoutherners is most noticeable in Figure 2.7: the decrease in voting participation is present for both groups, but it is more pronounced for the southerners. In summary, the pattern of volatility in the white electorate is not unique to the South or to the rest of the country. It is a pattern that is shared, both in its causes and in its consequences.

The Political Significance of Race

Why does race lead to levels of polarization that are so high relative to other social divisions? Why does race generate volatility within the electorate? A classic argument regarding the source of electoral stability within democratic politics provides part of the answer, suggesting that democratic stability is enhanced to the extent that important social divisions within the population intersect with each other (Lipset 1981). In an earlier era of American politics, Catholics were substantially more likely than Protestants to be Democrats, and members of the working class were more likely than members of the middle class to be Democrats. Yet a significant number of Catholics were members of the middle class, and a significant number of Protestants were members of the working class. Cross-cutting cleavages such as these serve to mute political conflict because they lead, inevitably, to increased ambiguity in the definition of interests within groups and to social interaction between individuals who hold opposite views and interests (Lazarsfeld, Berelson, and Gaudet 1968; Berelson, Lazarsfeld, and McPhee 1954).

One method for evaluating this argument is to compare changes in support for a party between two presidential elections across social boundaries. If elections exacerbate the political differences between groups, then as support for a party goes up in one group, support for that party in some naturally opposed group should go down. Analyses have typically shown, however, that while the rate of change may differ across opposed groups, the direction of change tends to be the same (Key 1966: chap. 3). Thus, somewhat indirectly, the evidence points to socially integrated groups within the population; that is, the absence of sharp political antagonisms suggests the presence of cross-cutting cleavages.

We undertake this type of analysis using data from the National Election Studies for the past five presidential elections. The data are displayed in Part A of Table 2.3 for the entire electorate, and in Part B of Table 2.3 for the

South alone. The percentages voting Democratic are relative to the entire population within each social category at each election—Democratic voters, Republican voters, other voters, and nonvoters. Three comments on the tables seem appropriate. First, the classic argument is well supported relative to the boundaries of class and sex. Movement between elections is in a uniform direction, and thus it would seem that group hostilities *are* suppressed by cross-cutting cleavages. Second, a comparison of black and white movement shows deviation from this pattern, especially between 1976 and 1980. Third, and perhaps most surprising, the pattern for the South is the same as the pattern for the nation as a whole.

Why is race different? Quite simply, cross-cutting cleavages are absent. Even when whites and blacks share the same religious denominations, class memberships, and party affliations, they worship at racially segregated churches, they live in racially segregated neighborhoods, and they conceive of their interests along racially structured lines. Racial conflict is more intense because racial groups in America are more separate, across a wide range of social experience. As a result, the potential is created for high levels of political polarization along racial lines and for political volatility driven by racial conflict.

Table 2.3. Percentage voting Democratic in presidential elections, 1968-84[a]

	1968	1972	1976	1980	1984	average *N*
A. The Nation						
Working class	30	19	33	31	32	862
Middle class	30	22	28	26	30	1,227
Whites	27	18	28	24	27	2,044
Blacks	61	45	43	60	58	234
Men	28	19	31	26	27	1,001
Women	31	22	28	29	33	1,322
B. The South						
Working class	22	17	33	34	30	225
Middle class	24	18	28	29	29	317
Whites	17	10	25	24	22	484
Blacks	59	42	45	61	57	117
Men	25	16	28	28	25	263
Women	23	17	30	33	33	351

[a]These percentages are relative to the total number of persons in that category in the survey sample, including nonvoters. For example, 30 percent of all working class respondents reported a Democratic vote in 1968.
Source: National Election Studies, 1968-84.

Racial Conflict and Partisan Decomposition

Weakened ties toward political parties, lowered levels of political enthusiasm and interest, and decreased levels of participation are all indicators that something is wrong in American electoral politics. The most common meaning ascribed to these events is that the motivating force behind the parties has worn thin through time. The basis of the cleavage between the parties has become irrelevant to changed social realities, and successive generations have only dim, third-hand appreciations of the reality that generated the partisan division in the first place. In this view, the country is ripe for political reinvigoration. New issues, new dramas, and new appeals might generate new lines of conflict between the parties and, perhaps more important, new commitment and enthusiasm on the part of the electorate.

We present a somewhat different view. Along with Kevin Phillips (1969, 1982) and others, we believe that the realignment has already occurred, that it took place in the aftermath of 1964, when a large segment of the normally Democratic white population became disenchanted with their party. However, this disenchantment was incomplete: it was not a repudiation of Franklin Roosevelt, or of the New Deal, or of the Democratic view of the American welfare state. Indeed, in survey after survey popular support for a generous social welfare policy is repeatedly shown (Ladd 1982). Rather, much of the white disenchantment with the Democratic party is fundamentally rooted in the politics of race. White voters across the country are ill at ease with a party that is fundamentally dependent upon, as well as responsive to, the American black electorate. This uneasiness is seldom articulated, except perhaps by an Archie Bunker caricature, and it seldom appears as virulent racism. Nonetheless, the black presence in the Democratic party has had a destabilizing effect upon white support.

The disaffection of working-class and lower-middle-class Democrats is, of course, not solely related to race. The Democratic party is out of touch with these voters on a wide range of issues — most particularly abortion rights and other issues of the New Left, or "post-material left," in American politics. Such issues are certainly part of the Democrats' problem, and we will give extended attention to them in a later chapter. Suffice it to say, however, that they are separable from what we believe to be the most crucial problem facing the Democratic party: conflict between whites and blacks in a working-class–lower-middle-class coalition.

The events of the mid to late 1960s are not typically recognized to be a realignment in American politics only because the popular and scholarly conception of realignment is static and mechanistic: a group that had previously supported the old party now switches to a different party. One static reality is subjected to a set of realigning events and a new static reality emerges. More important, one set of stable alignments gives way, over time, to a new set of stable alignments (Sundquist 1983).

This vision does not adequately capture the aftermath of 1964 even though it captures the essence of black behavior: as a result of Lyndon Johnson's bold actions, the ties of blacks to the Democratic party were solidified. It does not capture the essence of white behavior because, apart from race, nothing happened permanently as a result of the 1964 election to shake white voters free from the Democratic party. The Republican party did not become a party of New Dealers, the Democratic party did not repudiate the welfare state, and so on. Based upon a straightforward reading of public opinion polls, Johnson's actions were politically brilliant. He extended the welfare state and reached out to solidify the ties between blacks and the Democratic party.

Johnson's mistake lay in underestimating the incompatibility of blacks and whites in the same political coalition. He failed to take into account the group basis of politics in which the ability to achieve and maintain a biracial coalition is genuinely problematic. The result is not that whites have realigned to become Republicans. Rather the aftermath of 1964 is a white population that is continually and permanently at partisan disequilibrium. At the same time that the white population fails to be permanently attracted to a party whose image is antigovernment, it is also uncomfortable participating in a party coalition that depends significantly upon black support. Thus it is not that the aftermath of 1964 led to a new stable partisan equilibrium but rather that these realigning events have produced a politically adrift white electorate. A particular candidate in a particular election may be able to overcome this inherent instability, but the conditions that give rise to the instability are still present, and the Democratic coalition (or the Republican coalition) is continually on the verge of disintegration.

This view of the 1960s realignment helps to explain several different contemporary conditions often seen to be bizarre or perverse by political commentators. First, why does the electorate remain substantially Democratic in its loyalties when it fails to vote Democratic in presidential elections? With something close to relief, many analysts have pointed out that the partisan identification of the electorate was starting to become significantly more Republican after the 1980 presidential election, and again after the 1984 presidential election. For the most part, however, these gains were short-lived, and the current distribution of partisan identification does not appear significantly different from the distribution of ten years ago. The solution to this puzzle is straightforward: the balance has not shifted to the Republicans because the electorate is still substantially Democratic. To say that the Democratic coalition is permanently at disequilibrium is not to say that it no longer exists. Indeed, in many instances and for many purposes it is still quite vibrant.

Support for this position comes from research on party images held by members of the electorate. Confidence in the Democratic party has deteriorated on a number of counts, but the party maintains its credibility in terms of the groups that it is seen to represent. In reviewing more than twenty years of electoral survey data, Asher notes that "attitudes toward groups . . . have consistently favored the Democratic Party, with the most frequent positive comment referring to the Democrats as the party of the common man, in contrast to images of the GOP as the party of the more privileged elements of society" (1984:117). Most Americans favor the popular image of the Democratic party and the interests it is perceived to represent. As a practical matter, however, that support frequently unravels.

The unraveling consequences of racial conflict also help to solve a second puzzle: Why have the Democrats been able to maintain control of so many state-level electorates? They regained control of the Senate in 1986, they have maintained a slight edge in terms of gubernatorial offices, and they have a significant advantage in terms of state legislative control. We have addressed this discussion to one national electorate but this question requires that we consider fifty-one electorates: the national electorate and each state electorate; and if we address the vitality of Democratic candidates in local races, the number of electorates to be considered becomes even more significant. The important point is that group-based politics is environmentally specific to a particular setting. The severity of racial incompatibility within the coalition, and the attendant unraveling of the coalition, are dependent upon the relative size and intersection of racial groups in particular settings.

In Mississippi, where blacks make up a significant proportion of the eligible electorate, the Democratic party's dilemma is severe. In Minnesota, where blacks make up a minuscule proportion of the eligible electorate, the problems of race are less significant. In short, Democratic successes at the state level frequently occur because the dilemma of race is less pronounced, or because politicians within these states have learned how to cope with existing racial problems. As was seen in Chicago, however, even seemingly stable party coalitions can quickly come undone in the face of racial antagonism. In summary, we have argued that normally Democratic white voters have not left the party permanently to become Republicans; rather, their party ties are easily disrupted by racial antagonisms within the party. A large segment of the white working-class and lower-middle-class electorate has nominal Democratic loyalties, but it is at partisan disequilibrium, and thus the level of class voting is seriously impaired.

Appendix to Chapter 2

This appendix provides a more detailed description of the calculations leading to the fixed points exhibited in Figures 2.2 through 2.7. As a first step, respondents are classified as Republican voters, Democratic voters, and nonvoters in the presidential election that is current to the survey. In each survey, respondents also answered a question concerning their voting behavior and participation at the presidential election that occurred four years earlier. Thus, the recalled behavior coupled with the current choice implicitly defines a probability vector describing the conditional probabilities of Democratic voting, Republican voting, and nonvoting, contingent upon the same behaviors at the previous election. These vectors of conditional probabilities can in turn be used to construct a matrix of transition probabilities which define a regular Markov chain.

Operationally, frequencies were entered as column vectors for the three recalled partisan states. The sum across the three current election conditions for people who recalled voting Democratic four years earlier, for example, was used as an estimate of the distribution of Democrats from the prior election into the three categories of interest in the current election. A similar row vector estimates the distributions for prior Republicans and nonvoters. Several sources of error arise from this procedure. First, there is undoubtedly some error due to the respondents' inability to recall their votes correctly. Second, this procedure ignores third party candidates. For example, a 1972 Republican voter who reports a vote for George Wallace in 1968 is treated as missing data.

Births and deaths are only partially incorporated within the calculation of the transition probabilities. Because the deceased cannot be interviewed, they are explicitly omitted from these calculations. In contrast, newly come of age voters are included. A respondent who had not reached the requisite voting age at the the four-year-prior election is treated as a nonvoter in that election.

The procedures just described define a three-by-three matrix of frequencies. Row sums are then used to convert the row entries into estimates of transition probabilities, that is, each entry in a row is divided by the row sum. This procedure always produced an implied transition probability matrix which was regular—one in which passage between all states was possible over repeated elections. A property of regular transition matrices is that they imply a long run equilibrium distribution toward which the system moves, absent other influences. This long run probability vector is a fixed point for the Markov process thus defined.

For each election a transition probability matrix was constructed and a fixed point computed. The fixed point specifies the long run distribution into partisan categories under the hypotheses that the recalled information can be used to reconstruct the fixed probabilities of moving between states, that this process is undisturbed, and that the transition probabilities are fixed. Clearly, these numbers are useful only for analytic and theoretical purposes resting, as they do, on such fragile assumptions.

On the other hand, an important property of such processes is that convergence toward equilibrium is rapid—essentially being determined by raising the matrix of transition probabilities to successively higher powers (Kemeny and Snell 1960). A number between 0 and 1, especially when it is closer to 0, grows small rapidly when repeatedly raised to higher and higher powers. Thus the fixed point may very well be a good way of characterizing the current partisan situation because convergence of such processes is so rapid.

3 The Nature of Racial Conflict in Electoral Politics

Racial conflict in electoral politics is not simply a consequence of individual attitudes and predispositions. Many Americans are indeed racists and racist attitudes are central to racial conflict, but neither fact *explains* racial conflict. Were there significantly fewer racists in Chicago during the 1979 mayoral election than during the 1983 mayoral election? Probably not, but conditions in 1983 provoked levels of racial animosity that were unimagined four years earlier. This is an extreme case, but it serves to underline an important point: racial conflict is fundamentally a group phenomenon, subject to environmental and structural properties that are variable through time. Thus, the pattern and consequence of racial conflict in electoral politics must be understood in terms of particular groups at particular times in particular places.

The Group Basis of Racial Conflict

Discussions of American electoral politics are seldom conducted in terms of group boundaries, group cohesiveness, and group conflict. Rather, conventional explanations for voting behavior rely upon individual interest, individual motivation, individual characteristics, and individual opinions. Thus, it frequently is difficult to conceptualize electoral conflict between races in a wholly satisfying manner because racial conflict in electoral politics is group-based.

Evidence for the group basis of racial conflict comes from a variety of sources. Lipset (1981) argues that the (white) Southern vote in the 1860–61 secession referenda was structured by the racial mix of the local environment: Southern whites were more likely to support secession if they lived in counties with high-density black populations. In his landmark study of southern politics, Key (1949) demonstrated that increased political consciousness among whites was provoked by the presence of blacks: whites were more likely to vote if they lived in counties with high concentrations of blacks. Wright's (1976, 1977a) investigation of the 1968 George Wallace presidential candidacy extended the Key thesis: southern rural whites were more likely to vote for Wallace if they lived in black counties. Finally, Matthews and Prothro (1963) studied black voter registration prior to the 1965 Voting Rights Act and concluded that blacks were more likely to be disenfranchised when their relative strength in the population was higher—in situations where they posed a threat to white political hegemony.

Several of these findings warrant further attention. Wright's work demonstrates that the individual probability of engaging in a racially hostile act—such as voting for Wallace in the context of the 1968 national election—varied across whites as a function of county black densities, even when individual characteristics of whites were taken into account. Thus, participation in racial hostilities cannot be explained simply as an individual level phenomenon, even though the racially hostile act is carried out at the individual level, because it also depends on social densities. Racial hostilities are generated by the intersection of racial groups, and racial conflict is a consequence, acted out individually, of aggregate social organization.

The Matthews and Prothro results underscore this argument quite vividly. White antipathy toward blacks, and white efforts to disenfranchise blacks, have not been uniform across the South. Rather, white hostility was a direct function of black densities and the attendant potential for political dominance by blacks. It is the politically significant presence of blacks that produces a racially hostile response on the part of a white power structure.

The group basis of racial conflict becomes even more apparent when we consider the evolution of the political coalition led by Mayor Richard Daley of Chicago. First, it is important to understand that the population of Chicago underwent profound racial transformation during Daley's tenure. Five years before Daley became mayor in 1955, the population of Chicago was 13.5 percent black; four years after he died in 1976 its population was 39.5 percent black. Blacks and Latinos together accounted for 51.5 percent of Chicago's voting age population in 1980 (Kleppner 1985). Thus, Daley became mayor of a city with a small black minority, but he died as mayor of a city in which non-Hispanic whites constituted a minority.

The backbone of Daley's early support came from the black population, but during his time in office the black basis of his support declined as the white ethnic basis grew (Kleppner 1985: chps. 3 and 4). Why? The role of blacks in the Daley coalition changed because the relationship between blacks and whites changed in the city of Chicago. In the early 1950s the black community provided a valuable political resource with no threat attached. Blacks were residentially segregated, which meant they did not threaten white neighborhoods and they could be readily organized. Furthermore, the black population was large enough to provide a powerful voting bloc when blacks voted cohesively, but it was not large enough to elect its own candidates to city wide office.

This all changed, of course, as the Chicago black population continued to grow. Growth meant several things. First, blacks were still segregated residentially, but the growing size of the black community increasingly proved a threat to white neighborhoods. Second, especially in combination with Latinos, blacks were increasingly able to form a voting bloc with citywide aspirations. As the black presence in Chicago grew, the role of blacks in the Daley coalition began to change. Daley and his political machine were clearly not vehicles for the larger aspirations of the black community. Indeed, the mayor's support among white ethnics grew as he came to be perceived as a friend and supporter of racially embattled and defensive white ethnic communities. Even Daley, the great boss, had trouble accommodating both blacks and whites in the same electoral coalition.

In summary, important structural conditions changed in the city of Chicago as the relative densities of white and black populations changed, and as the level of racial hostilities increased. The splintering of the old Democratic coalition and the 1983 election of a black mayor may have occurred earlier than expected, but it was hardly surprising given the racial transformation of the city.

Conflict and Competition

The most important factors underlying the racial fissure in American politics revolve around the competitive positions of black and white voters. When black voters pose no perceived threat to white hegemony, politics is not structured in terms of race, and racial polarization within the electorate becomes less likely. Conversely, when white dominance is threatened, political appeals are much more likely to take on either covert or overt racial significance, and the electorate—particularly the lower-class electorate—is fractured by race.

Under what circumstances is white dominance likely to be threatened? Most obviously, white dominance is threatened when the numerical position of black voters is relatively enhanced. Recognizing this simple fact was the evil genius behind the solid Democratic white South: even in the face of numerically superior black populations, white dominance could be preserved so long as blacks were disenfranchised. And the best opportunity for maintaining the disenfranchisement of blacks was to make them politically irrelevant by eliminating partisan competition among whites—by eliminating democracy.

Racial hostility is at least in part a function of structural conditions. When blacks become sufficiently concentrated within a population to occupy strategically important positions within electoral coalitions, then the conditions potentially obtain to produce racially conscious politics and racial polarization within the electorate. We have frequently underestimated the structural potential for this sort of racial polarization because we all too often focus upon the density of blacks in the population rather than the density of blacks within the Democratic party. If an electorate is 25 percent black, and if blacks uniformly vote Democratic, then a minimum winning Democratic coalition will be equally dependent upon blacks and whites. Furthermore, blacks clearly occupy a strategically crucial role, and thus pose a threat to white dominance, long before they gain numerical equivalence within a coalition. Thus, even minority black populations, so long as they vote cohesively, are fully capable of threatening white hegemony within party coalitions.

Racial polarization is not simply a function of social structure, however. It is also a function of political choices and strategies that are consciously articulated and deliberately selected. In 1983 two ultimately successful black mayoral candidates, one in Chicago and the other in Philadelphia, were engaged in electoral contests with white candidates. The political circumstances, strategies, and personalities in Chicago made racial conflict virtually inevitable, while in Philadelphia racial polarization was largely avoided, even though the white candidate made a determined effort to focus the white electorate's attention on race.

A numerically threatening black population is neither a necessary nor a sufficient condition for racial conflict to occur in democratic politics. Far too many examples exist of frenzied white populations objecting to the presence of even insignificant black minorities. Rather, we argue that the prospects for racially polarized politics are increased in circumstances where the black population occupies a strategically important presence within one of the political party's electoral coalitions.

Time, Space, and Racial Conflict

Racial conflict in electoral politics was more straightforward in the era of the one-party South. In that environment the white population adhered to the Democratic party, and blacks were not allowed to participate. Politics became more complicated when this system of racial oppression broke down. In particular, the advent of blacks as a significant element within the national Democratic coalition has presented a dilemma for many white Democrats, for the Democratic party, and ultimately for the electorate as a whole. The depth of the dilemma varies across the country and across elections. In some places and at some times the black role in the party has been particularly objectionable to white Democrats. In other places and at other times black and white party constituencies have been better able to cooperate. Thus, time and space take on special significance in explaining the national politics of race.

The South provides an excellent example. White support for the national party's ticket has been very difficult to secure in the South, at the same time that many statewide Democratic candidates have been able to thrive in the bipartisan aftermath of 1964. In his ultimately successful attempt to become governor of Georgia, Jimmy Carter's core constituency came from the state's lower-class whites. His fundamentally populist appeal was able to incorporate blacks at the time of the general election, although he was clearly their second choice in the Democratic primary. Like many other successful southern Democrats, Carter's political career in Georgia revolved around the ability to incorporate black voters as part of his coalition without offending the white core constituency upon which he depended for electoral success.

In evaluating the politics of Alabama, Senator Howell Heflin (Dem.) argues that: "Southern politics are changing . . . Basically, it's become a situation of groups. You've got about 25 percent blacks, and they're liberal Democrats; about 25 percent Republicans, and they're hard-core conservatives; and the rest I call independents. They aren't as right-wing, but they're basically conservative in nature . . ." (Washington Post Weekly, Sept. 21, 1987, p. 14). In such an environment, successful Democratic party candidates must locate themselves strategically to win the support of the moderately conservative, white "independents" who are otherwise willing to support the Republicans. At the same time, however, the candidate must maintain the support of the black population. Often this means some combination of social conservatism, hawkish attitudes on defense, support for social welfare measures, and a populist appeal on economic matters. Indeed, a variation of this formula led to the political resurrection of Governor George Wallace and even made him the candidate of blacks in Alabama.

Yankee journalists frequently attempt to understand this new (post-1964) breed of southern Democratic politicians by labeling them southern conservatives. It is important to realize, however, that they are radically different from the southern conservatives of the pre-1964 period. Subject to the confines of their white core constituencies, they must secure the support of the black population in order to win elections. Within the contexts of the southern states, they are about as far to the left as the political market will bear, and their conservatism is selective in content—it more consistently has to do with defense and social issues than with economic matters. Finally, and perhaps most important, they are the only politicians in America who, with any regularity, enjoy the support of a biracial coalition of blacks and lower-class whites. The new southern Democrats are able to win elections by combining nearly unanimous support among black voters with substantial, but less-than-majority support among white voters (Petrocik 1987).

Racial Conflict in 1984

Democratic presidential candidates who try to secure the southern white vote are frequently aligned too closely with blacks (and with liberals) to be credible political alternatives. While such an appeal may win electoral votes in Massachusetts or Minnesota, it is not well suited to Mississippi or Louisiana. Thus we give particular attention to spatial patterns of racial conflict in the 1984 presidential election. The 1984 election is especially appropriate to our study of racial conflict in presidential politics in view of the record levels of racial polarization present in the national electorate at that time. Race was clearly and crucially related to voting behavior, and it is important to examine whether the significance of race varied in spatially meaningful ways. We make use of CBS–*New York Times* exit poll data obtained from separate state surveys conducted in eighteen states on election day. Three questions naturally arise: Does the level of white Democratic voting vary as a function of black presence in the state-level Democratic electorates? Does the effect of the black presence within the party vary across social class groups within the white population? What are the consequences of these potential patterns of effects for class cleavages within the white population?

In the absence of a more useful measure, we employ self-reported income as an indicator of social class for the white survey respondents. This is probably appropriate given the relatively high levels of voting differences reported between low- and high-income whites for the election. Part A of Figure 3.1 gives the Democratic proportion of the vote among low-income white voters in the 1984 presidential election across 18 states, arrayed by the percentage of the state's Democratic vote that was obtained from blacks. The figure shows a pronounced decrease in the level of support for Walter Mondale among low-income whites as the percentage of blacks in a state's Democratic coalition increased. Part B of the figure gives the Democratic proportion of the vote among high income white voters arrayed by the black percentage of the state's Democratic electorate. Once again, the level of support for Mondale among white voters decreased as the density of blacks among Mondale supporters increased, although the magnitude of the effect is not so pronounced. Putting the two individual-level effects together, we see an important aggregate effect: the political differentiation between white income groups is much greater in low black density states — in states where blacks make up a smaller proportion of the Democratic electorate.

Whites are less likely to vote Democratic if blacks make up a larger proportion of their state's Democratic coalition — if the state party relies more heavily upon black voters. This effect is much more pronounced among low-income whites, who are very likely to vote for Mondale in low black density states. The net effect is that class voting among whites is pronounced

Figure 3.1. Percent voting Democratic in the 1984 presidential election within states by individual income and the racial composition of the state Democratic vote.

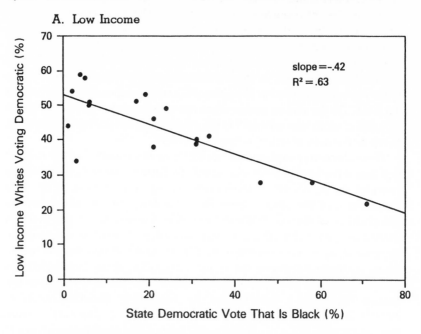

A. Low Income

slope=-.42
R² =.63

State Democratic Vote That Is Black (%)

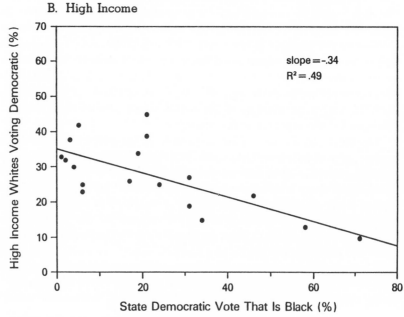

B. High Income

slope=-.34
R² =.49

State Democratic Vote That Is Black (%)

Source: 1984 *New York Times*–CBS state exit polls.

in low black density states but is nearly extinguished in high black density states. In short, race drove out class in some areas in the 1984 election because, where it was relevant, the politics of race took precedence over the politics of class among white voters. Racial conflict was therefore a systematic consequence of the intersection between racial groups and had the predictable effect of undermining class politics.

This argument can be evaluated more rigorously by addressing a series of alternative explanations for these relationships: Is this pattern of effects due to the regional distribution of partisanship and conservatism at the individual level? Do the effects persist when the liberal-conservative environment of states is taken into account? Is the relationship an artifact of South-non-South differences in states' political cultures?

These alternative explanations are addressed by reanalyzing the state exit poll data at the level of individual voters. In Table 3.1 we use a logit model to consider the likelihood of Democratic voting as a function of the racial composition of the state's Democratic coalition, the liberal-conservative composition of the state's white electorate, whether states are southern, individual party identification, and individual liberalism-conservatism. Separate analyses are undertaken for low-income and high-income respondents. As Table 3.1 shows, the racial composition of the Democratic vote within states only produces a satisfactory *t*-value for its effect upon low-income white voters, even though the direction of the effect meets our expectations among high-income white voters as well. The only measures that consistently generate unsatisfactory *t*-values are the dummy variable for whether a state is southern and the proportion of a state's electorate that identifies itself as conservative. The consistent absence of an adequate *t*-value for the southern dummy variable is crucial because it suggests that the racial structuring of partisan politics is perfectly general. It is sometimes more noticeable in the South, not because the South is unique or idiosyncratic, but rather because that region has high concentrations of black citizens. (An alternative specification of the model, which sustains these results, is discussed in the appendix to this chapter.)

Our chief concern lies in the magnitude of the effect due to the racial composition of state level Democratic coalitions after the alternative explanatory factors are taken into account. This concern is best addressed by holding all these additional variables constant at their mean population values while observing the consequence of variations in racial composition of the coalition upon low-income and high-income whites. The procedure yields Figure 3.2, which displays the probability of a Democratic vote among low- and high- income whites as a function of the racial mix in the states' Democratic coalitions. The chief substantive difference between Figure 3.1 and Figure 3.2 is that the latter takes account of these alternative explanations.

As Figure 3.2 clearly shows, none of the alternative explanations serve to

Table 3.1. Logit model for individual vote choice in the 1984 presidential election by individual partisanship, individual liberal-conservatism, state-level liberal-conservatism among whites, South-non-South, and racial composition of the state's Democratic coalition, for low- and high-income white voters (t-values are in parentheses)

$$\text{Mondale vote} = 1/(1 + e^f)$$
$$f = a_0 + a_1X_1 + a_2X_2 + \ldots$$

	Low-income whites	High-income whites
Constant	4.549	6.008
	(7.01)	(7.85)
Individual partisanship	−1.69	−1.76
	(27.87)	(23.16)
Individual liberal-conservatism	−0.72	−1.17
	(11.31)	(13.97)
State conservative proportion	0.0089	−0.020
	(0.49)	(0.94)
South-non-South	−0.348	−0.344
	(1.15)	(0.92)
Racial composition of Democratic party	−0.021	−0.0059
	(5.08)	(1.06)
N	3,400	2,994

Individual partisanship = 1 if Democrat, 2 if Independent, 3 if Republican.
Individual liberal-conservatism = 1 if liberal, 2 if moderate, 3 if conservative.
State conservative proportion = percentage of respondents in the state who called themselves conservative (range = 31-53).
South-non-South = 1 if South, 0 if non-South.
Racial composition of Democratic party = percentage of state Democratic vote that came from blacks (range = 1-71).
Source: 1984 *New York Times*–CBS state exit polls.

diminish the message conveyed by Figure 3.1. Whites are less likely to vote Democratic to the extent that the Democratic party in their state relies upon the votes of blacks. The effect is especially pronounced among lower-income whites. Thus, the level of class voting among whites, measured as the vertical distance between the two probability plots, is virtually extinguished as a function of Democratic reliance upon black voters.

Figure 3.2. Individual probability of voting Democratic in 1984 presidential election as a function of black presence in state level Democratic coalitions, controlling for individual partisanship, individual liberal-conservatism, South/nonSouth, and state level conservative proportion.

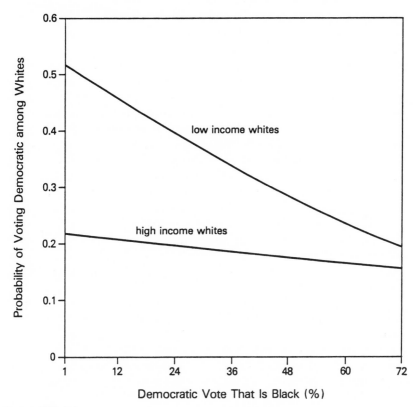

Source: Table 3.1.

Methodological Issues

Some readers may be concerned that an alternative explanation accounts for the relationship shown here. The increased reliance of the Democratic party upon blacks might be explained on the basis of white defections rather than black support. Thus, the observed relationship might be seen as an artifact of the manner in which the black reliance measure is constructed—that is, its magnitude is increased by lower levels of white Democratic support. According to this argument, white defections produce higher levels of black reliance on the part of the Democratic party, rather than higher levels of black reliance producing lower levels of white support.

This alternative explanation is unsatisfactory for several reasons. First, it fails to account for the differential effects of black reliance by the Democratic party among low-income and high-income whites. If the effect is an artifact, why is it stronger among lower-class whites and why does it serve to extinguish class politics? Second, the defection of whites from the party and the consequences of their departure for the further reliance of the party upon blacks are important parts of our argument regarding the racial unraveling of the Democratic party. The effort to recruit blacks serves as the initial stimulus for this unraveling, but the subsequent defection of whites serves to accelerate the process and ultimately leads to racially polarized politics.

As a measurement exercise, it is possible to respecify the model to eliminate this problem. For the 1984 presidential election the proportion of a state's Democratic voters who are black correlates very highly with the proportion of all voters in the state who are black and vote Democratic ($R^2 = .96$). Table 3.2 repeats the logit model of Table 3.1, but the original black reliance measure is replaced with this new measure. The new model yields very comparable results, contingent upon the changing metric of the variables (see also Figure 3.3). More important, the new model is not subject to the same criticism because as white voters switch from Democratic to Republican support, the proportion of all voters who are black and Democratic is unaffected.

Thus, the original results cannot be explained simply on the basis of black steadfastness and white defections. White voters frequently object to the reliance of the Democratic party upon black voters, and at least in 1984, these objections appear to have resulted in varying levels of white support across the states. The original analysis shows this most clearly, but the basic result is sustained when an alternative contextual measure is substituted.

Racial Unraveling: White on White, Black on Black

The group basis of racial conflict is not only the consequence of animosities and conflict between whites and blacks but also a direct result of reinforcement within racial groups. Similarly, the political polarization between whites and blacks is not simply a matter of social relations between whites and blacks but also a matter of social relations within the white and black populations. Interracial animosities thus provide the wedge, while a powerful combination of relations both within and between racial groups produces the unraveling effect that serves to magnify the political consequences of a racially conscious segment of the population.

Evidence for the social interdependence of political behavior within racial groups is widespread and persuasive. People do not arrive at political choices

Table 3.2. Alternative specification of logit model: Individual vote choice in the 1984 presidential election by individual partisanship, individual liberal-conservatism, state level liberal-conservatism among whites, South-non-South, and the black Democratic proportion of the state's electorate, for low- and high-income white voters (*t*-values in parentheses)

Mondale vote $= 1/(1 + e^{-f})$
$$f = a_0 + a_1X_1 + a_2X_2 + \ldots$$

	Low-income whites	High-income whites
Constant	4.78	6.04
	(7.47)	(7.95)
Individual partisanship	−1.69	−1.76
	(28.16)	(23.16)
Individual liberal-conservatism	−0.72	−1.17
	(12.00)	(13.96)
State conservative proportion	0.00076	−0.023
	(0.04)	(1.04)
South-non-South	−0.45	−0.43
	(1.50)	(1.19)
Black Democratic proportion of state electorate	−0.034	−0.0038
	(4.20)	(0.34)
N	3,400	2,994

Individual partisanship = 1 if Democrat, 2 if Independent, 3 if Republican.
Individual liberal-conservatism = 1 if liberal, 2 if moderate, 3 if conservative.
State conservative proportion = percentage of respondents in the state who
    called themselves conservative (range = 31-53).
South-non-South = 1 if South, 0 if non-South.
Black Democratic proportion of state electorate = percentage of state electorate
    that is black and votes Democratic (range = 1-31).
Source: 1984 *New York Times*–CBS state exit polls.

in an isolated manner, just as politics is not the end result of independent acts and judgments. Rather, citizens in a democracy arrive at choices that are socially contingent upon the choices of other citizens. Members of the working class are more likely to vote Democratic if they are surrounded by other workers. Voters are more likely to obtain socially transmitted information with a Democratic bias if they are surrounded by Democrats. More

Figure 3.3. Individual probability of voting Democratic in 1984 presidential election as a function of black Democratic presence in the state electorate, controlling for individual partisanship, individual liberal-conservatism, South/nonSouth, and state level conservative proportion.

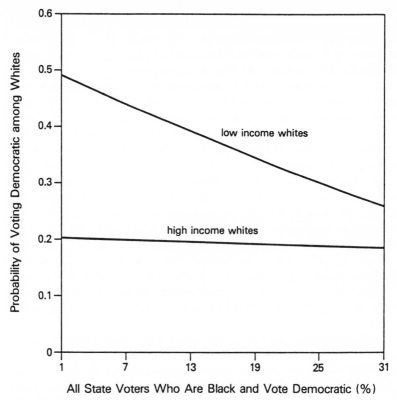

All State Voters Who Are Black and Vote Democratic (%)

Source: Table 3.2.

highly educated citizens are more likely to participate in politics if they live among other more highly educated citizens, while citizens with lower levels of education are more likely to participate in politics if they live among other citizens with lower levels of education. Further examples of interdependence abound, and all point to an inescapable conclusion: the end product of decision making in a democracy is truly collective in nature, not simply because votes are aggregated to determine winners and losers, but also because political activity is group-based and fully subject to processes of social influence (Huckfeldt 1986).

The specific mechanisms of social influence are not easily traced because social influence is diffuse, pervasive, and varied. Social influence in politics is perhaps best understood as a learning process in which people test their judgments against social interaction: some judgments and preferences tend to be reinforced positively and others negatively, with the end result that spatially varied reinforcement schedules produce spatially structured patterns of preferences (Sprague 1982). In practical terms, white Democratic voters in Mississippi had to look long and hard for other whites who agreed with their preference in the 1984 presidential election; as a result, Democratic preferences had a difficult time surviving in such a context.

Other social influence mechanisms can be seen to operate as well, and a relevant example is provided by Heard (1952) in his analysis of the prospects for two-party politics in the South. According to Heard, as a result of social ostracism, political repression, and economic coercion, white southerners who might have supported the Republican party did not do so: "Consider the secretary of the Democratic state committee in one state. He said, quite simply, that he would like to vote Republican. Most Americans who think and live and act as he does are Republicans. The Democratic Party has become, according to him, the party of Negroes, labor, and all the people who can't or won't make a living. They're not his kind. But if he voted Republican once, he says, and even if the Republicans won in that election, he might as well 'turn in his papers' and abandon any ambition for a successful law practice" (1952: 75). In this instance a voter had a clearly articulated preference that was repressed on the basis of a rational calculus: acting on the preference had the potential to produce his own economic demise.

A seminal demonstration of the social interdependence underlying political preferences can be found in the work of Warren Miller (1956). In an analysis of nonsouthern voting behavior he shows that the local political environment has had important consequences for the votes of county residents. The normally expected relationships between the vote and various partisan motivations (party identification, issue positions, candidate evaluations) were less pronounced among people who held a minority preference. "Just as the minority party seldom elects its 'fair share' of candidates for office, so in the phenomenon with which we are concerned the minority fails to receive its 'fair share' of votes if the relative incidence of supporting motivations is used as the criterion of fairness" (Miller 1956: 715). Rather than being resolute and determined in their preferences, minority voters demonstrated less unity and more heterogeneity than the majority. In short, absent a socially supportive environment (Putnam 1966), minority preferences face an uphill struggle if they are to survive (Huckfeldt and Sprague 1988).

Political preferences are not constructed or sustained in a social vacuum;

instead, they depend upon the social support of others who hold the same preferences. Prior to the events of the postwar period it was difficult for Republican preferences to survive among white southerners. Now, in the late 1980s, it has become difficult for Democratic preferences to survive within many segments of the white electorate. In states like Mississippi it has undoubtedly become socially unacceptable for many whites to support the Democratic party.

The Social Magnification of Racial Conflict

How does social interdependence within and between racial groups lead to the unraveling of political coalitions, even when individual level racial antagonisms are of low or moderate intensity? Reconsider the white South and its resistance to the incorporation of blacks within the Democratic party. Assume that 30 percent of all whites are unwilling to vote for a Democratic party that depends upon the support of the black community. Under these circumstances the Democratic party could continue to win elections by maintaining even a minority of white support in combination with the gains it has realized from the enfranchisement of black voters. Perhaps this was the reasoning of Lyndon Johnson and other party strategists prior their embrace of civil rights legislation in the 1960s. While the strategy frequently succeeds at the state level (Petrocik 1987), it has repeatedly failed to win the support of southern states for the Democratic party's presidential ticket.

Now assume that within the white population there is some distribution of levels of willingness to defect from the Democratic party. We know that 30 percent would defect automatically, and let us suppose that, at the other extreme, 10 percent would never defect under any circumstances. The remaining 60 percent are therefore open to persuasion—their willingness to defect depends in part on the weight of white public opinion. Perhaps when 40 percent decide to vote Republican, another 10 percent are persuaded to become Republicans; when 50 percent willingly vote Republican, another 5 percent are persuaded to become Republican, and so on. Further assume that the white voters who make up this middle 60 percent are not only susceptible to the weight of white public opinion, but are hesitant to support a party that is, in their view, excessively dependent upon black support. We might expect that within this population there is some distribution of viewpoints regarding the level of black participation in the coalition that is "excessive." Some will not participate in a Democratic coalition that is more than 40 percent black, others will not participate in a coalition that is more than 50 percent black, and so on. As more whites defect from the Democratic party, however, it is necessarily the case that the party becomes proportionally more dependent upon black votes. Thus we see the possibility of a second dimension to the threshold phenomenon: at a particular level of reliance upon black support, some whites are moved to defect from the party, and when they do so the party becomes more reliant upon black support, causing more whites to defect, and so on.

The end result of such a process depends, of course, upon the particular distribution of levels of willingness, or defection thresholds, within the population (Granovetter 1978; Schelling 1978). The process would reach an equilibrium somewhere between 30-percent and 90-percent Republican, and for present purposes it does not really matter where the equilibrium might lie. There are two important points here. First, the process can only magnify rather than diminish the initial presence of racist impulses in the population. Second, racial polarization need not be solely a product of racism. Some white voters support Republican candidates because they think these candidates are likely to maintain national pride and keep the nation standing tall. Other whites vote Republican because they cannot tolerate a Democratic candidate who appeals to black voters or who shares a podium with a black candidate—for example, Jesse Jackson. Still others vote Republican because they have been socially persuaded to do so. Clearly the more whites who vote Republican for any reason, the more likely other whites are to vote Republican as the result of social influence.

Appendix to Chapter 3

This appendix addresses the specification of the logit model in Table 3.1, and in particular the method for treating the statistical interaction effect between white income levels and Democratic reliance upon black voters. We estimated the model separately for low-income and high-income white voters, and this analysis shows that the effect of black densities in the Democratic party is greater among low-income whites than among high-income whites. The main disadvantage of this procedure is that it fails to consider the effect among moderate-income white voters.

An alternative specification is presented in Table 3.3. In this table a single equation is estimated for the entire white sample. In addition to the variable which measures Democratic reliance upon black voters, the equation also includes the variable which measures white respondent income on a five-point scale, and a variable which measures the multiplicative interaction between white income and the Democratic party's reliance upon black voters. As the table shows, the coefficients for two of the three variables possess *t*-values which inspire confidence. Only the interaction variable produces a marginal *t*-value. More important than *t*-values, when white income levels are held constant at appropriate levels, the model generates probability plots across levels of Democratic reliance upon black voters that closely mirror the plots of Figure 3.2.

Table 3.3. Alternative specification of logit model: Individual vote choice in the 1984 presidential election by individual income, individual partisanship, individual liberal-conservatism, state-level liberal-conservatism among whites, South-non-South, racial composition of the state's Democratic coalition, and interaction between individual income and racial composition of the state's Democratic coalition (*t*-values are in parentheses)

Mondale vote $= 1/(1 + e^{-f})$ $f = a_0 + a_1X_1 + a_2X_2 + \ldots$	
Constant	5.85
	(22.02)
Individual partisanship	−1.64
	(66.37)
Individual liberal-conservatism	−0.90
	(34.20)
State conservative proportion	−0.019
	(2.59)
South-non-South	−0.057
	(0.47)
Income	−0.14
	(6.14)
Racial composition of Democratic party	−0.020
	(7.08)
Interaction variable	0.0011
	(1.27)
N	22,646

Individual income = scale ranging from 1 (low) through 5 (high).
Individual partisanship = 1 if Democrat, 2 if Independent, 3 if Republican.
Individual liberal-conservatism = 1 if liberal, 2 if moderate, 3 if conservative.
State conservative proportion = percentage of respondents in the state who called themselves conservative (range = 31-53).
South-non-South = 1 if South, 0 if non-South.
Racial composition of Democratic party = percentage of state Democratic vote that came from blacks (range = 1-71).
Interaction = racial composition of Democratic party multiplied by individual income.
Source: 1984 *New York Times*–CBS state exit polls.

Finally, we have run the logit model of Table 3.1 separately for all five white income groups. The results show a strong effect for black reliance on the part of the Democratic party that is only diminished in the highest income groups.

4 Postmaterialism and the Politics of Race

The motivating thesis behind our argument is that the role of class in American politics has been traditionally and consistently submerged by the pervasiveness of race in politics and political arrangements. More particularly, the reinvigoration of class in American politics during the presidency of Franklin Roosevelt was undermined when the Democratic party became the vehicle for American black liberation. The increasing significance of race has thus led to the eclipse of class as a major dividing line between American political parties, and thus race, not class, has become the major structural setting for the issues and debates of American politics.

The decline of class in American politics and in the politics of other Western democracies is a widely recognized phenomenon in the postwar period, and many efforts have been made to explain the source of this decline. Our own explanation is sufficiently different from those commonly offered to warrant an examination of the most popular alternative—postindustrialism, the rise of postmaterial values, and the resulting decline of class as the main cleavage in democratic political systems.

The Postindustrialism Thesis

According to the postindustrial society argument, politics and social life have been transformed in many Western democracies by changes in social and economic realities since the end of World War II. Perhaps most important, a basic shift has occurred in the occupational structure of many advanced nations: the industrial work force has stopped growing, or it has actually declined in size, and the service and professional sectors have increased rapidly. These changing structural realities, in turn, have important consequences for the influence of organized labor within advanced nations and even for underlying systems of political values.

Particularly in western Europe, but also in the United States, rising levels of prosperity and a continued freedom from severe economic depression and political turmoil have fostered a new set of postmaterial political values. Especially among the young in these societies, "economic security may be taken for granted, as the supply of water or the air we breathe once could." And thus, for these younger and more privileged age cohorts, "a new set of 'post-bourgeois' values, relating to the need for belonging and to esthetic and intellectual needs, would be more likely to take top priority" (Inglehart 1971: 991–92).

This shifting focus of concern, which has been especially profound among post–World War II age cohorts, is well documented by the work of Ronald Inglehart (1971, 1977, 1981) and others. Most of Inglehart's work compares the value that people place upon four different goals: maintaining order in the nation, giving people more say in important political decisions, fighting rising prices, and protecting freedom of speech. The first and third of these goals are material and acquisitive in nature, while the second and fourth are postmaterial or postbourgeois.

The results of the various analyses are quite impressive. A strong age-cohort effect is present not only in the United States and western Europe but in Japan as well, though different measures are employed in the Japanese context. Younger age cohorts are much more likely to place a higher priority on nonmaterial values. The data are, unfortunately, much less complete for the United States than for the European nations, but there is little reason to expect a strikingly different pattern in North America. As collective memories of political turmoil, severe economic distress, and social dislocation grow faint, individuals turn their attention toward other matters. These other concerns rest upon the assumption of social and economic well-being; hungry stomachs are not inclined to deeply felt concerns regarding freedom of speech.

What are the political consequences of this shift in attention from material to nonmaterial concerns? According to Lipset (1981) it has led to the creation of two lefts in democratic politics. The old left is the material left, concerned with the whole spectrum of social welfare issues so crucial to the relatively disadvantaged in any society: national health insurance, the protection of collective bargaining rights, full employment, and other issues related to the standard of living. The new left takes many of these issues for granted and focuses instead upon quality-of-life issues, such as freedom of speech, women's liberation, abortion rights, and the environment.

Lipset argues that the two lefts are not easily accommodated and reconciled within the same party coalition. Thus, the party of the left is in danger of being fractured, and class-based cohesiveness in electoral politics is undermined. This is especially true to the extent that the old-left agenda has a working-class constituency, and the new-left agenda has a middle-class constituency. Workers will be loathe to support a party that is identified with the new-left agenda, because many new-left issues such as abortion rights are repugnant to value positions widely held in the working class, and others such as the antinuclear movement, are potentially damaging to economic well-being within the working class.

One of the best examples of a fractured left has been unfolding over the past ten years in West Germany. The advent of the Green party has been structured around the new-left agenda, and particularly around environmentalism. The rise of new-left issues, and the rise of the Greens, has in turn produced a political crisis within the Social Democratic party related to a division between those who are sympathetic to the new-left agenda of the Greens and those who would maintain the old-left agenda. The conflict is best symbolized in terms of the nuclear power issue as it has been played out in West Germany and Sweden. To the new left, nuclear power is a symbol of all that is dangerous and evil in modern, technocratic society. To the old left it is a means to cheap energy which will, in turn, generate prosperity and produce more jobs. As Inglehart would predict, conflict over these sorts of new-left agenda items tends to be structured along lines of age, with younger cohorts being more sympathetic to the new-left agenda than older cohorts.

Postindustrialism in the United States

To what extent does the postindustrialism thesis account for the decline of class politics in the United States? It certainly accounts for several widely recognized and recurring problems in the Democratic party. Anyone who has watched a Democratic National Convention on television cannot help but be impressed by the disjuncture between the political constituencies represented by labor leaders on the one hand and by Gloria Steinem on the other. Internal party conflicts such as these are well accommodated by the postindustrialism thesis.

At the same time, this explanation falls short on several counts. The most serious conflict within the Democratic party occurs over black interests. The new-left–old-left dichotomy is largely irrelevant to most blacks because their own agenda includes issues of concern to both. That is, blacks are more likely to be poor, thus they will necessarily focus upon social welfare issues that the new left might take for granted. However, blacks also suffer from entrenched discrimination in American society, and thus the black agenda also focuses upon civil liberties issues more easily accommodated by the new left than by the old left.

Furthermore, the postindustrialism thesis provides a better fit to the experience of advanced European nations than to the experience of the United States. Peculiar features of American politics place severe limitations upon the applicability of this cross-national explanation in the American context. First, while overall levels of affluence are higher in the United States than in advanced European nations, levels of poverty are also higher. At the end of its second century, for many of its citizens, the United States is still an underdeveloped nation. Many Americans still live under corrugated metal roofs, in states with startling levels of illiteracy and appalling infant mortality rates; many others live in urban areas where civil disorder (otherwise known as street crime) turns parts of the city into an uninhabitable "free-fire zone." The United States is not Sweden, and large portions of the U.S. population have not emerged into the warm glow of postindustrial affluence. The American experience certainly has parallels to the experience of other advanced Western nations, but it also shares much in common with the experience of underdeveloped nations—high rates of crime, poverty, infant mortality, and so on.

Second, a large portion of the American working class is either unemployed or underemployed, and another large segment fears this fate. Current low levels of reported unemployment should not deceive the astute observer. The definition of unemployment has been modified so that these currently "low" levels are actually quite high when measured by traditional yardsticks. Furthermore, while unemployment *has* decreased since the early 1980s, many of the most lucrative working class jobs are gone forever, with many more under threat of extinction. Just as important, the loss of a job is not buffered by an extensive system of retraining, financial support, and reintegration into the labor force. Therefore, losing a good job often spells calamity for the victim. When unemployment levels rise in the advanced nations of western Europe (as is currently the case in West Germany, for example), a more extensive social welfare system protects the unemployed from the more disastrous consequences of job loss.

Third, a series of persuasive studies have called into question the standard wisdom regarding the relationship between affluence and working-class consciousness. In response to the pop suburbanization literature of the 1950s, which asserted that suburbanized workers were being transformed into Republicans, a horde of investigators descended upon affluent working-class communities in an effort to learn whether the new wealth served to undermine the old class consciousness. It was generally found that affluence alone did not turn workers against their class, and thus the "embourgeoisement" thesis was discounted (see Berger [1960] and Goldthorpe et al. [1968]; for a reinterpretation see Huckfeldt [1986]).

Fourth, an important part of the postindustrialism argument rests upon the relative decline of industrial jobs in the economy and the concomitant rise in service-sector jobs within the overall occupational structure. But the decline of the Democratic party has not occurred simply because the working class has been outnumbered. Rather, it has occurred because the working class has lacked cohesion, even when offered the opportunity to vote for an old-left candidate of organized labor. In the 1984 presidential election, the leadership of organized labor vigorously supported its endorsed candidate, Walter Mondale, and the rank and file barely gave Mondale a majority of their vote. In its own defense, the labor leadership pointed out that this level of support compared favorably to the support obtained from the population at large. That was small consolation in view of the fact that labor invested all its political resources in a very solid prolabor candidate, while Ronald Reagan, during his first term as president, dealt with the union movement in an aggressive and belligerent fashion.

Fifth, many of the new jobs in the expanding service sector are warmed-over assembly-line jobs. Operating a computer terminal in a parts warehouse is not much different from operating a drill press, and working in a fast-food stand is not much different from sweeping factory floors. A variety of factors make it difficult to unionize these positions, but many of these jobs share much in common with the old, nonunionized working-class jobs: low skill, vulnerability to economic fluctuations, close control by a supervisor, unrewarding activities, low pay. In short, even for many in the new postindustrial order, the warm glow of affluence has yet to appear. Many of the new postindustrial jobs are lower-middle-class occcupations with low levels of benefits and pay, and the people occupying these positions should be receptive to a party that represents lower-class interests.

Revealing light is cast on this problem by Ginzberg (1979: 31–39), who makes several crucial points regarding postwar changes in the American occupational structure: (1) Rapid growth in the American working-age population was matched by equally rapid growth in employment opportunities provided by the American economy. (2) Much of the growth in the labor force was due to the entry of women into the job market. (3) Throughout this period unemployment remained at high levels because new jobs were occupied by new entries into the labor force, many of whom were married women and young people reaching working age. (4) Many of the new jobs were bad jobs or poor jobs — jobs in the service sector with lower salary and benefit levels. (5) The concentration of bad jobs among newly created jobs was especially high in the private sector, where Ginzberg estimates that two-and-a-half times as many poor jobs were created as good ones.

Given this bleak picture, why have we not seen greater labor militancy, particularly among workers in the service sector? According to Ginzberg:

> The most plausible answer is that most of the new jobholders were "secondary" workers, whose earnings supplemented the income of the family's principal breadwinner. Of the 28 million individuals added to the employed work force between 1950 and 1976, by far the largest category — about 12 million — consisted of married women whose husbands were employed and living at home. A second large increase, amounting to 5.9 million, took place among single people, for the most part young, many of whom were still in school and therefore content with less than full-time work. About 10 million of the 28

million new jobholders were heads of households: 6 million men with nonworking wives and 4 million men or women who shouldered family responsibilities without spouses. (1979:39)

Postwar employment growth in the private sector cannot be given credit for the increase in postwar affluence. Instead, two factors are largely responsible. First, the public sector has created a great many good jobs—jobs with high salary and benefit levels. Second, people who did not traditionally work have now entered the labor force. Most often this means married women, but not the chic, liberated, upper-middle-class women of the Virginia Slims' commercials. Rather, significant growth has occurred among the women who populate the enlarged service sector in a wide range of less-rewarding positions. In simple terms, so-called middle-class affluence is typically the result of two-wage-earner families, and postwar affluence is often achieved on the back of two salaries, at least one of which is likely to come from a bad job. The price of postwar affluence has been the restructuring of the American family and the economic mobilization of American women, frequently into substandard employment.

We do not argue that workers were better off in the 1920s than they are in the 1980s. Neither do we argue that there is still fire in the belly of American labor. The working class is more affluent today than ever, even if that affluence is increasingly endangered and built upon an edifice of two wage earners with one-and-a-half incomes. The fire in the belly of organized labor has certainly been extinguished, but it was not put out by the wonders of affluence, the presence of which does not really go very far in explaining political complacency. Rather, we look toward race as the responsible factor.

Race and Postmaterial Values

Important changes have occurred in American political values, and these changes are most profound within the political left. Furthermore, changes associated with a postindustrial society have important and far-reaching consequences for contemporary American politics, but their significance must be seen within the context of racial conflict. Thus, several questions immediately arise: What are the effects of race and class upon postmaterial values in the United States? What is the effect of these values upon partisan choice in American elections? How does the rise of postmaterial values intersect with the rise of race to undermine the New Deal (class) basis of the Democratic party?

The relationship of postmaterial values to electoral politics is considered using 1972 and 1976 data from the National Election Studies conducted by the Center for Political Studies. The analysis is based upon Inglehart's previously described index, which included two material and two nonmaterial political goals. Respondents were asked which of the four goals is most important and which is second in importance. Respondents who chose two postmaterial goals were categorized as postmaterialist, those who chose two material goals were categorized as materialist, and the nonmissing remainder was categorized as mixed.

Table 4.1. The percentage of respondents who held various political values, by race and occupational class, in 1972 and 1976

1972	Whites	Blacks	Professional-managerial	Clerical-service-sales	Working class
Post-materialist	9	8	14	9	8
Mixed	55	64	55	53	55
Materialist	36	28	31	38	38
N	924	96	299	191	406
1976					
Post-materialist	10	9	13	10	8
Mixed	59	61	58	58	61
Materialist	31	30	29	31	31
N	1,629	149	541	371	662

Source: 1972 and 1976 National Election Studies (unweighted).

As Table 4.1 shows, there is virtually no difference across either race or class groupings in terms of postmaterial values in the 1976 election. However, slight differences do appear in the 1972 data. The working class was somewhat more likely to hold material values than either the clerical-service-sales or professional-managerial occupational categories. Similarly, whites were somewhat more likely than blacks to hold material values. A logit analysis, not shown here, sustains these results when simultaneous consideration is given to several factors: occupational class, age, race, and (in 1972) attitudes about Vietnam troop withdrawal. The only factor that consistently shows a statistically discernible effect is age: older people were consistently more likely to hold materialist values across the two elections. According to these measures, then, postmaterial values are not explained by either race or class. Rather, they add another layer of attitudinal structure upon an electorate already structured by race and class. Because the attitudes are heterogeneous within both racial and class groupings, they have the potential to fracture class-based and even racially based coalitions. This is not likely to occur among blacks, given their close ties to the Democratic party, but it might happen more readily among whites and within both class groupings.

The elections of 1972 and 1976 provide an excellent opportunity to assess the role of postmaterial values upon American electoral politics. These two elections presented distinctly different sets of alternatives to the American voter. George McGovern was widely perceived to be a candidate of the new left within the Democratic party, while Jimmy Carter's candidacy was perceived as being much closer to the traditional New Deal coalition. This is not to say that either candidate was correctly perceived, only that they appealed to very different elements of the party.

Table 4.2 shows the relationship between post-material values and vote choice in the two elections, expressed as the percentage of two-party voters who cast a Republican ballot. The table clearly shows that postmaterial values were related to vote choice in 1972, but not in 1976. In 1972 voters who held postmaterial values were much less likely to vote for Nixon, while in 1976 there was virtually no difference in the votes cast by those who held different sets of values. Further analyses not shown here used a logit model to test these relationships while controlling for multiple individual characteristics: age, occupational class, race, and attitudes about Vietnam troop withdrawal in 1972. Even when individual controls are introduced, postmaterial values are related to the vote in 1972 but not in 1976.

Table 4.2. Percentage of likely voters[a] who voted for the Republican presidential candidate in 1972 and 1976, by political values

	Materialist	Mixed	Postmaterialist
1972 (Nixon)	70	61	38
N	262	397	79
1976 (Ford)	47	46	48
N	404	794	129

[a]Likely voters may have not voted, but on the basis of pre-election interviews, they were thought to be considering whether or not to vote.
Source: 1972 and 1976 National Election Studies (unweighted).

These results indicate that a particular candidate pairing (McGovern vs. Nixon) in a particular political environment—characterized in this instance by "acid, amnesty, abortion," and the Vietnam War—can lead to significant polarization between those holding material and postmaterial values. Clearly there was also conflict between new-left and old-left visions of the Democratic party. The depth of the internal party conflict between these two visions in 1972 is well demonstrated by Miller, Miller, Raine, and Brown (1976), who have shown that internal dissension within the normally Democratic electorate succeeded in at least temporarily driving a wedge between old-left and new-left constituencies. The collision between these differing agendas disintegrated the Democratic coalition in 1972, greatly diminishing the level of class voting within the electorate. Indeed, the disaffection of the working class from McGovern in 1972 led to the lowest recorded level of class voting within the electorate during the postwar period (see Figure 1.1). While the power of this old left–new left split is certainly impressive, the speed with which the old coalition recovered is impressive as well. Four years later, when the Republican and Democratic candidates were virtually indistinguishable on new-left issues such as abortion and the ERA, the salience of postmaterial values completely disappeared. As a result, the Democratic party was not torn in two, and class voting was reinvigorated. While the new left political agenda still has the potential to fracture the Democratic party, such a fracture is certainly not inevitable. After splitting the party and losing in a landslide characterized by nonexistent levels of class voting in 1972, the Democrats were able to put together an admittedly inexact replica of the traditional party appeal which reinvigorated the class basis of politics and led to a narrow Democratic victory in 1976.

Race and the New-Left Agenda

The importance of the new left–old left division within the Democratic party must be seen within the larger issues of race and class in American politics. First, the black agenda intersects with both left agendas, even though it is also separate and distinct from both. Because blacks are disproportionately disadvantaged, their interests are intimately tied up with the old left, materialist agenda of the Democratic party. However, other sets of black concerns, such as affirmative action, equal rights, and so on, are not easily accommodated by the old-left constituencies.

Similarly, the black agenda has much in common with the new-left agenda in terms of equality and civil rights, but the match is less than perfect. Finally, fundamentally, new-left concerns are the concerns of economically secure citizens and tend to overlook the needs and aspirations of the disadvantaged. Furthermore, many blacks are not sympathetic to major elements of this agenda. Abortion rights have never become a popular issue within the black community, and women's liberation among blacks often signifies a different set of issues and concerns than those supported by the white (middle class) women's liberation movement.

The Democrats' dilemma can be seen as the difficult, perhaps impossible task of trying to accommodate three only partially overlapping constituencies: blacks, the white old left, and the white new left. Assuming that black support is crucial to electoral success, the party probably has one of two alternatives: it must put together either a new-left appeal with black support, or an old-left appeal with black support.

The first option, combining new-left whites with blacks has been carefully studied in the context of city politics by Browning, Marshall, and Tabb (1984, 1986). Their argument is simple. The best hope of black incorporation within the political structure rests upon the possibility of a coalition of blacks with white liberals. The most notable example they found of such a strategy was in Berkeley, California. In a fascinating symposium a group of scholars examined the thesis relative to the experience of major American cities (Browning et al. 1986). Interestingly, none of the authors discuss the implicit displacement of class-based electoral conflict as a viable alternative. Rather, it is taken as a given that blacks and disadvantaged whites cannot successfully participate in the same coalition. Perhaps this is true, but it produces an unlikely coalition of interests in American politics. Blacks are mostly disadvantaged and liberal whites are mostly affluent. Thus it would appear that the glue holding such a coalition together must be altruism on the part of white liberals. We are led, unwillingly, back to some variation of the unsatisfactory conclusion offered by Banfield and Wilson (1963): namely, must we rely upon the public-spirited ethos of the white middle class for the realization of the public good?

Actually, at least at the local level, there are reasons to expect that material interests may in part explain the coalition between the white liberal middle class and the black population. Urban political conflict ultimately revolves around issues of space and location and public facilities, and these are the issues that so often keep disadvantaged whites and blacks apart in local politics—the unwillingness of disadvantaged whites to share public services and living space with blacks is well documented. Upper-middle-class white liberals can often afford to be altruistic because they do not experience the same sort of threat.

The factors that make black coalitions with white liberals possible at the local level do not necessarily exist on the national level. First, at the national level the threat of shared living space becomes less relevant, and thus threat and self-interest do not necessarily propel blacks and middle-class liberal whites into the same coalitions. Second, and even more important, the density of liberals in Berkeley, for example, is higher than the density of liberals in the country as a whole. As George McGovern found out in 1972, a coalition between blacks and new-left whites does not win presidential elections. It is not entirely clear that blacks are enthusiastic over such a coalition, but even if they were, the size of the white liberal population is simply insufficient to make such a coalition successful in national politics.

The second option, a coalition between blacks and working-class–lower-middle-class whites, would seem to hold out more hope of success, simply because there are no inherent *class* tensions within such a coalition. The problem, of course, is that of *racial* tension. Populists since Tom Watson have looked longingly toward a coalition between whites and blacks based on common economic interests and concerns. The difficulty has always been, and continues to be, racial animosity and competition among the disadvantaged.

The problems inherent in putting together a coalition of blacks and lower-class whites has repeatedly surfaced in American politics and will be discussed further in Chapter 5. Suffice it to say that it is often tempting for Democratic party politicians to take the first option and pursue a coalition of blacks and liberal whites. But as enticing as such an option might seem, it does not win national elections. The old left is failing in several advanced European nations, in part because affluence and material security have undermined the natural constituency for materialistic politics. Perhaps ironically, America may have an adequate constituency of voters to sustain a coalition based upon the materialist agenda and to win elections on that basis. The American problem is not a shortage of disadvantaged voters, or at least not a shortage of voters who feel the hot breath of economic deprivation. Rather, the problem of the old left in America is that it combines two sets of voters who have historically had great difficulty participating within the same political coalition: blacks and lower-class whites.

5 Populism, Class, and Biracial Politics

> The key to building any new majority in American politics is a
> coalition of self-interest between blacks and low- and moderate-
> income whites; the real division in this country is not between
> generations, or between races, but between the rich who have power
> and those blacks and whites who have neither power nor property.
> Newfield and Greenfield, (1972: 9)

The populist analysis of politics is an old one that echoes through the years of American electoral politics. The heroes and patron saints of the populist tradition trace at least to Andrew Jackson, if not to the great Thomas Jefferson himself. The tradition extends through the history of the republic to include names as diverse as Tom Watson, William Jennings Bryan, Franklin Roosevelt, Harry Truman, Huey Long, Robert Kennedy, George Wallace, and Jimmy Carter. Two features of populism are especially important to our analysis. First, populism is fundamentally rooted in the politics of class, comprising the distinctively American effort to bring considerations of class to bear on the political process. Second, at least since the Civil War, populist movements and candidates have been vulnerable to the disintegrative effects of race upon lower-class coalitions.

At the outset it is important to emphasize that the populist tradition in America is politically variegated and culturally diverse. It includes race baiters, patronizing upper-class advocates for the disadvantaged, a few genuine political heroes and heroines, and more than a few scurrilous demagogues. Nonetheless, it is impossible to talk about the role of class in American politics without addressing the role of populism. Indeed, class has never been successfully introduced into the political process in this country without a populist appeal. It is possible to conceive of a class-based political movement that does not rest upon a populist appeal. Such movements in Europe have roots that often extend deep into national histories, with appeals that are articulated in the vocabulary of Marxism.

In the United States, however, American populism rests upon a curious amalgam of common interests among disadvantaged groups and a cultural heritage that extols the virtues of common people in American social life. Populism combines American democratic symbols with lower-class self-interest. In view of this fact, it is curious that the popular press and most political commentators have successfully painted populist appeals in such a bad light. The words "populist" and "demagogue" are spoken in tandem so often that they finally appear to be part of the same phenomenon. Indeed, part of our effort here is to help reestablish the acceptability of class-based politics and populism as part of the American political vocabulary.

The real enemy of populism and class-based politics has not been a middle-class press but a deep racial fissure within the natural constituency of the populist appeal. We begin this chapter by giving special attention to the demise of populism in the post–Reconstruction South before turning to the difficulties of class-based politics in the post–World War II era.

Populists, Bourbons, and Blacks

Blacks in the post–Reconstruction South were presented with at least two political options: join in a political coalition with the conservative, upper-class Bourbons or join in a coalition with the radical, lower-class populists. The advent of Jim Crow legislation and black disenfranchisement at the turn of the century removed even these options for blacks. This brief interlude in southern political history between the end of Reconstruction and the rise of Jim Crow is interesting, however, because it places the difficulties of racial politics in bold relief.

At first consideration the political affinity of blacks and poor whites seems obvious. Both occupied similar economic roles in a system that favored the few over the many. Both were tied to the land in ways that were almost feudal in terms of economic relationships. Finally, both were the victims of severe poverty and extreme material hardship.

In many instances, poor Southern whites were conscious of their disadvantaged status and resentful toward the power and influence of the Bourbon elite. The solid, white Democratic South was built upon a white population that was characterized by class cleavage, hard feelings, economic discontent, and political animosity. This theme, the class basis of southern white society, is documented again and again by analyses of southern politics. Key's (1949) examination of Mississippi politics underscores the fracture between the poverty of the hills and the affluence of the delta and illustrates the manner in which this great divide gave rise to race baiting, Bilbo-style politics. Williams's (1969) analysis of Huey Long emphasizes the politics of class in the political cleavage between the Long faction and the anti-Longs: the controversial senator may have been assassinated by a madman, but that madman viewed Long as a class enemy. Indeed, even interviews with veterans of the Confederate army yield strong evidence of important class cleavages among white southerners (Bailey 1985).

Any analysis of southern politics that ignores the important class cleavages within the white population of the South thus also ignores a crucial ingredient in the region's complex political structure (Gaither 1977). The only cleavage more important within the rigidly stratified Southern social structure was the great divide of race, and abundant evidence suggests that the racial fissure was most complete between blacks and lower-status whites.

The animosity between poor whites and blacks during this period was both economically and socially based. Not unlike lower-class and working-class populations elsewhere, lower-class whites in the South were exposed to economic competition from a new group of social outcasts — recently emancipated southern blacks. Not surprisingly, they often reacted in an aggressive, violent fashion to the source of competition. For example, in 1909 the Georgia Railroad began hiring black firemen at a lower rate of pay, leading to a strike by eighty white firemen who were members of the Brotherhood of Locomotive Firemen and Enginemen. The strike inflamed passions, generated mob violence, and led to the complete halt of railroad service by the company (Matthews 1974).

The economic and social bases for the animosity were inextricably tied together. Indeed, had the railroad workers allowed blacks into the union, they might have avoided such difficulties altogether. As Woodward (1966:50) shows, the impetus for Jim Crow came not from upper-class whites but from lower-class whites who felt threatened by the presence of blacks sharing public facilities. In view of the heightened sense of racial hostility felt by lower-class whites, and in view of the repeated acts of violence committed by lower-class whites against blacks, it was not surprising that the seemingly natural coalition between blacks and whites failed to materialize. Certainly, long-term economic rationality should have led to a lower-class coalition between whites and blacks, but lower-class whites were not acting on the basis of any long-term rational calculus.

Given this level of racial animosity, blacks faced threats that extended far beyond matters of class concern. According to Chafe (1968:418), the populist movement failed to incorporate blacks because economic interests alone did not guide black choices:

Negroes and whites had different perceptions of reality and therefore different perceptions of self-interest. The primary concern of the white person was economic . . . . The primary concerns of the Negro, on the other hand, were prejudice and violence. He sought security, stability, and status from the white community, things which in the past the rich and well-born had been more willing to give than the poor. It was not in the Negro's self-interest to attack a class that had traditionally befriended him. It was in his self-interest, however, to seek protection and security wherever he could find them.

In the words of Woodward (1966:51), it was not "sentimentality for 'Ole Marster'" that encouraged blacks to choose a coalition with the Bourbons rather than the populists but "the hot breath of cracker fanaticism they felt on the back of their necks."

Conditions in the late nineteenth century were ripe for a political coalition between blacks and poor whites, but the disintegrative effects of race undermined this potential. Tom Watson, the great Georgia populist, began his political career as an advocate of political freedom for blacks as well as a lower-class biracial coalition. By the end of his career, frustrated with his inability to combine blacks and poor whites into a political movement based upon common self-interest, Watson became a rabid race baiter. His solution, which was inevitably adopted, was to remove blacks from politics altogether. His unfulfilled hope was that politics might focus upon economics and class rather than race once blacks were absent from the political process. So long as blacks were disenfranchised, they could not occupy a strategic position with respect to the conflicts within the white population. But the same institutionalized machinery that removed blacks from politics also proved injurious to the political interests of lower-class whites.

Class Politics in the Postwar South

For the first half of the twentieth century, class was submerged in the one-party South because there was no partisan vehicle for class conflict. So long as everyone voted Democratic there could be no partisan differentiation along class lines. This is not to say that class never made itself felt in southern politics. Key (1949) shows that the politics of class was expressed repeatedly within the internal factional politics of the Democratic party in the southern states. With respect to *national* politics, however, the South served as an impediment to the development of class-based coalitions because, at least in congressional and presidential elections, all southerners were Democrats.

For a time in the early part of the century, the Republican party had tried to construct a southern coalition that incorporated blacks and conservative whites. The dismal failure of this experiment was proof to many that blacks simply could not be included in the politics of the South, or perhaps in the politics of the nation. White voters simply would not tolerate it.

All that began to change in the aftermath of World War II, however. Roosevelt's Democratic party (as well as Truman's) was fundamentally a party with a class-based appeal, and in the end the southern wing of the party had to address that new reality. In predicting the revival of two-party politics in the South, Alexander Heard (1952: 226) rightly pointed toward the crucial role played by blacks: "It was not merely that the new Negro voters held out a danger as well as a hope to any party that claimed them, as Republican history had demonstrated. They also stood to strengthen the lower reaches of Democratic voters and in the long run would contribute to the fundamental reconstitution of the southern Democratic party that would in turn revitalize its opposition."

The uneasy coalition of blacks and Bourbons had always been rooted in paternalism, but the Democratic coalition of Roosevelt and Truman was ultimately incongruous with such a relationship. The New Deal and the Fair Deal were about collective bargaining *rights* for unions, social security as a *right* of citizens, economic regulation as an *obligation* of government. In short, the new Democratic party was not about charitable attitudes toward social inferiors. It was the stuff of rights, obligations, and the egalitarian treatment of citizens as a matter of course in democratic politics. Thus, while there was little room for the Bourbon in the new Democratic party, the larger question was: could the party accommodate both blacks and lower-status whites?

Class and Race in the Postwar South

At the time of Heard's (1952) postwar analysis, the Republican party was on the rise in urban areas across the South, and as he predicted, the class-based cleavage in southern society was being reorganized along partisan lines. At the same time, however, blacks began to emerge in southern politics. Particularly after the landmark civil rights legislation of the 1960s, blacks became active participants in democratic politics. Thus the postwar South offers a unique opportunity to analyze the vulnerability of lower-class biracial coalitions to the disintegrative effects of race.

Our analysis of postwar coalition evolution in the south makes use of data compiled by Bartley and Graham (1978) that include election returns for twenty-four southern cities from 1948 through 1972. We omit the 1948 presidential election returns for several reasons: returns are unavailable for many of the cities, and when available they are often not helpful; the national Democratic ticket did not appear on the ballot in Alabama and in several other states the national ticket had to compete against Strom Thurmond and the Dixiecrats, as well as Thomas Dewey and the Republicans. These factors combine to make the 1948 presidential election very difficult to analyze in conjunction with the rest of the period, even though that election is a dramatic illustration of the problems encountered by the new Democratic party in the South.

Bartley and Graham provide voting percentages and numbers of reported votes for each election in each city. These voting data are reported for five categories of precincts—all black precincts, and four categories of white precincts as precinct social status varies from low to high. The white precincts are divided into categories on the basis of socioeconomic status (SES) quartiles using census data, with equal weight assigned to median family income, median house value, and median years of education. Whenever any precinct could not be classified according to race, or whenever any white precinct could not be classified according to status, that precinct was omitted from the analysis. (The cities included in the data set, along with the presidential election years available for each city, are in Table 5.1.)

Table 5.1. Cities included in the southern cities data set, with presidential elections

Montgomery, Ala. (1952–68)	Greensboro, N.C. (1952–68)
Birmingham, Ala. (1952–68)	Charlotte, N.C. (1960–72)
Little Rock, Ark. (1952–68)	Charleston, S.C. (1952–72)
Miami, Fla. (1952–72)	Columbia, S.C. (1952–72)
Jacksonville, Fla. (1952–72)	Nashville, Tenn. (1956–72)
Atlanta, Ga. (1952–72)	Memphis, Tenn. (1960–72)
Macon, Ga. (1952–72)	Fort Worth, Tex. (1952–72)
Baton Rouge, La. (1952–72)	Houston, Tex. (1960–68)
New Orleans, La. (1952–72)	Waco, Tex. (1952–72)
Shreveport, La. (1952–72)	Norfolk, Va. (1952–68)
Jackson, Miss. (1956–68)	Richmond, Va. (1952–68)
Raleigh, N.C. (1952–68)	Roanoke, Va. (1952–68)

Source: Bartley and Graham (1978)

As Figure 5.1 shows, class voting among whites was readily apparent in the 1952 election. The Democratic proportion of the vote in low-status white precincts was considerably higher than the Democratic proportion of the vote in high-status white precincts. Subsequently, during the 1950s and 1960s, the level of Democratic support in both high-status and low-status white precincts declined, but it declined most rapidly in the low-status white precincts. As a consequence, the level of class voting is very nearly extinguished by the end of the period. At the same time that white support for the Democratic party was deteriorating, the Democrats' reliance upon *black* support was increasing. As Figure 5.1 also shows, the average proportion of Democratic votes coming from black precincts went from barely more than 10 percent in 1956 to approximately 50 percent in 1968. This increased reliance upon black voters was a result of the declining rate of white support,

Figure 5.1. Class and race in twenty-four southern cities from 1952–72, for presidential elections.

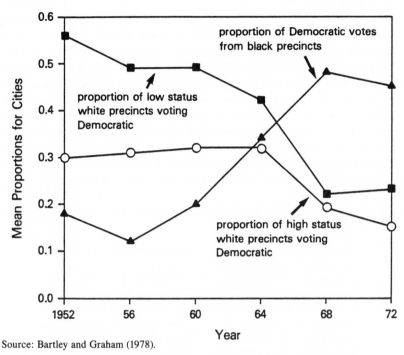

Source: Bartley and Graham (1978).

the increasing rate of black support, and the rapidly increasing *number* of black voters during the 1960s.

Thus it is important to emphasize that the increased reliance of the Democratic coalition upon black voters was not simply an artifact of white defections from the party. As the Democratic party mobilized black voters in the 1960s, it necessarily became more dependent upon black votes quite independently of white voter behavior. Indeed, Democratic reliance upon black voters has regularly increased in both ways—as a result both of defecting whites, and of mobilization efforts among blacks. To reiterate our earlier argument, an unraveling process often results: As the Democratic party mobilizes black voters the party becomes more dependent upon black support causing many whites to leave the party. When whites defect, the Democratic coalition becomes still more dependent upon black votes, resulting in more white defections, and on it goes.

Once again, the election of 1964 looms large. It was in this year that Democratic reliance upon blacks began increasing rapidly, and it was also in 1964 that class voting, as well as overall white support for the Democrats, began decreasing rapidly. (For discussions of the crucial role of 1964 see:

Carmines and Stimson, 1989). This same pattern is sustained when we look at two individual cities, Atlanta and New Orleans, in Table 5.2. As before, the 1960-68 period is the watershed in which class voting among whites nearly disappeared and the Democrats become reliant upon black votes.

Table 5.2. Democratic proportion of the presidential vote in low-status and high-status white precincts by the proportion of the Democratic vote coming from black precincts, for Atlanta and New Orleans, 1952-72

	Low-status white precincts	High-status white precincts	Vote coming from black precincts
NEW ORLEANS			
1952	.51	.27	.32
1956	.45	.27	.16
1960	.64	.40	.12
1964	.43	.33	.30
1968	.21	.17	.45
1972	.19	.17	.48
ATLANTA			
1952	.76	.36	.16
1956	.76	.46	.04
1960	.64	.40	.18
1964	.42	.45	.46
1968	.19	.32	.50
1972	.17	.19	.58

Source: Southern cities data (Bartley and Graham 1978).

White Participation in a Blackening Coalition

Rather than considering the manner in which the significance of class and race change through time, in this section we demonstrate the manner in which class is driven out as a function of race. Figure 5.2 plots the Democratic vote proportion in a city's low-status white precincts as a function of Democratic reliance upon black votes within that city. Democratic reliance on black support is measured as the proportion of all Democratic votes coming from black precincts for each city in each election. Thus the horizontal axis measures the reliance of each city's Democratic coalition upon votes from the black community. Each point in the scatterplot of Figure 5.2 represents the low-status white precincts in a particular city for a particular election. Figure 5.3 is the same scatterplot for high-status white precincts. The lines drawn diagonally through the plots are the least squares

Figure 5.2. Democratic voting in low status white precincts as a function of black presence in the Democratic coalitions, for 24 southern cities, 1952–72.

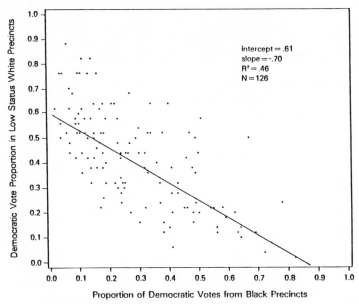

Source: Bartley and Graham (1978).

Figure 5.3. Democratic voting in high status white precincts as a function of black presence in the Democratic coalitions, for 24 southern cities, 1952–72.

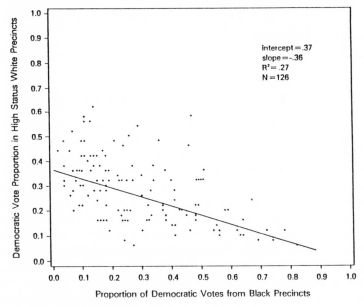

Source: Bartley and Graham (1978).

lines fitted to the plots. Both figures show that white Democratic support declines as a function of increased Democratic reliance upon black support, with the effect being most pronounced in low-status white precincts. Thus, these figures sustain an argument that race was driving out class in southern cities during the postwar period.

Figures 5.2 and 5.3 demonstrate that these two time-ordered trends are closely related, but a more rigorous test of our argument is to examine each relationship in the absence of the trends. The trend in each time series is readily removed by taking first-order differences for each series: that is, rather than examining the level of Democratic support in lower-status white precincts, we examine election-to-election changes in this support; and rather than examining Democratic reliance upon voters from black precincts, we examine election-to-election changes in that reliance. The results of the two different analyses are presented in Table 5.3. The left-hand column gives the results of a least squares regression of Democratic reliance upon black votes on the proportion of white voters who voted Democratic. (These least squares lines are drawn in on Figures 5.2 and 5.3). The right-hand column gives the same results for the differenced data. Part A of the table reports the analysis for low-status white precincts, and Part B reports the analysis higher-status white precincts. The *n*-size for the right-hand column is reduced because one observation in time is lost for each city due to differencing.

Table 5.3. Democratic proportion of the presidential vote in low-status and high-status white precincts by the proportion of the Democratic vote coming from black precincts, for twenty-four southern cities, 1952-72 (*t*-values are in parentheses)

	Original data	Differenced data
A. Low-status white precincts		
Intercept	0.61	−0.06
	(26.36)	(3.79)
Slope	−0.70	−0.34
	(10.44)	(3.41)
R^2	0.46	0.10
N	126	102
B. High-status white precincts		
Intercept	0.37	−0.02
	(20.66)	(1.86)
Slope	−0.36	−0.17
	(6.81)	(2.70)
R^2	0.27	0.07
N	126	102

Source: Southern cities data (Bartley and Graham 1978).

The analysis of the differenced data supports the analysis of the original data. As would be expected, fit is reduced from the original to the differenced data, but the magnitude difference for the coefficients and the direction of coefficient signs are both maintained. Once again, the effect of a blackening coalition is almost twice as pronounced upon lower-status whites as it is upon higher-status whites, and thus the net effect of black participation in the coalition is to reduce white support, as well as the level of class voting.

A more direct test of the effects that black participation has upon class voting among whites can be obtained by constructing a summary measure of class voting. We arrive at such a measure by subtracting the proportion of Democratic voters in higher-status white precincts from the proportion of Democratic voters in lower-status white precincts. Thus, higher positive numbers indicate higher levels of class voting and negative numbers indicate an inversion of class voting where higher-status voters are more likely to vote Democratic. This is graphically demonstrated in Figure 5.4, as each point on the scatterplot represents the level of class voting relative to Democratic reliance upon black votes within a particular city at a particular election. The pattern is again clear: class voting declines as a direct function of black presence in the Democratic party coalition. Table 5.4 provides the regression results for this analysis, using both the original data and the differenced data.

Figure 5.4. Class structure of white Democratic voting as a function of black presence in the Democratic coalition, for 24 southern cities, 1952–72.

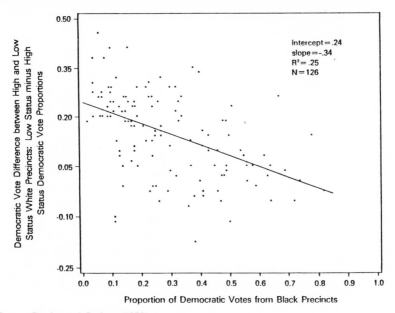

Source: Bartley and Graham (1978).

As before, the measures of fit are less impressive for the differenced data, but the direction of the slope coefficient is sustained, as is an adequate t-value for the slope coefficient.

Table 5.4. Democratic proportion of the presidential vote in low-status white precincts minus the Democratic proportion in high-status white precincts by the proportion of the Democratic vote coming from black precincts, for twenty-four southern cities, 1952-72 (t-values in parentheses)

	Original data	Differenced data
Intercept	0.24	−0.04
	(12.94)	(3.29)
Slope	−0.34	−0.16
	(6.48)	(2.11)
R^2	0.25	0.04
N	126	102

Source: Southern cities data (Bartley and Graham 1978).

These results suggest that two party politics structured along class lines was emerging in southern urban areas at the beginning of the 1950s. But the full emergence of class based politics was aborted by the mobilization of the black population. Quite simply, the Democratic party was not big enough to accommodate both blacks and whites. Racial hostility, particularly on the part of lower-status whites, meant that race served to splinter the Democratic coalition.

Methodological Issues

Some readers may be concerned about the construction of the black reliance measure, arguing that the increased reliance of the Democratic party upon blacks is explained by white defections rather than by increased levels of black support. Several factors stand in the way of accepting this argument. First, the argument fails to account for the class-based differential effects among whites of the Democratic party's reliance upon black voters. If the relationship is an artifact of construction, why is it stronger for lower-status white precincts, and why does it serve to diminish class politics?

Second, the combined, interdependent effect of black recruitment and white defection serves both to heighten the Democratic party's reliance upon black voters and to produce the progressive unravelling of the party's biracial coalition. According to the construction of our measure, an increased level of Democratic reliance upon black voters does not logically depend upon a decrease in the proportion of whites voting Democratic. Rather, this is an open question subject to empirical scrutiny. In southern cities between 1952 and 1972, the Democratic party became more reliant upon black votes independent of white political behavior. We fully acknowledge that a decrease in the level of Democratic voting among whites will increase the party's reliance upon black voters, assuming that blacks remain steadfast in support of the party. Indeed, the effect of white defections upon the Democrats' reliance upon black votes is a crucial element in our theoretical argument. As the party becomes more reliant upon black support, more whites defect, the party becomes more reliant upon black support, and so on.

Finally, it is possible to offer further empirical support for our position that Democratic reliance upon black votes has a corrosive effect upon white support that is independent from the party's overall level of support. Unlike the analysis in Chapter 3, in this instance the proportion of Democratic voters who are black does not correlate as highly with the proportion of all voters who are both black and Democratic supporters. Black participation increased dramatically during the 1952–72 period, and blacks demonstrated significant levels of bipartisanship during parts of the period. These two facts combine to suppress the correlation, and thus we cannot simply substitute measures. This is an important point because it speaks directly to our argument. It is not simply the level of black Democratic support that is the crucial theoretical property of interest; rather it is the level of black Democratic support relative to political support levels among whites.

As a reformulation of the statistical model in Table 5.5, we introduce an additional explanatory variable—the total number of Democratic votes. This is, of course, the denominator for the original explanatory variable—the proportion of all Democratic votes that come from black precincts—and thus it serves as a control that takes into account fluctuations in overall support as a factor separate from the extent to which the Democratic party depends upon black voters. The introduction of this control requires two more changes in the model to avoid the contaminating effects of city population size. First, the two dependent variables become *numbers* of votes from low-status and high-status white precincts. Second, all variables are measured as first differences in time. Thus, the model is expressed as

$$\Delta Y = a + b\Delta(B + W) + c\Delta(B/[B + W])$$

where

Y = the number of voters who vote Democratic, first in low-status white precincts and then in high-status white precincts

B = the number of voters from black precincts who vote Democratic

W = the number of voters from white precincts who vote Democratic

Δ = an election-to-election difference operator, such that ΔY equals Y_{t+1} minus Y_t.

Table 5.5. Alternative model specifications for white response to the proportion of Democratic votes coming from black precincts and from opposite-status white precincts. (All data are differenced, with *t*-values in parentheses)

	Dependent Variables:	
	Number of Democratic votes from low-status white precincts	Number of Democratic votes from high-status white precincts

A. WHITE RESPONSE TO THE PROPORTION OF DEMOCRATIC VOTES COMING FROM BLACK PRECINCTS.

Explanatory Variables:

Intercept	−50.17	128.16
	(0.56)	(1.854)
Total number of	0.15	0.22
Democratic votes	(10.96)	(20.31)
Proportion of Democratic votes from black precincts	−2568.72 (4.25)	−2078.72 (4.47)
R^2	.56	.80
N	102	102

B. THE WHITE RESPONSE TO THE PROPORTION OF DEMOCRATIC VOTES COMING FROM OPPOSITE STATUS WHITE PRECINCTS.

Explanatory Variables:

Intercept	−216.09	−35.42
	(2.43)	(0.47)
Total number of	0.14	0.21
Democratic votes	(9.80)	(18.27)
Proportion of Democratic votes from opposite-status white precincts	−1255.08 (0.96)	−1269.74 (1.11)
R^2	.48	.77
N	102	102

Source: Southern cities data (Bartley and Graham 1978).

Part A of Table 5.5 shows that this procedure supports our original results. Overall support for a candidate is strongly related to support in both high-status and low-status white precincts, and thus the proportion of explained variation increases dramatically in comparison to Table 5.3(B). As might be expected, controlling the size of the total vote reduces the extent to which the effect of black reliance is stronger in low-status white precincts. Most important, the effect of the party's reliance upon black voters is maintained: white voters are less likely to support a Democratic candidate who relies more heavily upon black votes.

Could this result also be an artifact of model construction? To answer this question we consider the class composition of the party's coalition (see Table 5.5[B]). The results are much less impressive in terms of coefficient magnitudes and *t*-values. It would appear that low-status white voters are much more sensitive to the density of blacks in the Democratic coalition than they are to the density of high-status whites. Similarly, it would appear that high-status white voters are much more sensitive to the density of blacks than they are to the density of low-status whites. The results for class sensitivity become even weaker (in an analysis not shown here) when we broaden our definition for low-status whites to include voters from low- and moderately low-status white precincts and when we broaden our definition for high-status whites to include voters from high- and moderately high status white precincts.

In summary, these results support the independent importance of black densities within the Democratic coalition for levels of Democratic support among white voters. Increased Democratic reliance upon black voters is not merely a function of white Democrats who have left the party for reasons unrelated to race; the increased reliance of the Democratic party upon black voters is the engine that drives the relationship between levels of white Democratic support and the proportion of Democratic supporters who are black.

Can the Effects be Explained by Divergent Interests?

Could it be that the inability of the Democratic party to construct a coalition of lower-status whites and blacks was not due to racial animosity but rather to the presence of divergent interests? An alternative explanation of the data is that black interests and lower-status white interests ran in opposite directions during the postwar period. If the party served lower-status white interests it could not serve black interests, and vice versa.

Figure 5.5 plots the proportion of voters in lower-status white precincts voting Democratic against the proportion of voters in black precincts voting Democratic. Assuming that the political incompatibility between blacks and lower-status whites was based upon objectively defined interests, then we should expect to obtain a strong negative relationship to the extent that the

Figure 5.5. Democratic voting in low status white precincts as a function of Democratic voting in black precincts, for 24 southern cities, 1952–78.

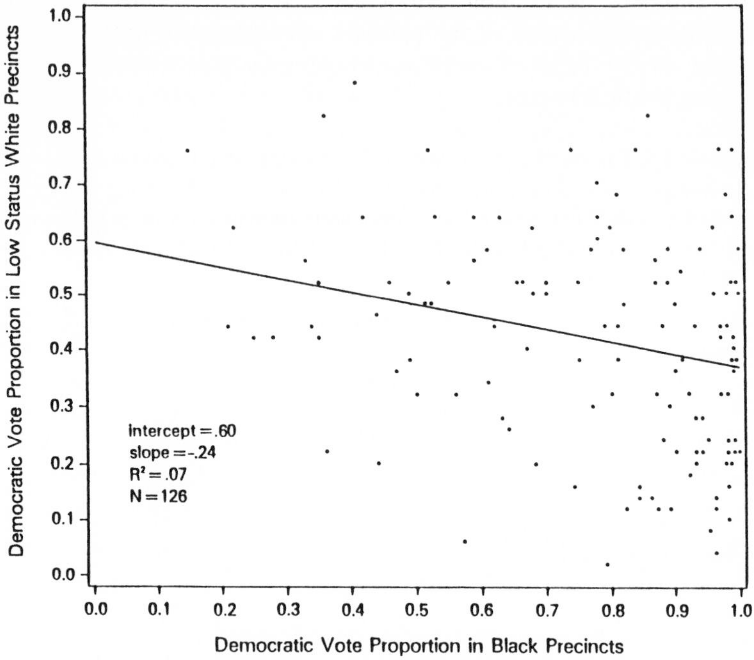

Source: Bartley and Graham (1978).

divergent interests are expressed with a partisan vote. That is, when blacks vote Democratic, lower status whites should not, and vice versa. In fact, while the relationship in Figure 5.5 is negative, it is much weaker than the relationship exhibited in Figure 5.2, measured according to the criterion of explained variation.

A more thorough comparison of these effects is obtained through a multiple regression of the proportion of lower-income whites voting Democratic on the racial composition of the Democratic coalition as well as the proportion of blacks voting Democratic. Results for this regression are reported in Table 5.6, both for the original data and for the differenced data. The most important result from these regression models is that the effect of racial composition persists even when controlling for divergent interests between blacks and whites. Indeed, the t-values and the coefficients are much more impressive for racial composition. Furthermore, this analysis suggests that the interests of blacks and low-income whites are not divergent at all! Once the effect of racial composition is taken into account, the direction of the relationship between white interests and black interests is reversed. Higher proportions of black support are *positively* related to higher proportions of low-income white support. Thus, we can only conclude that it is the *presence* of blacks in the Democratic coalition to which lower-status whites object. The nature of the political incompatibility is much better explained on the basis of racial hostility rather than on the basis of conflicting political interests.

Table 5.6. Democratic proportion of the presidential vote in low-status white precincts by the proportion of the Democratic vote coming from black precincts and by the Democratic proportion of the vote in black precincts, for twenty-four southern cities, 1952-72 (*t*-values are shown in parentheses)

	Original data	Differenced data
Intercept	0.51	−0.05
	(11.30)	(3.60)
Black proportion of	−0.82	−0.51
Democratic vote	(10.05)	(4.56)
Democratic proportion of	0.17	0.17
black precinct vote	(2.48)	(2.95)
R^2	.48	.16
N	126	102

Source: Southern cities data (Bartley and Graham 1978).

Race, Class, and the New Bourbons

These results run at least partially counter to those obtained by Murray and Vedlitz (1978). In their study of voting patterns in five southern cities from 1960 to 1977, they conclude that "in all cities save Atlanta, black-supported candidates received more support from lower SES whites than from upper or middle SES whites" (p. 36). How do our results differ? First, Murray and Vedlitz use a considerably different data set. They examine 106 elections at the local, state, and presidential levels in the cities of Atlanta, New Orleans, Memphis, Dallas, and Houston. The time period of their study straddles the great divide of 1964, but it does not reach as far into the past as the southern cities data employed here. Also, we are only concerned with presidential politics and the racial coalitions in support of presidential candidates at the local level during the critical and tumultuous period of 1952 through 1972.

Our results are not entirely at odds with their study, however. Rather, we have posed different questions, which can be seen most clearly in Figure 5.4 by drawing a line parallel to the horizontal axis which intersects the vertical axis at zero. Points above this line generally meet the Murray-Vedlitz criterion for class voting, that is, lower-status white precincts are more likely to vote for the Democratic candidate, who is generally the black-supported candidate as well. Clearly, most of the observations fall above this imaginary line; thus, Murray and Vedlitz are correct in their assertion that lower-status whites are more likely to support the black supported candidate, even using the Bartley and Graham (1978) data.

Our own concern is not with the presence of class voting among whites, but rather with the extent of class voting. The results of this chapter suggest that class voting has become less extensive among whites as the Democratic Party has come to rely increasingly upon blacks for electoral support. Thus, we do not argue that class voting is absent among whites, but only that it is less extensive due to racial conflict within the lower-class coalition.

The Murray-Vedlitz results speak directly to the much-discussed inversion of class voting in the post–New Deal era. According to an argument offered by Ladd (1982), Burnham (1970), and others, race and the continued evolution of electoral coalitions have produced a reversal of the class basis for liberalism within the white population. Lower-status whites are less likely to be liberal than higher-status whites, and the end product is thus a top-bottom coalition of middle-class white liberals and blacks. In a sense these white liberals occupy the role once filled by the southern Bourbons—an affluent section of the white population not threatened by the presence of blacks and fully willing to enter into a politically cooperative relationship. What are the prospects for this coalition between blacks and the new Bourbons?

As we noted previously, this coalition has been particularly successful in its ability to elect black mayors in black minority cities—the most notable example being Tom Bradley in Los Angeles. Two factors combine, however, to decrease its chances of more widespread success. First, abundant evidence suggests that there are not, in general, enough white liberals to produce a winning coalition. While these coalitions may sometimes succeed in local politics, they have little chance for nationwide or even statewide successes. After two losses in statewide races, Tom Bradley would be the first to agree that there are just not enough white liberals, even in California. Second, when a class inversion does occur, it is likely to be due to the extreme deterioration of support among lower-class whites rather than to any increase in support among upper-class whites. Our analysis suggests that southern white urban residents do not easily cooperate in biracial coalitions regardless of their class, even though lower-class whites resist such coalitions more strenuously. At least in national politics, the presence of a class inversion only speaks to the dismal potential for a successful biracial political coalition.

The hope for a political coalition favorable to lower-class interests rests with the lower class. Political salvation is not likely to be imposed from the outside. Neither the old Bourbons nor the new Bourbons have been sufficient in numbers or intensity or altruism to serve as sponsors for such a movement. At the same time, however, race continues to be the *internal* impediment to the forging of a lower-class coalition. Thus the lower-class party—the Democratic party—continues to stumble along, with solid support from blacks, symbolic support from affluent white liberals, and only a fragment of the support it needs from the white working class to become a truly majority party.

Conclusion

What are the prospects for a political rapprochement between blacks and lower-status whites? To answer this question we must first seek the source of conflict. As a group, blacks occupy a material, economic role roughly the same as working-class and lower-middle-class whites. Our analyses suggest, however, that lower-class whites are precisely the group that rejects class politics, the group most sensitive to the presence of blacks and most unwilling to cooperate with them in the same political coalition. Several different social mechanisms might account for this reluctance. It may simply be that the social background of lower-class whites makes them less tolerant of blacks and more reluctant to join in a biracial political effort. In other words, lower-class whites might be bigots in comparison to the more enlightened attitudes of upper-class whites. But even if this were an accurate descriptive statement—and its accuracy is problematic at the very least—it would explain nothing. The natural question would be: What factors in the social background of lower-class whites make them less tolerant?

One answer to this question is that lower-class whites are socially and economically threatened by blacks in a way that upper-class whites are not. Much is concealed in the statement that lower-class whites do not like blacks because blacks are economically threatening. The processes that assign similar class interests to blacks and lower-class whites are also the processes that induce racial hostility and ultimately produce its political manifestations in partisan behavior. When a white hod carriers' union is required to admit blacks, the threat is economically real and socially visible. The two groups clearly become closer in their objective economic position in the order of production, but that is not what becomes most immediately visible to white hod carriers. The common interpretation is, undoubtedly, that the government is taking their jobs away and giving them to blacks. Even when an employer begins to hire blacks absent government coercion, the political interpretation may not be as clear, but the social interpretation of losing white jobs to blacks still holds.

If lower-class whites are more sensitive to these easily seen, short-run economic events than they are to the increases in common class interests obtaining between themselves and blacks, then the political consequences are not likely to be far behind. And who doubts that is the case? The perennial challenge of left mobilization has always been to convince the lower classes of their objectively defined class interests and to encourage political behavior along these common class lines. The precipitate of modern economic development may very well be steadily increasing similarities between the objective economic interests of blacks and lower-class whites. The processes creating that similarity, however, are precisely those that elevate race over class in the organization of contemporary Democratic party politics. The structural mechanisms reducing material inequality are socially visible and immediate. The common class interests of blacks and lower-class whites remain obscure.

Finally, it may be the case that more sinister and personalized forces are at work generating the fissure between blacks and lower-class whites. The vulnerability of a biracial, lower-class coalition frequently becomes apparent to participants in electoral politics, and it is not beyond the capabilities of political opponents to exploit the inherent vulnerability of such a coalition. In the context of the post–Reconstruction South, this meant that upper-class whites may have been less enthusiastic supporters of Jim Crow because they realized, perhaps subliminally, the potential of racial conflict, encouraged by racially shared facilities, to disrupt a lower-class coalition that was opposed to their interests. Allowing blacks to ride in second-class railway cars with whites had no direct effect on their level of social comfort—they rode first class anyway—but it did serve to exacerbate the tensions between blacks and lower-class whites.

We need not reach back to Reconstruction in our search for political efforts to exploit race as a disruptive wedge within lower-class coalitions. Consider the 1986 gubernatorial race in South Carolina. According to David Broder,

> Rep. Carroll A. Campbell, Jr. (R-S.C.), a bright and aggressive younger-generation Reaganite, was asked how he expected to win the South Carolina governorship. Democrats have held it for all but four years in the past century. The answer, he said, was to find an issue that would drive a wedge into what he described as the "unnatural" and "unstable" Democratic coalition. That coalition here, as in most other Southern states has twin bases: blacks and low-income, mainly rural, whites. Campbell was asked for examples of "wedge issues." He mentioned several, including the purely symbolic question of flying the Confederate flag over the state capitol, which still bears the scars of Sherman's artillery. (*Bloomington Herald-Telephone*, October 19, 1986, p. A12)

It would be a mistake to push this line of reasoning too far. Sinister forces are certainly capable of exploiting racial conflict, but the source of the racial fissure lies much deeper within the logic and fabric of social, economic, and political organization. Thus, it is not enough to indict the villains, even though there are more than enough villains to indict. Rather, a solution to the problem requires the identification of a set of strategies for overcoming the structural basis of racial conflict in American politics, an end to which the remainder of this book is dedicated.

6 Party Dynamics and Racial Hostility

In previous chapters we offer a set of arguments regarding the racial basis of electoral politics, as well as empirical support for these arguments. This chapter develops our theoretical argument as a precisely stated verbal model that can, in turn, be translated into a mathematical form. The central features of our thesis are both interdependent and simultaneous, and the model is designed to capture the essentials of the theoretical argument in a manner that facilitates an assessment of the complex consequences of this interdependence. With the model in hand, deductive implications of our thesis may be obtained and the phenomenon of racial politics more fully assessed. The text is devoted primarily to a verbal development of the model, while the mathematical translation is accomplished in the accompanying tables and appendix.

Time and Space

The theory developed here is explicitly dynamic and locational. A time-ordered logic is employed to portray the interdependence between races and parties in electoral politics. This logic sets forth rules of change, which in turn dictate both long-term and short-term consequences for electoral conflict and for the shape of party coalitions. Thus we are concerned here with change and with the dynamic consequences of an electoral process embedded within a racially polarized society.

The theory is locational in its reliance upon social structure. Because the dynamic of the theory is played out within the context of a particular racial mix, location circumscribes politics by determining racial composition. In some instances the relevant location is a precinct, in others a state or the nation. The important point for our argument is that politics occurs within a social structure that is peculiar to a particular setting.

The theory and its associated model are *not* deterministic: similar settings might produce very different political outcomes, depending upon the strategies and decisions adopted by parties and politicians and the effectiveness with which the strategies are pursued. Indeed, a major contribution of the theory developed here is to locate party strategies within the context of a dynamic process, circumscribed by a set of structural constraints that are both political and social.

The Participants in the Process

The theoretical focus is upon the politically eligible, voting-age population, which can be distributed across social and political groups in a number of analytically useful ways. First, some proportion of the eligible population is completely disengaged from politics and therefore lies beyond the reach of parties and candidates and their mobilization efforts. Verba and Nie (1972) set this figure at slightly in excess of 20 percent for an American national population in the middle 1960s. Taking this fact into account, four population characteristics provide the social structure for the theory: eligible whites, eligible blacks, politically engaged whites, and politically engaged blacks.

All of these population characteristics are treated independently of the theory's time-dependent logic. This does not mean that they do not change, or even that they do not change systematically across time. It does mean that they are not subject to the political dynamic being specified in the theory. This is perhaps most troubling in terms of political engagement, because the challenge to parties and candidates is that of engaging more and more elements of the population in their cause. Specifying the engaged population as fixed for purposes of analysis may be viewed as specifying upper bounds on possible participation levels. This assumption proves to be very useful and does no great harm in analyses of particular electoral epochs.

Turning to political groups, the model allows for Democrats, Republicans, and nonvoters among both blacks and whites. Furthermore, thirty years of survey research lead us to believe that some portion of a party's coalition is not subject to defection. Whether they are straight ticket voters, or strong identifiers, or voters who have made a standing decision to support one party or the other, these people comprise the hard core of support upon which each party can depend. Thus it makes good sense to assume that some segment of each racial group's support for each party is insulated from changes due to the dynamic being set forth in this theory.

The relevant social and political groups, as well as the possible dynamics between groups, can be more easily visualized by consulting Figure 6.1, which lays out a modified Venn diagram of the population. This representation characterizes the relevant social groupings as areas of the plane, with movements between groups represented by arrows across boundaries. As a first step, the population is divided into two races, whites and blacks, thus ignoring the distinctive size and importance of Hispanics as well as other ethnic and racial groups. Within the population of each race, noneligibles such as children and felons are then excluded. The two resulting populations, white eligibles and black eligibles, provide the basis for our analysis. The politically disengaged segment of each population is designated and might vary proportionally across blacks and whites. The two remaining populations of blacks and whites represent the politically engaged population— those who might potentially participate.

Further inspection shows the principal partisan divisions within the politically engaged segment of each racial group to be Democrats, Republicans, and the uncommitted. These partisan definitions vary across substan-

Figure 6.1. A social and political partitioning of the population.

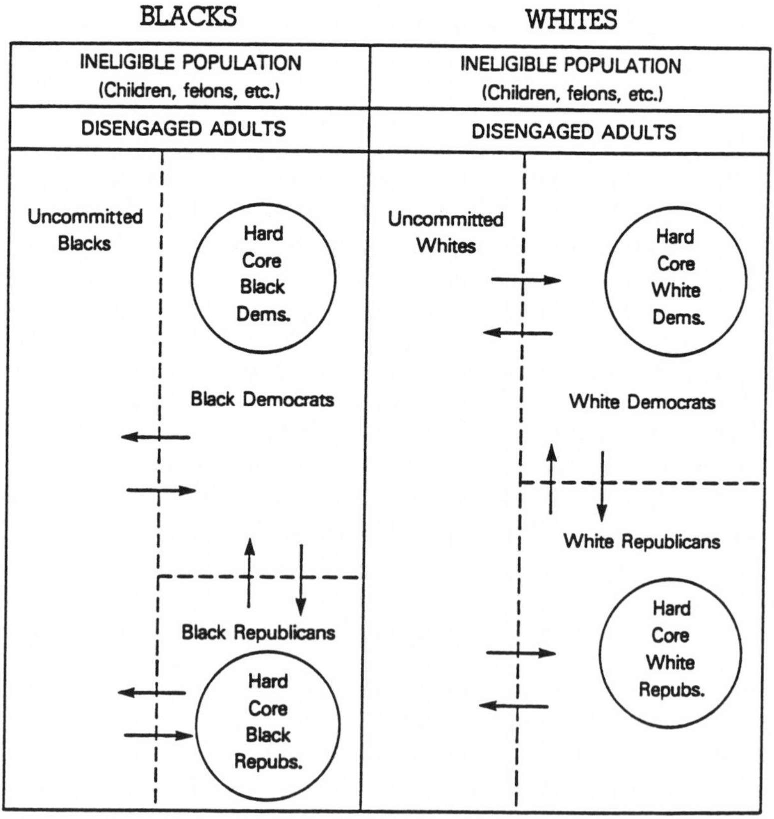

tive contexts. For example, in the context of an election campaign, the categories might refer to a vote intention. In the context of party identification, they might refer to Democratic identifiers, Republican identifiers, and independents. In the context of election day, they might refer to Democratic voters, Republican voters, and nonvoters. Included as a subset of each partisan grouping for each race is a circle representing the hard-core supporters of a particular party within a particular race. These hard-core supporters are a subset of the political grouping; they are included, in the set theoretic sense, in the membership of the group within which they are located.

In order to assess the possible paths for political dynamics, the boundaries of groups in Figure 6.1 should be examined. Borders across which movement is possible are specified by arrows. For example, movement into the space of black Democrats from the space of uncommitted blacks is possible, just as is the reverse. The arrows specify the direction of possible flows, with magnitudes determined by other considerations in the complete specification of the model. No arrows are found on the border between blacks and whites; similarly, and perhaps more subtly, there are no arrows on the borders of the circles representing hard-core partisans in each racial group. We argue that hard-core partisans contribute to partisan dynamics, but they are not themselves subject to those dynamics — they move others but are not themselves moved.

The essential logical requirements for a model of partisan dynamics can also be determined from the diagram in Figure 6.1. Twelve flows are present, and rules of change must be established to specify the dynamic contribution of each. These rules fall into three categories: (1) partisan *mobilization* — from uncommitted status to partisan support for one of the parties; (2) *conversion* — from partisan support for one party to partisan support for the other; and (3) *defection* — from partisan support to nonsupport. In the development of the logic underlying these rules, the uncommitted in each racial group constitute a residual state of the system whose dynamic is defined by the explicit rules specified for the four groups of central interest: black Democrats, black Republicans, white Democrats, and white Republicans (mathematical definitions for all groups in the process are given in Table 6.1).

The Dynamic Logic: Rules of Partisan Transformation

What are the sources of change in the current level of support *within* a particular racial group *for* a particular party? The party might: (1) lose support it previously enjoyed; (2) convert supporters from the opposite party; and (3) mobilize support from the ranks of the uncommitted. We consider each of these sources in reverse order.

Table 6.1. Key to participants

B_e = proportion of the politically eligible population that is black
W_e = proportion of the politically eligible population that is white
L_b = proportion of politically eligible blacks who are engaged by politics
L_w = proportion of politically eligible whites who are engaged by politics
P_b = proportion of the politically eligible population that is black and politically engaged: $L_b B_e$
P_w = proportion of the politically eligible population that is white and politically engaged: $L_w W_e$
BD_t = proportion of the eligible population at time t that is both black and supports the Democratic party
WD_t = proportion of the eligible population at time t that is both white and supports the Democratic party
BR_t = proportion of the eligible population at time t that is both black and supports the Republican party
WR_t = proportion of the eligible population at time t that is both white and supports the Republican party
$P_b - BD_t - BR_t$ = proportion of the eligible population at time t that is black, politically engaged, and uncommitted
$P_w - WD_t - WR_t$ = proportion of the eligible population at time t that is white, politically engaged, and uncommitted

The Nature of Mobilization. People are mobilized when they are recruited to the support of a party from the ranks of the uncommitted. In terms of election day, mobilization involves the recruitment of previous nonvoters to vote for a particular party or candidate. Mobilization need not be wholly subservient to electoral politics, however. When Ronald Reagan goes to the people via his weekly radio messages, he is attempting to mobilize public support in his role as president and Republican party leader. When President Nixon made his trip to China in 1972, or when President Johnson orchestrated the Gulf of Tonkin Resolution in 1964, the underlying goal was to mobilize political support. The crucial ingredient of mobilization is its tactic of seeking commitment from the uncommitted, and involvement from the uninvolved.

The chief concern here is with electoral politics. Thus mobilization is important both as a short-term tactic during a particular election campaign aimed at winning a particular election and as a long-term component of party systems and the coalitional bases of individual parties. In its short-term version, mobilization has to do with voter registration drives, get out the vote campaigns, and seeking support from the undecided. It also has to do with candidates who construct appeals that will, in the words of Schattschneider (1960), broaden or limit the scope of conflict to encourage or discourage higher rates of participation among various population groups.

In its long-term variant, mobilization has to do with the nature of political coalition construction. The mobilization of the northern, urban, European ethnic vote by the Democratic party in the late 1920s and early 1930s fundamentally restructured American politics, and the effects of that mobilization have still not disappeared (Lubell 1956). The mobilization of black voters by the Democratic party in the period from 1948 to the mid-1960s similarly reconstructed American politics and set into motion a dynamic logic that brings us to the present day.

Mobilization in the long-term does not occur in an instant, even though it can be set into motion at a critical juncture or by a critical decision. For example, the Democratic party was unable to adopt an anti–Ku Klux Klan plank in its 1924 platform, yet four years later it not only adopted the anti-KKK plank but also nominated an Irish-American Catholic from a New York City political machine to be its presidential candidate. That action put a framework into place for the incorporation of urban white ethnics into its coalition (Key 1955). In general terms, crucial strategic decisions set the stage for sustained efforts on the part of a party to mobilize and incorporate particular groups within their coalitions, usually over a time period of several elections. This occurred with the Democratic party and the populist movement in 1896, with the Democrats and European ethnics in the 1920s, with the Democrats and blacks in the 1940s, and some observers believe it may be occurring now with the Republicans and large portions of the white population.

The first two significant twentieth century mobilization efforts were carried out by the Democratic party, and they were characterized by very different political strategies. In the first case, that of white urban ethnics, the party provided the group with a set of reasons for becoming Democrats—Al Smith at the head of the ticket, support for industrial labor unions heavily populated by urban ethnics, and a range of social welfare measures that appealed to this predominantly working-class constituency.

In the second case, blacks in northern and southern cities and in the rural South, the strategy was twofold. Once again the party provided a set of reasons, both real and symbolic, for blacks to become Democrats—its civil rights plank in the 1948 party platform, Truman's desegregation of the armed forces, Kennedy's phone call to Coretta Scott King while her husband was in a Birmingham jail, the 1964 Civil Rights Act, and the 1965 Voting Rights Act. In addition Democrats attacked the set of legal obstacles that stood in the way of mobilizing southern blacks, and therein lies the special significance of the 1965 Voting Rights Act. Without this act southern blacks could not be mobilized, and thus the act set the stage for the transformation of the Democratic party by allowing the mobilization effort to proceed. In terms of our model, the Voting Rights Act served to increase the pool of politically engaged blacks, moving them directly toward partisan political behavior.

Legal obstacles to mobilization are not new phenomena in democratic politics, and the removal of these obstacles has frequently set the stage for large-scale mobilization efforts by a political party, resulting in a transformation of democratic politics and party coalitions. It was this sort of transformation that occurred in most European nations during the nineteenth and early twentieth centuries and is currently being resisted in vigorous fashion by proponents of apartheid in South Africa.

The Causes of Mobilization: Mobilization Rules. Once the legal obstacles to mobilization are removed, what are the factors that cause mobilization to occur? Our theory points to two interrelated factors: the intrinsic effectiveness of a party's appeal to relevant groups in the population and the extent to which that appeal has been successful in the immediate past. In terms of intrinsic appeal, no party in 1924 could construct a truly effective appeal to Catholic ethnics if it repudiated an anti-KKK plank, and no party could effectively mobilize blacks in 1964 if it failed to support the Civil Rights Act. The intrinsic appeal of the party lies at the heart of effective mobilization, but it is not enough by itself.

Effective mobilization depends not only upon the party's intrinsic appeal but also upon the party's preexisting basis of support in the population. Voters are rational in responding to the appeals of candidates and parties, but they do not act in isolation (Downs 1957:229). Rather, democratic rationality is collective in nature. Rational voters receive information and advice from other voters, and voters who disagree with their friends and associates are subject to subtle and not so subtle forms of social coercion. As a result, a party's intrinsic appeal will be more effective among nonvoters and uncommitted voters if the party receives a higher level of support within the population. In short, the act of voting cannot be understood in social isolation because the behavior of voters is fundamentally interdependent.

This interdependence of voter behavior has been empirically established and reestablished in numerous investigations of democratic politics, perhaps never more effectively than by Warren Miller's (1956) study of one-party politics and its effect on voter preference. As Miller shows so persuasively, the majority party in a particular setting is benefited because it *is* the majority party, quite apart from the issue positions and partisan predispositions of individual voters. Individual voters are encouraged to support a party and its candidates by the sheer weight and direction of public sentiment, regardless of their own idiosyncratic preferences.

The fundamental interdependence of voting becomes even more pronounced under conditions of racial polarization and competition in electoral politics. The implicit dynamic underlying C. Vann Woodward's (1966) classic argument is that, under conditions of racial polarization, lower-class whites in particular cannot overcome the anxiety that is produced by their political separation from other whites. That simple observation explains the demise of populism in the South during the late nineteenth and early twentieth centuries.

Our model incorporates this theoretical argument by representing the mobilization rate as a weighted function of a party's appeal to a particular race, where the weight is the party's level of support within the politically engaged segment of that racial group. Thus, the success of the Democratic party in recruiting uncommitted blacks, the mobilization rate, is proportional to the product of (1) the party's intrinsic appeal to uncommitted blacks and (2) the current level of Democratic support among politically engaged blacks.

Mobilization rates are formulated similarly for the remaining racial-partisan groups. Each racial group has a characteristically different parameter reflecting the intrinsic appeal of the party to the group, and each mobilization rate also reflects the level of support given to the party by the politically engaged members of the racial group. Thus, for all groups mobilization of the uncommitted will be proportional to the current size of the racial-partisan group, with an intrinsic appeal parameter differing across groups on the basis of other substantive considerations (see mathematical definitions in Table 6.2).

The most obvious and intuitive time metrics for these dynamics are the

Table 6.2. The nature of mobilization

A. Rates of Mobilization

$M_{BD_t} = a(BD_t/P_b)$ = rate at which uncommitted blacks are mobilized to support the Democratic party

$M_{BR_t} = e(BR_t/P_b)$ = rate at which uncommitted blacks are mobilized to support the Republican party

$M_{WD_t} = m(WD_t/P_w)$ = rate at which uncommitted whites are mobilized to support the Democratic party

$M_{WR_t} = r(WR_t/P_w)$ = rate at which uncommitted whites are mobilized to support the Republican party

where

a = intrinsic appeal of the Democratic party among uncommitted blacks

e = intrinsic appeal of the Republican party among uncommitted blacks

m = intrinsic appeal of the Democratic party among uncommitted whites

r = intrinsic appeal of the Republican party among uncommitted whites

BD_t/P_b = proportion of politically engaged blacks who support the Democratic party

BR_t/P_b = proportion of politically engaged blacks who support the Republican party

WD_t/P_w = proportion of politically engaged whites who support the Democratic party

WR_t/P_w = proportion of politically engaged whites who support the Republican party

B. Who Might Be Mobilized?

politically engaged, uncommitted blacks = $P_b - BD_t - BR_t$

politically engaged, uncommitted whites = $P_w - WD_t - WR_t$

day-to-day metric of an election campaign and the election-to-election metric of a particular electoral epoch. The processes of interest, however, go on continuously across election campaigns, elections, presidencies, and epochs. Thus we develop our argument in the metric of continuous time, even though we make specific applications to the metrics of elections and election campaigns in the chapters that follow.

An additional subtlety is also present in the matter of time metrics. The theoretical argument we have constructed specifies a fairly complex set of interdependencies among the principal racial and partisan groupings. Marginal effects and first-order effects in the short run often conceal ultimate consequences when the logic is allowed to play itself out over the long run. In subsequent chapters we analyze the sometimes hidden and counterintuitive long-run consequences of what appear to be quite obvious and innocuous short-run dynamic specifications.

The motivation for the construction of this model is the ability to assess the longer run results due to a complex set of interdependent political behaviors. The model will allow us to consider the long-run consequences of short-term strategies and thus to separate what is good for the party in the short run from what may be counterproductive in the longer run. A readily manipulated logic is essential to such an undertaking, and it is this logic which our model provides.

The Nature of Conversion. True conversions do not come easily in electoral politics. Old habits are changed slowly, especially because their durability is anchored in a supporting set of social relationships and social loyalties. In the strict sense, conversions occur when voters with consistent voting histories abruptly change the direction of their support or when voters change their preferences during an election campaign. These sorts of conversions are relatively rare. Empirical research shows that voters who express a voting intention early in the campaign generally do not change that preference during the campaign. More impressive still, research on rapid partisan realignment in American politics points toward the importance of new voters rather than old voters (Beck 1976). Indeed, the political revolution of the 1930s was probably the result of new voters who were overwhelmingly mobilized in a Democratic direction (Andersen 1979, supporting the original hypothesis of Lubell 1956). Thus, sudden realignments do not generally appear to result from conversions of former adherents of one party to the other, although cataclysmic events (such as the American Civil War) and dramatic alterations in group interests (such as blacks in the context of the New Deal) are able to produce such an outcome.

The concept of conversion being employed here carries no cataclysmic overtones. We are not so much interested in dramatic and permanent alterations in deep seated political loyalties, or even in voters who change their minds, as we are in voters who regularly reassess their political options at each succeeding election. Indeed, this latter type of behavior is, according to Key (1966), the lifeblood of democratic politics. Aggregate vote totals that vary within a relatively narrow range disguise the amount of individual change taking place in the electorate. Conversion occurs in both directions and thus tends to be self-canceling when the focus of attention is upon net change. By comparing survey respondents' current voting preferences with their voting preferences four years earlier, Key calls attention to the important role played by conversion and converts in American electoral politics.

On the basis of this strategy, Key is able to pull apart a party's aggregate vote total and determine the contribution of new voters, standpatters, and switchers—our converts—to party victory in presidential elections. For example, Key's estimates show that Kennedy and Nixon each received 14 percent of their 1960 support from voters who had not voted in 1956. In contrast, 30 percent of Kennedy's support, but only 8 percent of Nixon's, came from converts—people who had voted for the opposite party's candidate in 1956. Thus, in Key's analysis it was the conversion rates between 1956 and 1960, rather than the mobilization of new voters, that explained the outcome of the 1960 election.

In Key's view it is the voters who switch preference to whom the parties must address their efforts, and thus democratic politics frequently turns on the behavior of potential converts. The short-term impact of conversions between parties is problematic: it may be self-canceling, it may produce a defeat for the majority party, or, as in 1960 it may reinstate the candidate of the majority party. Over the long haul, however, even slight differences in rates of conversion, if they are systematic and sustained, have profound consequences for the shape of party coalitions in American politics.

A great deal of intellectual energy has been spent in an attempt to understand Key's (1955) concept of critical elections, while less attention has been paid to his subsequent discussion (1959) of secular change: slow but steady and persistent shifts in aggregate voter preference. While it is not central to the argument, our strong inclination is toward the view that critical elections are rooted in rapid and sustained mobilization, while secular change is rooted in long-term conversion patterns.

The Causes of Conversion: Conversion Rules. Why do voters convert (and reconvert) from one party to another? Our argument is that voters are converted for the same interrelated reasons that the uncommitted are mobilized—intrinsic party appeal and past party success within a relevant group. Indeed, a failure to appreciate this social dimension underlying the voting histories of particular groups has led to some misplaced interpretations of American electoral politics. Ladd and Hadley (1978) discount a class-based interpretation of the New Deal coalition on the basis of strong political loyalties that cut across class lines within the northern white population. In particular, they point to the durability of Republican loyalties among white working-class Protestants, and on this basis they argue that the New Deal's appeal was fundamentally rooted in ethnicity and religion rather than class.

Their otherwise informative analysis is not compelling on this point. In the 1930s, white northern Protestants were predominantly middle class and Catholics were predominantly working class. Due to the *social* interdependence of political preferences, it was easier for the New Deal to convert a working-class Catholic than it was to convert a working-class Protestant. The social frame of reference for Catholics was other (mostly working-class) Catholics, just as the social frame of reference for Protestants was other (mostly middle-class) Protestants. Thus, the same working-class appeal produced a higher rate of conversion among Catholics because it received a higher level of social support within the relevant social group.

The working-class appeal of the New Deal simply cannot be ignored. Even a cursory review of campaign memorabilia from the period shows an appeal toward workers that seems fairly radical by contemporary standards and underscores the extent to which the Democratic party has middle-classified its appeal since that time. The phenomenon of middle-class Democrats among the Catholics and working-class Republicans among the Protestants becomes easily explained once we take account of the historic class densities within these religious groups and the social support (and nonsupport) for particular political preferences that has been engendered by them.

Once again, the role of social support takes on added importance when we examine racially polarized politics. Even when southern blacks were effectively excluded from the polls and registration lists, it often took an act of extreme courage for a white southerner to become a professed Republican (Key 1949). Quite apart from the behavior of other groups, a voter's own group plays an important role in encouraging or discouraging political conversion.

Our model specifies a party's conversion rate as the product of that party's intrinsic appeal among potential converts (a fixed parameter) and the level of support given to the party by the politically engaged members of the relevant racial group. Thus, the rate of Democratic conversion among potential black Republican converts is the product of (1) the Democrats' intrinsic appeal among potential black converts and (2) the level of Democratic support among politically engaged blacks (see Table 6.3).

Who are the potential converts and to whom does the conversion rate apply? The conversion rate is antecedent to a defection rate from the opposite party. That is, some proportion of the opposite party defects, for whatever reasons, and from this pool of potential converts some proportion is converted. Those who defect without being converted become uncommitted, and thus it is crucial to consider the sources of defection.

The Nature of Defection. Parties lose supporters for a great variety of reasons, which we summarize in two categories: (1) racial disaffection, our central concern, and (2) all other sources of defection.

Table 6.3. The nature of conversion

A. Who Might Be Converted?
1. Black defectors from the Republican party might be converted to Democratic support.
2. Black defectors from the Democratic party might be converted to Republican support.
3. White defectors from the Republican party might be converted to Democratic support.
4. White defectors from the Democratic party might be converted to Republican support.

B. Rates of Conversion?

$C_{BD_t} = b(BD_t/P_b) =$ rate of Democratic conversion among black Republican defectors

$C_{BR_t} = f(BR_t/P_b) =$ rate of Republican conversion among black Democratic defectors

$C_{WD_t} = n(WD_t/P_w) =$ rate of Democratic conversion among white Republican defectors

$C_{WR_t} = s(WR_t/P_w) =$ rate of Republican conversion among white Democratic defectors

where

$b =$ intrinsic appeal of the Democratic party among black Republican defectors

$f =$ intrinsic appeal of the Republican party among black Democratic defectors

$n =$ intrinsic appeal of the Democratic party among white Republican defectors

$s =$ intrinsic appeal of the Republican party among white Democratic defectors

$BD_t/P_b =$ proportion of politically engaged blacks who support the Democratic party

$BR_t/P_b =$ proportion of politically engaged blacks who support the Republican party

$WD_t/P_w =$ proportion of politically engaged whites who support the Democratic party

$WR_t/P_w =$ proportion of politically engaged whites who support the Republican party

---

These other sources of defection are given time precedence in the model. We assume that party supporters defect because of economic downturns, wars, scandals, corruption, and so on, and that among those who remain some additional supporters defect because they are disaffected from a party that relies too heavily upon the opposite race.

These nonracial sources of defection are treated as a constant factor that is fixed within a particular analytic time frame. In contrast, racial defections *must* vary through short-run electoral time as the direct logical consequence of the dynamic underlying racially structured politics. As the members of one race become disenchanted with the racial mix supporting their party, some of them defect. But this serves to alter the composition of the party, and thus the process is self-accelerating. Under conditions of racially polarized politics, disaffection is stimulated by racial antagonism, but racial antagonism alters the composition of the coalition, thereby leading to an unraveling through time. Racially polarized politics is not a simple function of individually based racist impulses. It is also the product of the progressive transformation of party coalitions that is consequent on these antagonisms (Granovetter 1978; Schelling 1978).

The Causes of Defection: Defection Rules. The attractiveness of parties and candidates has already been treated in the discussion of conversion, but what causes racial disaffection from a party? First, of course, racial disaffection depends upon the level of racial sensitivity within a population. Some populations are acutely sensitive to matters of race while others are not. The frequency of racist attitudes among white southerners, for example, has been the subject of novels, popular discourse, and serious academic investigation. This dimension of racial disaffection relates to the distribution of racial attitudes within some population group, but other factors give rise to racial hostility as well.

A second factor is closely related to the first, but it underscores the importance of politics and politicians rather than the distribution of racial attitudes within a population. Parties and candidates have a great deal to do with racial sensitivity among party supporters. According to Schattschneider (1960:chap. 4), the threat of populism encouraged white conservatives to transform the nature of political conflict in the late nineteenth century. They shifted the focus of political debate and the basis of political conflict away from matters of class and toward matters of race. As Schattschneider argues so persuasively, control over the basis of conflict determines who will win and who will lose in politics. Southern conservatives could win a political conflict structured by matters of race, but they were destined to lose a conflict structured around class. Skillful practitioners of politics attempt to choose a battlefield where the odds for victory are highest.

How do political practitioners control the definition of conflict? In a culture where racially oriented fears and anxieties are never far below the surface, it often takes very little on the part of politicians to shift the focus of public attention toward race. Campaign complaints about welfare fraud and food stamp abuse carry racial overtones that are none too subtle, but more extreme examples are available as well.

Philadelphia's black mayoral candidate, Wilson Goode, came from a political background that gave his white opponent, Frank Rizzo, little opportunity to exploit race as an issue in the 1983 Democratic mayoral primary. Goode had been the antithesis of a black militant. His background in city administration gave him impeccable credentials of middle-class respectability and professionalism. Such a situation called for a high level of creativity and resourcefulness, and Rizzo made every attempt to rise to the occasion. If Goode's image stymied his efforts to raise the issue of race, black Chicago mayoral candidate Harold Washington provided a more vulnerable target. Rizzo took time off from his own Philadelphia campaign to lecture voters on the dangers that Washington presented. Unfortunately for Rizzo, Philadelphia voters cast their votes on the basis of Philadelphia candidates rather than Chicago candidates.

The appeal to race need not be overt, just as the focus upon race need not be intended. White politicians who run against blacks frequently assert that race is irrelevant to the election and that they do not want racially oriented votes. These statements may be sincere and well intended, but the more they are uttered the more they focus public attention on the racial divide. Neither is racial politics the sole domain of white politicians. Appeals to race and to racial solidarity are frequently made by black politicians in an overt manner. Our political culture generally views such appeals as appropriate on the part of a black minority but inappropriate on the part of a white majority. Indeed, the black experience in America more than legitimates the identification and pursuit of explicit black interests in the political system. A central concern here is: What strategy serves those interests best? Does the overt identification and pursuit of black interests within the electoral process undermine the success of those interests? Are short-run and long-run consequences at odds with each other?

Racial sensitivity is not only due to the presence of racist attitudes among a white majority or to the presence of black consciousness on the part of a black minority. It is also the direct result of politicians who make race an important basis of conflict within an election. Given the level of racial distrust and hostility within the electorate, the politician's focus upon race is sometimes unintended and oftentimes unavoidable. At other times, however, the focus upon race is more sinister. More important, the ascendance of race as the basis for conflict in electoral politics has inevitable consequences for the nature of public debate and for the course of public policy within this country. In the language of Schattschneider, the subordination of class to race has been a classic strategy of politicians in the political development of the United States. The displacement of class by race has served to reorient the lines of conflict in American politics in a manner that is harmful to the interests of lower classes, black or white. Indeed, we argue that it may be ultimately harmful to the interests of upper classes as well.

The Context of Racial Politics. The politics of race does not simply take place in the heads of voters and the appeals of politicians. Conversely, the absence of racially oriented politics does not necessarily mean that voters are racially enlightened or that politicians are principled regarding matters of race. Rather, the politics of race is intimately tied up in the relative size of racial groups, the extent to which racial groups have been mobilized politically, and the degree to which racial groups are concentrated within political parties and party coalitions.

The model we develop specifies a rate of defection due to racial disaffection among party supporters who belong to a particular race. This rate is the product of (1) the group's racial sensitivity and (2) the presence of the other race in the same party. Thus, using white Democrats as an example, the rate of defection due to racial disaffection is heightened either because racial sensitivity increases among white Democrats or because the proportional level of black Democratic support increases. Recall, however, that defection is not only due to racial disaffection but also to a variety of other factors. The defection rate is conceived as a fixed rate due to nonracial factors plus a time-dependent rate due to racial disaffection operating upon those who do not defect on the basis of nonracial factors (see defection rates in Table 6.4).

Finally, each party has supporters within each race who will not defect, who are immune to the appeal of the opposite party and are not subject to racial disaffection. Party strategists frequently rely upon such supporters. For example, Johnson's hope in 1964 must have been that hard-core supporters among whites, coupled with newly mobilized black voters, would allow the Democratic party to offset losses due to white racial disaffection, thereby maintaining a position of political dominance. We return to this matter in the pages that follow.

A Summary of the Rules of Change

The rules of change are summarized in Figure 6.2. Some proportion of each race is politically uncommitted, and each party makes some attempt to mobilize these uncommitted citizens. At the same time, some proportion of each party's base of support is defecting within each race. Finally, and once again simultaneously, some proportion of these defectors are converted to support the opposite party, while the remainder join the

Table 6.4. The nature of defection

A. Nonracial Rates of Defection

c = rate at which black Democrats defect for reasons unrelated to race
g = rate at which black Republicans defect for reasons unrelated to race
p = rate at which white Democrats defect for reasons unrelated to race
u = rate at which white Republicans defect for reasons unrelated to race

B. Who Might Defect for Reasons Unrelated to Race?

All supporters of the party, minus the hard-core supporters, within each race.

C. Rates of Defection Due to Racial Disaffection

dWD_t = rate of defection due to racial disaffection among black Democrats
hWR_t = rate of defection due to racial disaffection among black Republicans
qBD_t = rate of defection due to racial disaffection among white Democrats
wBR_t = rate of defection due to racial disaffection among white Republicans

where

d = racial sensitivity among black Democrats
h = racial sensitivity among black Republicans
q = racial sensitivity among white Democrats
w = racial sensitivity among white Republicans

D. Who Might Defect Due to Racial Disaffection?

If we ignore the role of hard-core supporters, any supporter who has not defected for nonracial reasons.

E. Aggregate Rate of Defection for Racial and Nonracial Reasons Operating upon All Supporters Who Are Not Hard-Core Supporters (D_{it})

$c + d(1 - c)WD_t$ = aggregate rate of defection among black Democrats
$g + h(1 - g)WR_t$ = aggregate rate of defection among black Republicans
$p + q(1 - p)BD_t$ = aggregate rate of defection among white Democrats
$u + w(1 - u)BR_t$ = aggregate rate of defection among white Republicans

ranks of the uncommitted. All twelve flows previously identified in Figure 6.1 are accommodated within these three sources of change: mobilization, defection, and conversion. Each source of change depends upon the intrinsic appeal of a party and the political behavior of racial-political groups in the population. Thus, we have specified political change to be both inherently social and inherently political. Politics matters, and our model is driven by the political strategies and appeals of parties and candidates, but these strategies and appeals occur within contexts that are both social and political.

Assessing the Model

Before turning to the model's accomplishments, we must ask what it fails to accomplish. We have not developed a general theory of

Figure 6.2. Rules of Change.

FOR BLACKS WHO ARE POLITICALLY ENGAGED:

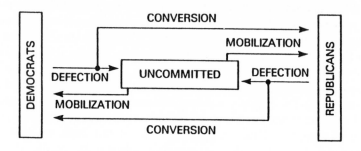

FOR WHITES WHO ARE POLITICALLY ENGAGED:

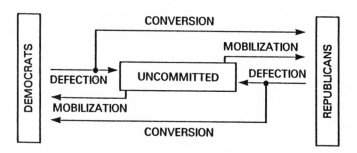

political change, and our model does not incorporate all that is interesting in democratic politics. It is, for example, irrelevant to issues of presidential popularity, to the effect of economic conditions upon voting, and to many other important issues. Thus, the model fails to give a comprehensive account of all the factors that are germane to democratic politics.

The intent of our theoretical argument has not been to offer an inclusive explanation for the myriad events of political campaigns and elections. Rather, it is intended to pull apart the dynamic logic of electoral conflict structured along racial lines. What is the source of racial polarization in electoral politics? Is it possible to avoid racially polarized politics in a racially polarized society? Is it possible to maintain two-party competition within both races? Is it possible to maintain two-party competition within a single race if the opposite race is bunched within a single party? What is the relationship between race and class in a racially polarized society? How does the dynamic logic of class differ from that of race in democratic politics?

These questions are addressed in the chapters that follow through the use of the model constructed here. The model does not require much in the way of suspended disbelief on the part of readers, as it is not based upon wild statements, nor dependent upon repugnant normative views, nor does it ask the reader to accept the empirically implausible. The theoretical arguments embodied in the model are constructed from a set of reasonable statements regarding the nature of change in party coalitions under conditions of racial polarization. The primary accomplishment of the model is to provide a deductive framework within which the nature of contemporary racial politics may be explored. Thus, in the remainder of this book we exploit this framework to analyze the consequences inherent in racially structured politics.

Appendix to Chapter 6

Our theory can be written as a system of four differential equations ($\dot{x} = dx/dt$):

$$\dot{BD_t} = M_{BD_t}\,(P_b - BD_t - BR_t)\ + C_{BD_t}(D_{BR_t}BR_t)\ - D_{BD_t}BD_t \quad (6.1)$$

$$\dot{BR_t} = M_{BR_t}\,(P_b - BD_t - BR_t)\ + C_{BR_t}(D_{BD_t}BD_t)\ - D_{BR_t}BR_t \quad (6.2)$$

$$\dot{WD_t} = M_{WD_t}\,(P_w - WD_t - WR_t) + C_{WD_t}(D_{WR_t}WR_t) - D_{WD_t}WD_t \quad (6.3)$$

$$\dot{WR_t} = M_{WR_t}\,(P_w - WD_t - WR_t) + C_{WR_t}(D_{WD_t}WD_t) - D_{WR_t}WR_t \quad (6.4)$$

In this algebraic form the dynamic logic parallels the graphic presentation of Figure 6.2. In terms of mobilizing the uncommitted, Democrats and Republicans focus their efforts upon the same populations. Two separate pools of uncommitted blacks and whites are available to both parties.

uncommitted blacks $= P_b - BD_t - BR_t$

uncommitted whites $= P_w - WD_t - WR_t$

This means, in turn, that at any instant, the sum of the two mobilization rates must lie in the unit interval in order to produce a descriptively realistic characterization of the mobilization process.

$0 \le M_{BD_t} + M_{BR_t} \le 1$

$0 \le M_{WD_t} + M_{WR_t} \le 1$

That is, at any instant it is not possible to mobilize more than the population of nonsupporters.

Some proportion of each party's support within each racial group defects, and some proportion of those defectors are converted. The two processes, defection and conversion, occur simultaneously. Indeed, for many citizens the processes are indistinguishable, and thus the decision to quit supporting the Democrats in favor of supporting the Republicans becomes a single decision. Analytically, it is useful to separate the two stages; logically it must be the case that defection takes precedence over conversion. Defection absent conversion produces uncommitted nonsupporters. In contrast, and by our definitions, defection serves as a necessary condition for conversion because no citizen can simultaneously support both parties.

Democrats and Republicans of each race therefore defect at some rate, and the opposite party is able to convert those defectors at some rate. This means that the population of potential defectors is the same as the population of party supporters, and the population of potential converts is the same as the population of defectors. It also means that at any instant each of the conversion and defection rates must lie in the unit interval.

$0 \leq$ each conversion rate $(C_{it}) \leq 1$

$0 \leq$ each defection rate $(D_{it}) \leq 1$

The defection rate is actually the sum of two component defection rates: the nonracial defection rate, which is a fixed constant that operates upon the population of supporters; and a second rate, which is a function of racial competition, and operates upon party supporters who do not defect for nonracial reasons. Thus, each of the component defection rates operate upon an identifiable population, and at any instant in time each must be bounded in the unit interval.

Given our definition of mobilization, conversion, and defection rates the model is rewritten as

$$\dot{BD_t} = a(BD_t/P_b)(P_b - BD_t - BR_t) \qquad \text{mobilization}$$
$$+ b(BD_t/P_b)(gBR_t + hWR_t(1-g)BR_t) \qquad \text{conversion}$$
$$- cBD_t - dWD_t(1-c)BD_t \qquad \text{defection} \qquad (6.5)$$

$$\dot{BR_t} = e(BR_t/P_b)(P_b - BD_t - BR_t) \qquad \text{mobilization}$$
$$+ f(BR_t/P_b)(cBD_t + dWD_t(1-c)BD_t) \qquad \text{conversion}$$
$$- gBR_t - hWR_t(1-g)BR_t \qquad \text{defection} \qquad (6.6)$$

$$\dot{WD_t} = m(WD_t/P_w)(P_w - WD_t - WR_t) \qquad \text{mobilization}$$
$$+ n(WD_t/P_w)(uWR_t + wBR_t(1-u)WR_t) \qquad \text{conversion}$$
$$- pWD_t - qBD_t(1-p)WD_t \qquad \text{defection} \qquad (6.7)$$

$$\dot{WR_t} = r(WR_t/P_w)(P_w - WD_t - WR_t) \qquad \text{mobilization}$$
$$+ s(WR_t/P_w)(pWD_t + qBD_t(1-p)WD_t) \qquad \text{conversion}$$
$$- uWR_t - wBR_t(1-u)WR_t \qquad \text{defection} \qquad (6.8)$$

This form of the model highlights the nature of dynamic interdependence in the flow of support between parties. Mobilization and conversion rates are accelerated and diminished as a function of political support levels within relevant racial groups, and defection rates are accelerated and diminished as a function of racial competition and disaffection within parties.

The full model, as it is written in 6.5 through 6.8, is a system of four nonlinear differential equations in four system states. Nonlinear differential equations present unique analytic problems because, unlike linear systems, solutions are not readily obtained and in most situations are not available (Huckfeldt, Kohfeld, and Likens 1982). Thus, in the appendix to Chapter 8 we develop our analytic strategy.

It would be possible to incorporate the concept of hard core supporters within the algebraic statement of the model. We have decided against such a strategy because it both complicates and trivializes the mathematical analysis. Placing a floor under white Democratic support levels means that the Democrats can always count upon support from the white population, but such a statement is not enlightening. This is not to say that the concept of hard-core supporters is substantively unimportant; rather, it should be addressed verbally and substantively instead of mathematically, a strategy we pursue in our argument.

7 The Politics of Class and Race: Alternative Forms of Interdependence

In this chapter we explore alternative forms of interdependence between parties and groups as they are specified in our model of the racial basis for party dynamics. Under conditions of racial hostility, what is the nature of the electoral relationship between white Democrats and white Republicans and between black Democrats and black Republicans? What is the nature of the relationship between white and black Democrats and between white and black Republicans? To answer these questions, precise distinctions must be drawn between electoral relationships that differ in important ways. Building upon these distinctions, attention is focused upon two political relationships of interest: competition and predation within and between political parties and racial groups.

The Nature of Interdependence

The competition label is used frequently to describe a variety of relationships in politics that might fruitfully be labeled differently and with greater precision. For example, it is often asserted that Democrats are in direct competition with Republicans, but the relationship between political parties actually takes on several different forms of interdependence. Competition is one of these forms, but it is certainly not the only one, or even the most important. For this book we adopt the vocabulary of ecology to distinguish between several different types of dynamic interdependence (May 1974).

In some instances the Democratic and Republican parties engage in activities that involve direct conflict over scarce resources, a situation in which one side must lose if the other side is to win. Coalition governments are not part of American politics, and thus either one party or the other must control the focal point of modern American government: the presidency. Such a relationship is properly labeled *competition* in its pure sense. If the Republicans succeed, then the Democrats must fail, and vice versa. A competitive relationship is present when the well-being of one party has a negative impact upon the well-being of the other party—a theoretical parallel to the zero-sum game.

When competition is defined in this more precise manner, it fails to capture the variety of relationships that occur in two-party democratic politics. Indeed, the relationship exactly opposite to competition is symbiosis, which frequently occurs between the two major parties. To cite an obvious example, the parties regularly cooperate to sustain the two-party system by supporting arrangements to ensure that third parties have a difficult time participating fully in electoral politics. In this instance the parties' interests run in a uniform direction, and the effect of increased well-being for the Democrats is also to increase Republican well-being, and vice versa.

Finally, the relationship between political parties might take on predatory qualities, wherein one party's well-being has a negative effect upon the other party's well-being, but the latter's well-being has a positive effect upon the well-being of the former. We will show that an increase in Republicans is generally bad news for the Democratic party but, given particular forms of interdependence between parties and groups, more Democrats may not always work to the ultimate disadvantage of the Republican party.

The specification of mobilization, conversion, and defection rates determines the extent of interdependence within the theory. Although each racial-political group is subject to a dynamic that is affected by the three other groups, special attention will be devoted to the relationships between members of the same racial group but the other party, as well as members of the same party but a different race. Particular concern rests upon the manner in which levels of white Democrat support change with respect to levels of both black Democratic support and white Republican support.

Racial Interdependence Within a Party

Our model of party dynamics can be manipulated to examine the relationship between coalition partners: the separate marginal effects of one race upon another within the confines of the same political party. These marginal effects are discussed here in terms of the relationship between blacks and whites in the Democratic party, but the same relational components would also, as a logical matter, be present between black and white Republicans as well. Indeed, close observers of the Republican party have already begun to detect some middle-class manifestations of racial conflict among the Republicans.

First consider the marginal effect of black Democratic densities upon changes in white Democratic densities (see Table 7.1). This marginal effect is derived from the specification of our model, and its substantive interpretation is that higher proportions of black Democratic support have a greater negative impact upon white Democratic support to the extent that there are: (1) higher levels of racial sensitivity among white Democrats (q); (2) higher levels of white Democratic support (WD_t); and (3) lower rates of white defection from the Democratic party to the Republican party for nonracial reasons (p). Similarly, the marginal effect of white Democrats upon black Democrats and its substantive interpretation runs in a parallel fashion. Higher proportions of white Democratic support have a greater negative impact upon black Democratic support to the extent that there are: (1) higher levels of racial sensitivity among black Democrats (d); (2) higher levels of black Democratic support (BD_t); and (3) lower rates of black defection from the Democratic party to the Republican party for nonracial reasons (c).

Table 7.1. Marginal effects of race within the Democratic party

Marginal Effects of Black Democrats Upon Changes in White Democrats
$$\text{Marginal effect of } BD_t \text{ upon } \dot{WD_t} = -qWD_t(1 - p)$$
Marginal Effects of White Democrats Upon Changes in Black Democrats
$$\text{Marginal effect of } WD_t \text{ upon } \dot{BD_t} = -dBD_t(1 - c)$$
where
BD_t = proportion of the eligible population at time t that is black and supports the Democratic party
WD_t = proportion of the eligible population at time t that is white and supports the Democratic party
q = racial sensitivity among white Democrats
p = rate at which white Democrats defect for nonracial reasons
d = racial sensitivity among black Democrats
c = rate at which black Democrats defect for nonracial reasons

Several features of these marginal effects deserve emphasis. The relationship between races within a party is always competitive. An increase in the density of black Democrats reduces the density of white Democrats, and vice versa. This feature of the model captures the critical qualitative element of our argument—animosity and suspicion characterize racial politics. A somewhat surprising feature of the marginal effect of black Democrats upon white Democrats is that it increases as the density of white Democrats increases. Similarly, black Democrats are more affected by the density of white Democrats as the density of black Democrats increases.

Our theory points toward a set of circumstances under which racial polarization in electoral politics is likely to be most severe. Electoral environments marked by high levels of racial sensitivity certainly produce more extensive competition between races. More interesting, however, is the role played by the political composition *within* a given race. Even if racial hostility is held constant, the effects of competition become more severe to the extent that races become politically homogeneous. Thus, the solid white Democratic South was especially vulnerable to the competitive effects of race because it was so heavily reliant upon the Democratic party. Similarly, the effect of racial competition upon black Democrats might be potentially heightened by the fact that blacks are so heavily reliant upon the Democratic party. In short, political heterogeneity within a race helps to offset racial competition within a party.

Much as a defective valve can cause a pressure cooker to explode, so a political party whose adherents have no alternative can lead to a politically explosive situation within the party. The logic of political competition between races indicates that the disintegrative effect of such competition might be offset if both competitors possess political alternatives. In very practical terms, the Democrats should not necessarily fear Republican appeals to the black voter or, for that matter, to the white voter. To the extent that political alternatives exist, both groups are less likely to defect from the party on the basis of racial disaffection.

The presence of political alternatives is, of course, a two-edged sword. Too many defections might, at the same time that they reduce racial conflict within the party, lead to the disintegration of the party's base of support. Such a danger does not compromise the basic principle: parties with the captive support of one racial group are more vulnerable to the disintegration of support as the result of racial competition. Thus the difficulties of racial conflict internal to the party might be mitigated by the presence of political alternatives for both races.

This analysis calls into question a bedrock assumption underlying many analyses of political coalitions. The spatial-modeling tradition (Downs 1957; Hirschman 1970) has frequently assumed that a party coalition is strengthened to the extent that coalition members have no place to turn. The lack of a politically palatable alternative, it is thought, cements the bonds between the party and the members of its coalition. The present analysis suggests, however, that the lack of an alternative may exacerbate competitive tendencies within the party and thereby inevitably weaken the unity and integrity of the party.

Political Interdependence Within a Race

The model can also be used to understand the nature of the relationship between parties within a race and the manner in which this relationship is transformed under conditions of racial competition. The intraracial relationship between parties is best illustrated by focusing upon whites, remembering that the relationship between parties is symmetric within both races. Thus, assuming that the Republican party eventually develops an appeal to the black middle class, the same logic would hold among blacks as well.

Based upon the model of party dynamics, the marginal effect of white Democrats upon the change in white Republicans may be expressed mathematically (see Table 7.2). Interpreted substantively, the mathematical form of this marginal effect suggests that increased levels of white Democratic support lead to decreases in white Republican support to the extent that the Republican party relies upon a mobilization strategy among whites and increases in white Republican support to the extent that (1) the defection rate among white Democrats is higher and (2) the Republican party is successful at converting white Democratic defectors. That is, to the extent that the Republican party seeks to mobilize nonvoters, increased levels of Democratic support injure Republican prospects. In contrast, to the extent that the Republican party seeks to convert defecting Democrats, increased levels of Democratic support provide the Republicans with increased opportunity.

Table 7.2. Marginal effects of party support among whites

Marginal Effect of White Democrats Upon Changes in White Republicans

Marginal effect of WD_t upon $\dot{WR}_t = -r(WR_t/P_w) + s(WR_t/P_w)[p + qBD_t(1 - p)]$

$$= -M_{WR_t} + C_{WR_t}D_{WD_t}$$

Thus, the marginal effect is negative if $M_{WR_t} > C_{WR_t}D_{WD_t}$

Marginal Effect of White Republicans Upon Changes in White Democrats

Marginal effect of WR_t upon $\dot{WD}_t = -m(WD_t/P_w) + n(WD_t/P_w)[u + wBR_t(1 - u)]$

$$= -M_{WD_t} + C_{WD_t}D_{WR_t}$$

Thus, the marginal effect is negative if $M_{WD_t} > C_{WD_t}D_{WR_t}$

where

M_{WD_t} = Democratic rate of mobilization among white nonvoters
C_{WD_t} = Democratic rate of conversion among white Republican defectors
D_{WR_t} = rate of defection among white Republicans
M_{WR_t} = Republican rate of mobilization among white nonvoters
C_{WR_t} = Republican rate of conversion among white Democratic defectors
D_{WD_t} = rate of defection among white Democrats

The marginal effect of white Republicans upon the change in white Democrats demonstrates the same logic (see Table 7.2). Increased levels of white Republican support lead to decreases in white Democratic support to the extent that the Democratic party relies upon a mobilization strategy among whites. Increased levels of white Republican support lead to increases in white Democratic support to the extent that (1) the defection rate among white Republicans is higher and (2) the Democrats are more successful at converting Republican defectors.

Consider the effect of white Republican support levels upon changes in white Democratic support levels. By providing a larger pool of potential converts, more white Republicans produce more white Democrats to the extent that the Democratic party depends upon a strong conversion appeal among white Republicans and to the extent that white Republicans defect from the party. More white Republicans result in fewer white Democrats to the extent that the Democratic party has a strong mobilization appeal to nonvoting whites, because more Republicans mean fewer nonvoters.

Perhaps the most important feature of the intraracial relationships between parties is that, unlike the intraparty relationship between races, the theory does not yield a determinant sign. Depending upon conversion and mobilization, and upon levels of defection, the relationship between parties within a race might conceivably be competitive, predatory, or symbiotic. In short, the relationship between parties depends upon the specifics of a particular political environment. What does this suggest regarding the relationships between parties in the post–New Deal period?

Whites and the Parties

Consider class politics absent racial hostility. What is the likely relationship between parties among whites? In such an environment, the Democratic party, as the party of the lower classes, is likely to be the party of mobilization: its primary task is to mobilize potential supporters and get them to the polls. In contrast, the Republican party, as the party of higher status groups, is likely to be the party of conversion as it concentrates its efforts upon winning away supporters from the Democrats. Parties of the lower classes tend to be parties of mobilization that seek to recruit the (mostly lower status) nonvoters, while upper-status parties are likely to be parties of conversion that seek to recruit support from the more conservative ranks of the lower-class party. Thus, under conditions of class politics, the relationship between parties is likely to be rooted in predation.

How is this predatory relationship likely to be altered by the politics of race? First, by recruiting blacks as well as whites, the Democratic party has produced racial disaffection among many of its white supporters, thereby leading to a higher rate of defection. In this way the politics of race is likely to reinforce predatory politics. Second, many defectors from the Democratic party do not become immediate converts to the Republican party, and thus the pool of nonvoting whites grows. This increased pool, which is not sympathetic to the Democrats, offers an unusual opportunity to the Republicans. The Republicans have the potential to pursue a successful mobilization strategy, and to the extent that such a mobilization strategy is pursued, the politics of predation may be replaced by the politics of competition. Such a scenario does not, of course, bode well for the Democrats, who are not only losing defectors at a high rate to the Republicans but who may be replaced as the party of mobilization among whites.

In summary, under conditions of class politics, higher densities of white Republicans are almost certain to have a negative effect upon the density of white Democrats. The general rule is that, in an environment where class is the crucial cleavage, Democrats do not regularly convert Republican defectors, while Republicans frequently convert Democratic defectors. Rather, in class-based politics, the Democrats will rely upon mobilization efforts among the generally lower status, nonvoting population. As a result, an increase in the ranks of Republicans has generally come at the direct expense of the Democrats.

The marginal effect of white Democratic support upon white Republican support may very well be positive under conditions of racial politics. At least in the longer term, an increase in Democratic support may not bode poorly for the Republican party. Upper-status parties do not typically attempt to increase turnout because, in the short-term, the differential effects of turnout tend to favor the lower-status party. Thus, the Republican mobilization appeal is likely to be low, and the Republican conversion appeal among Democrats is likely to outweigh significantly the Democratic conversion appeal among Republicans. Absent racial competition, the lower-status party becomes the party of mobilization, and the upper-status party benefits indirectly from these mobilization efforts because its pool of potential converts increases. This means that, under conditions of class politics and absent racial competition, the relationship between parties within a race is likely to be predaceous, where the upper-status party is the predator and the lower-status party—the party of mobilization—is the prey.

Thus, both parties benefit from the mobilization efforts of the lower-status party. The lower status party benefits directly, and the upper-status party benefits indirectly to the extent that it can convert voters from the lower-status party. The extent to which each party benefits and the point at which the benefits accrue are open to analysis. As the pool of nonvoting, but potentially mobilized, voters grows smaller, the prey—the lower status party—is in danger of extinction. This may indeed help to explain the decline of the old left in affluent Western democracies. Parties of mobilization are in a disadvantaged circumstance if the pool of potentially mobilized citizens grows small—hence the shift in relative positions between social democratic and conservative parties in several European nations may be a function of the decline in the size of the left's natural audience. In short, it is difficult to be the party of mobilization in an environment where there is no one to mobilize.

Such an explanation is less than satisfactory in the American context. When only 50 percent of eligible voters turn out to vote in the national spectacle of a presidential election, after the general population has been bombarded with political stimuli for nearly a year, it cannot be said that the pool of potentially mobilized citizens is nearing extinction. Rather, as we have said before, the decline of the Democratic party in American national politics must be explained on a different basis.

We now turn to the relationship between parties in a racially competitive electoral environment, where blacks tend to be Democratic and where white Democrats object to the presence of blacks in the party. The negative effect of white Republicans upon white Democrats becomes more severe because the pool of potential Republican converts is increased by racially disaffected defectors from the Democratic Party. Furthermore, racial hostility produces a larger pool of disgruntled, formerly Democratic, nonvoting whites subject to the mobilization efforts of the Republican party. Thus, under conditions of racial hostility, the Republican party is more likely to pursue a strategy of mobilization. Indeed, for the first time in recent history, voter mobilization efforts became a serious element of Republican strategy during the 1984 presidential election. In short, racial competition has the potential to transform the relationship between the parties from predation to competition by transforming the upper status party into a party of mobilization.

Competition and Predation Among Whites: 1948–80

To what extent do these expectations withstand the test of observation? It is possible to obtain estimates for mobilization, conversion, and defection rates among the white population for both parties throughout most of the postwar period. In every presidential election study from 1948 through 1980, the Center for Political Studies at the University of Michigan asked respondents whom they voted for in the recent and previous presidential elections. (Unfortunately, the queries of previous presidential voters were not included in the 1984 interview protocol.) Using these responses, it is a straightforward matter to estimate the rates between elections. Technically, this means that we are transforming our continuous-time representation of political change into a discrete-time representation. Rather than estimating continuous rates of change, we are estimating rates of change between presidential elections.

As a first step we examine the reliance of each party on a mobilization strategy versus that same party's reliance upon a strategy of converting defectors from the other party. Figure 7.1 plots the Democratic reliance, among whites, upon mobilization and conversion strategies through time.

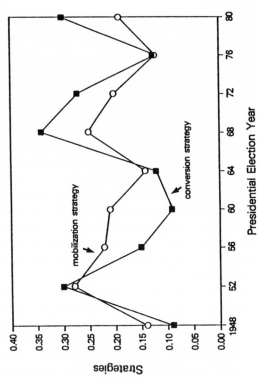

Figure 7.1. Mobilization strategy versus conversion strategy for the Democratic Party among whites, presidential elections from 1948–80.

white mobilization strategy = rate at which the Democratic party mobilized whites who did not vote at the previous election (M_{WD}). Average N size is 542. white conversion strategy = the product of 1. the rate at which whites who voted Republican at the previous election defected from Republican support (D_{WR}) and 2. the rate at which the Democratic party converted these defectors to Democratic support (C_{WD}). The average N sizes for the two rates are 677 and 195 respectively.

Source: National Election Studies, 1948–80.

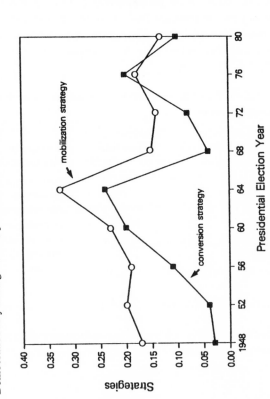

Figure 7.2. Mobilization strategy versus conversion strategy for the Republican Party among whites, presidential elections from 1948–80.

white mobilization strategy = rate at which the Republican party mobilized whites who did not vote at the previous election (M_{WD}). Average N size is 542. white conversion strategy = the product of 1. the rate at which whites who voted Democratic at the previous election defected from Democratic support (D_{WD}) and 2. the rate at which the Republican party converted these defectors to Republican support (C_{WR}). The average N sizes for the two rates are 635 and 215 respectively.

Source: National Election Studies, 1948–80.

The mobilization strategy is defined as the rate at which the Democrats mobilize whites who failed to vote at the previous election (M_{WD}). The conversion strategy is defined as the product of (1) the rate at which Republican voters in the previous election defect from Republican support and (2) the rate at which the Democrats are able to convert these defectors to Democratic support ($C_{WD}D_{WR}$). Only in one election does the conversion strategy surpass the mobilization strategy for the Democrats: the 1976 victory of Jimmy Carter over Gerald Ford.

The same procedure is employed to examine Republican efforts among white voters (see Figure 7.2). In this instance, however, the evidence is mixed. In the aftermath of 1964, the Republicans have relied predominantly upon a conversion strategy. Only in 1976 did the conversion strategy fail to surpass the mobilization strategy. In the period before 1964, the Republicans tended to rely more heavily upon a mobilization strategy.

On the basis of this information we can characterize the relationship between the parties among whites. When a party's mobilization strategy surpasses its conversion strategy ($M > CD$), the party is negatively affected by growth in the other party (see Table 7.2). When the conversion strategy surpasses the mobilization strategy, the party is positively affected by growth in the other party. The directions of these effects determine the nature of interdependence between the parties. Prior to 1964 the relationship was likely to be one of competition (see Table 7.3), while after 1964 it was likely to be one of predation, where the Democrats were the prey and the Republicans were the predators. Why? What had changed: conversion rates, defection rates, or mobilization rates?

Table 7.3. The nature of interdependence between the parties in the postwar period among whites

	Republican party effect upon Democratic party	Democratic party effect upon Republican party	Nature of relationship
1948	−	−	competition
1952	+	−	predation
1956	−	−	competition
1960	−	−	competition
1964	−	−	competition
1968	+	−	predation
1972	+	−	predation
1976	0	+	neither
1980	+	−	predation

The parties' mobilization rates among white nonvoters, displayed in Figure 7.3, reflect very little difference between the mobilization successes

Figure 7.3. Mobilization rates among whites by party, presidential elections from 1948–80.

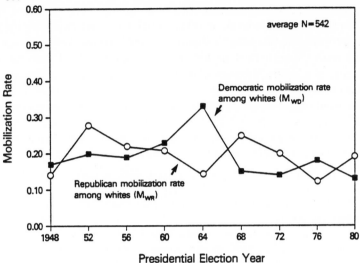

Presidential Election Year

white mobilization rate = the rate at which each party mobilized whites who did not vote at the previous election

Source: National Election Studies, 1948–80.

of the two parties. Indeed, if 1964 is omitted, the average mobilization rate is higher for the Republican party than it is for the Democratic party; whereas if 1964 is included, the averages are virtually the same. Figure 7.3 offers persuasive evidence for the demise of class in American politics. During the postwar period the Democratic party has ceased to be the dominant party of mobilization among whites.

These same data are not available for the New Deal period, so one must speculate regarding what the data would show, extended back to 1932. Several analyses offer strong evidence to suppose that Roosevelt's party was the party of mobilization—particularly in the period beginning in 1936 (Beck 1976; Andersen 1979; Brown 1987). Our data show quite clearly, however, that the Democratic mobilization advantage, which is the central feature of a lower-class party in a class-based system, disappeared in the postwar period.

Figure 7.4 compares the party defection rates between 1948 and 1980. In six of the nine elections, the Democrats held the dubious distinction of having a higher defection rate. The Dixiecrat walkout in 1948 and the Republican candidacy of Dwight Eisenhower in 1952 produced high rates of defection from the Democratic party, but these defection rates pale in comparison to those of more recent times. In the period following 1964, and especially in 1968, 1972, and 1980, the Democratic Party suffered extremely high rates of defection. In the aftermath of 1964, the white Democratic electorate began to hemorrhage.

The rates, among whites, at which parties convert defectors from the opposite party are presented in Figure 7.5, and it is especially instructive to focus upon the post-1964 period. Not only have white Democrats been defecting at a higher rate than white Republicans, but the Republican party has generally done a better job of attracting defectors. Only in 1976 does the Republican party conversion rate fall below the Democratic party conversion rate.

On the basis of this evidence, several statements can be made regarding the course of electoral politics among whites in the postwar period.

1. The Democratic and Republican parties cannot be significantly differentiated in their ability to mobilize nonvoting whites.

2. The Democratic party has been more reliant upon a mobilization strategy throughout the period.

3. The Republican party has become more reliant upon a conversion strategy in the aftermath of the 1964 presidential election, as it has taken advantage of substantial rates of defection from the Democratic Party.

4. As a result, the shift from competition to predation after 1964 is not due to a reinvigoration of class-based politics. Rather, it is the result of a hemorrhage in the white basis of support for the Democratic party.

In summary, the predatory politics of class was replaced by competitive politics in the immediate postwar period. The reorientation of American politics after 1964 reinstituted predatory politics, but it was predatory politics with a vengeance. No longer did the Democratic party have an edge over the Republican party in terms of mobilizing nonvoting whites. Rather, predation after 1964 was the result of increased levels of Democratic defection and Republican conversion. Ironically, we may be on the verge of reinstituting competitive politics, but it will be due to Republican dominance as the party of mobilization. This in turn means that the Republican party would be clearly dominant at both strategies: mobilization and conversion.

Blacks and the Parties

At least since 1964, the Democratic party has been extraordinarily successful among blacks, across all dimensions. Limited numbers of black respondents in the Center for Political Studies survey data keep us from engaging in a thorough analysis, but the general direction is clear. Quite simply, the Democrats have enjoyed a huge advantage among blacks across all dimensions: mobilization, conversion, and defection. Since the middle of the 1960s, the Democratic party has realized high levels of effectiveness in mobilizing nonvoting blacks (see Figure 1.3), while the Republican party has been relatively ineffective. The number of blacks sampled in the election

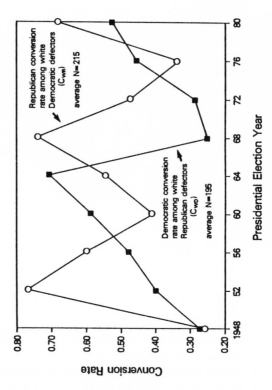

Figure 7.5. Conversion rates among white party defectors by party, for presidential elections from 1948–80.

white conversion rate = the rate at which each party converts the opposite party's defectors (for whites only)

Source: National Election Studies, 1948–80.

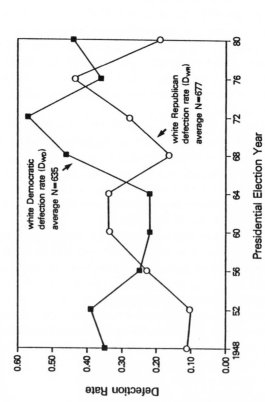

Figure 7.4. Defection rates among whites by party, presidential elections from 1948–80.

white defection rate = the rate at which each party's supporters in the previous election defected in the current election (for whites only)

Source: National Election Studies, 1948–80.

survey is often small, hence caution is in order (see Table 7.4). As the data for 1968–80 indicate, however, the average rate of Democratic mobilization among nonvoting blacks is .32, while the average rate of Republican mobilization is only .03.

Table 7.4. Mean defection, conversion, and mobilization rates among blacks, by party, 1968-80

	Average rate	Weighted average[a]	Average N
Democrats			
Mobilization	.32	.34	118
Conversion	.60	.55	10
Defection	.28	.23	130
Republicans			
Mobilization	.03	.02	118
Conversion	.14	.11	30
Defection	.86	.84	12

[a]The weighted average is the average of the yearly rates weighted by the yearly N.

The Democrats are not only the party of mobilization among blacks, they are also the party of conversion. In terms of defections, the average rate of defection among black Republicans in the period is a phenomenal .86; among black Democrats it is only .28. The Democratic conversion rate among black Republican defectors is .6, while the Republican conversion rate among black Democratic defectors is only .14. In summary, among blacks, the Republicans suffer from higher rates of defection than the Democrats. And the Democrats are more likely to attract Republican defectors than the Republicans are to attract Democratic defectors.

The success of the Democratic appeals among blacks has produced a situation in which the Democratic party is the predator and the Republicans are the prey. While the former has been very successful at mobilizing nonvoting blacks, the Democrats have done even better in terms of converting former Republican voters in the post-1964 period (i.e., $M_{BD_t} < C_{BD_t}D_{BR_t}$). This means that the marginal effect of an increase in black Republicans upon Democrats is (or at least would be) positive.

The effect of more black Democrats upon the vitality of black Republicanism is a different story. The Republicans tended to be slightly better at mobilizing black nonvoters during this period than they were at converting black Democrats (i.e., $M_{BR_t} > C_{BR_t}D_{BD_t}$). This means, in turn, that more black Democrats led to fewer black Republicans.

Among blacks, the relationship between the parties has come to be marked by predation, where the Democratic party is the predator. Since the crucial events of 1964, the Democratic party has enjoyed enormous success among the black population. This success has produced a situation in which the party is not only able to enjoy the advantage of huge Democratic majorities among black voters, but it is also able to prey upon the miniscule residual of black Republican support.

Conclusion

Absent racial competition, predation is the natural order of electoral politics in the presence of lower- and upper-status parties. Racial competition has the potential to reinforce and to disrupt this pattern: among Democrats it reinforces predatory politics to the extent that it leads to higher rates of defection from the party and to the extent that it produces a high rate of conversion of Democratic defectors by the Republican party. Racial competition within the Democratic party disrupts the predatory politics of class to the extent that the Republican party successfully seeks to mobilize the pool of politically disgruntled nonvoting defectors from the Democratic party. What difference does this make in the nature of electoral politics through time?

The most ironic consequence of these shifting strategies on the part of the Republican party is that the interests classically associated with that party are necessarily undermined. Republicans are not able to pursue a mobilization strategy or to convert racially disgruntled Democrats without significantly redefining their own appeal and thereby redefining the party's public policy vision. Consider the transformation of the party since Eisenhower, when it was economically conservative and probusiness. In spite of the furor his comments caused, Charles Wilson, a member of the Eisenhower cabinet, represented the Republican party well when he gave voice to the idea that the best interests of General Motors were coincidental with the best interests of America. At the same time, however, it was possible for a social liberal to belong to the party. On issues of civil rights, civil liberties, and individual freedoms, the Republican party was in many respects ahead of the Democratic party.

That Republican party is, for all practical purposes, a thing of the past. The new Republican party, sired by Barry Goldwater and sustained by Ronald Reagan, is an intentional or unintentional response to the politics of race, a curious blend of populist rebellion and conservative social backlash that frequently falls short of adequately representing the probusiness, upper-middle-class interests that formed the core of Eisenhower's party. The Democrats as well as the Republicans are currently scrambling to represent those interests—witness the "new industrial policies" advocated by the "neoliberal" Democrats. Neither party, however, possesses a coalition that neatly and logically incorporates the interests represented by the party of Eisenhower. In summary, it is not only the lower classes that suffer due to the demise of class politics. To the extent that class politics revolves around the crucial and legitimate interests of a society, interests at both ends of the class spectrum are likely to suffer.

It is also the case that the logic of class politics differs significantly from the logic of racial politics. One aspect of these differing logics is particularly important: the dynamic of predation is inherently more stable than the dynamic of competition. As we will demonstrate in the next chapter, the competitive logic of racial politics, the logic captured by our model, has considerable potential for undermining the stability of electoral politics.

8 The Prospects for Political Heterogeneity within Races

If democratic politics rests upon the preferences and choices of the people, is it possible to avoid racially structured politics when the people harbor racially competitive impulses? That is, is it possible to avoid a situation in which political preferences tend toward homogeneity within races? This question is important for several reasons. First, racially structured politics leads to a numerical mismatch: blacks and liberal whites do not constitute a winning coalition in national politics; indeed, they do not even constitute a competitive coalition. Second, racially structured politics is destructive of democracy—equal rights for blacks, and for all groups, must be supported by both parties. Race is not a legitimate basis for partisan conflict in democratic politics, and an electoral system structured in terms of race is destructive of democratic values.

The primary safeguard against racial polarization in electoral politics is the maintenance of political diversity among members of the same racial group. The danger of racially inspired politics is that other bases of political diversity might be overwhelmed and submerged by increasing political homogeneity within races. Thus, the maintenance of heterogeneous political preferences within racial groups serves to impose limits upon race as a structural component underlying mass politics. In this chapter we address the potential for stable, heterogeneous political preferences within a racial group. The discussion is carried out in terms of whites, but the same theoretical principles apply to blacks as well. Under what conditions can heterogeneous political preferences be maintained within a race? Does racial hostility or racial consciousness inevitably lead to the homogenization of political preferences within a race? These questions are addressed on the basis of the party dynamics model developed earlier. In anticipation of this analysis, two key issues must be discussed: (1) the nature of a party system equilibrium and (2) the conditions leading to stability and instability in party systems through time.

Party Systems, Intraracial Equilibria, and Stability

A party system is defined to be at an intraracial equilibrium when the proportional levels of support given to the parties remain constant within a race across time. Thus the system is at equilibrium among whites if the proportion of eligibles who are white and Democratic, and the proportion of eligibles who are white and Republican, remain constant in time. Of course, no party system maintains an equilibrium. Short-term forces constantly disrupt electoral politics, and thus an equilibrium is best seen as the long-term logic that underlies the brush fires and disruptions of day-to-day, week-to-week, and year-to-year politics. In this sense the concept of an electoral equilibrium is akin to Converse's (1966) conception of a normal vote—a long-term tendency rather than a deterministic rule.

An intraracial political equilibrium does not signify that either coalition must be static through time. A party system might be at equilbrium even though it suffers from high rates of defection and enjoys high rates of mobilization and conversion. There is an equilibrium so long as the *net* effects of mobilization, conversion, and defection are zero. Equilibrium does not mean an absence of change; rather, it requires that any change be balanced and offsetting (Smith 1974; Huckfeldt, Kohfeld, and Likens 1982).

Key (1955) defines a critical election as a "sharp and durable" change in voting behavior. Thus a critical election, or a critical election period (Niemi and Weisberg 1976), can be seen as a change from one equilibrium to another. In very approximate terms, the realignment of the 1890s produced a party system equilibrium in which the vast majority of the South was Democratic and vast majorities of the Midwest and Northeast were Republican. The realignment of the 1930s produced an equilibrium in which a large majority of both the Catholic ethnic working class and the white South were Democratic and a vast majority of the Protestant middle class outside the South was Republican (Ladd and Hadley 1978). Each of these realignments also ushered in a period of partisan dominance—a long-term period of ascendancy by one of the parties. In short, realignments have the potential to produce new equilibria that favor one party or the other.

Viewed in this light, the abstract relevance of an equilibrium becomes clear. If democratic politics is to possess logic and order, it is necessary that parties and candidates construct appeals and programs that persist through time, undergirded by a base of electoral support that is not only predictable in terms of its size but also in terms of its composition. Electoral realignments take on importance because they redefine the political landscape by redefining the party system equilibrium that underlies democratic politics.

This leads to an important characteristic of any partisan equilibrium, namely, its stability. A party system is stable if it returns to equilibrium after some set of short-term political circumstances has moved it away from equilibrium. The party system installed by Franklin Roosevelt and the New Deal appeared to possess a stable equilibrium when the Democratic party returned to its old position of presidential dominance in the 1960 election. The equilibrium appeared even more stable after the Johnson landslide of 1964. By 1970, however, Kevin Phillips (1969) was able to argue that Democratic dominance was the relic of a bygone era and that a new conservative majority was leading the Republicans to ascendancy.

According to this view, a stable political equilibrium favorable to the Democratic party began to disintegrate over a relatively short period of time, and the Democrats' ability to regain their position of ascendancy was rendered problematic. Democratic dominance had been disturbed in the past by a variety of factors: postwar economic turbulence, the fear of Communists within domestic politics, and a militarily victorious and personally attractive general at the head of the Republican presidential ticket. In previous instances, however, the Democratic party was able to recover its position of ascendancy. What had changed?

The most widely cited causes of the Democratic party's problems in the late 1960s and onward were Vietnam, racial disturbances in American cities, and new social issues—abortion, school busing, affirmative action, and so on (Scammon and Wattenberg 1970). All of these issues and problems are important, of course, but none of them in isolation explains satisfactorily the extreme levels of racial polarization demonstrated in earlier chapters. Furthermore, these commonly cited dilemmas for the Democratic party were essentially transitory in nature; while they might explain why the party faltered, they fail to explain why it could not be reconstructed.

The conditions that gave rise to the demise of the New Deal party system are more fundamental in nature and relate directly to the rise of race as an issue in American partisan politics—and particularly to the inability of coalition partners to achieve a sustained level of tolerance for one another. The Democratic coalition has been undermined as a direct result of its changing racial composition and the level of racial hostility that is present in American society. Ultimately, the party system itself has been dramatically altered.

If Phillips was correct, one stable equilibrium, favorable to the Democratic party, was replaced by another stable equilibrium favorable to the Republican party. But there is another potential explanation as well. It is at least possible that the new system possesses no stable equilibrium at all. And thus, electoral coalitions frequently unravel in a way that produces political homogeneity within races.

It is important to recognize that this unraveling process does not proceed in the same way in different places and at different times. In some places, for some elections, the Democratic party is alive and well and even thriving; in some places, for some elections, it is able to maintain a successful biracial coalition. Thus, we are analyzing a process that unfolds differently at different places and at different times. Our goal in this chapter and the next is to specify the structural and strategic ingredients (and their variation through time and space) that are responsible for the failures and successes of biracial politics.

Partisan Equilibrium Within a Race

The model set forth in Chapter 6 sheds light on the nature of partisan equilibrium within a race and the conditions that must be present for such an equilibrium to be stable, the set of circumstances under which heterogeneous political preferences can be maintained within a race. The discussion here focuses upon the prospects for maintaining political heterogeneity among whites, but the same principles apply to the potential for maintaining political heterogeneity among blacks.

What conditions must be present for *any* sort of equilibrium to be present, stable or unstable? According to our model, the dynamics of electoral politics are driven by three factors: mobilization, conversion, and defection to and from both parties, among both whites and blacks. Equilibrium exists among the members of a race when the three sources of change produce a net effect that is zero, both for the Democratic party and for the Republican party (see Table 8.1). Equilibrium is attained within the white population when, for both Republicans and Democrats, losses due to defections are offset by gains due to mobilization and conversion, so that net change is zero.

Two questions then arise: What conditions satisfy these equilibrium relationships? What are the political equilibria for the white population? To make our task manageable, we temporarily assume that racial competition is absent within both parties ($q = w = 0$). With this assumption, and with the definitions of defection, conversion and mobilization rates from Chapter 6, equilibria conditions are shown in Table 8.2[A]. These conditions take the form of two equations, where the first establishes conditions for a white equilibrium in Democratic support and the second establishes conditions for a white equilibrium in Republican support. In order for whites to be at a system equilibrium, both equations must be satisfied (Huckfeldt, Kohfeld, and Likens 1982).

Several features of these equilibrium conditions are particularly important. First, both conditions are satisfied by setting white Democratic support and white Republican support to zero. Second, if equilibrium in white Democratic support is attained by setting it to zero, another equilibrium in white Republican support can be attained by setting it to $[(r - u)Pw]/r$. Third, if

Table 8.1 Defining equilibria

The dynamics underlying political preferences among whites are restated as

$$\dot{WD_t} = M_{WD_t}(P_w - WD_t - WR_t) + C_{WD_t}D_{WR_t}WR_t - D_{WD_t}WD_t \text{ (for white Democrats)}$$

$$\dot{WR_t} = M_{WR_t}(P_w - WR_t - WD_t) + C_{WR_t}D_{WD_t}WD_t - D_{WR_t}WR_t \text{ (for white Republicans)}$$

where

M_{WD_t}, M_{WR_t} = mobilization rates among white nonvoters for the Democrats and Republicans, respectively

D_{WD_t}, D_{WR_t} = defection rates among white Democrats and white Republicans, respectively

C_{WD_t}, C_{WR_t} = conversion rates among white defectors from the opposite party for the Democrats and Republicans, respectively

In order for an equilibrium to be present among whites, it must be the case that $\dot{WD_t} = \dot{WR_t} = 0$.

Thus, the white equilibrium is defined as

$$0 = M_{WD_t}(P_w - WD_t - WR_t) + C_{WD_t}D_{WR_t}WR_t - D_{WD_t}WD_t \text{ (for white Democrats)}$$

$$0 = M_{WR_t}(P_w - WR_t - WD_t) + C_{WR_t}D_{WD_t}WD_t - D_{WR_t}WR_t \text{ (for white Republicans)}$$

equilibrium in white Republican support is attained by setting it to zero, another equilibrium in white Democratic support is attained by setting it to $[(m - p)Pw]/m$. In summary, three equilibria are identified where one or both support levels are at zero—that is, where political diversity, or heterogeneity, is eliminated among whites.

Finally, and crucially for this analysis, it is possible that a fourth, nonzero equilibrium might be present, an equilibrium in which heterogeneous political preferences are present among whites. Returning to Table 8.2, a fourth equilibrium is present for white political preferences if both equations in Part B are satisfied. These equations are important because they have the potential to produce an equilibrium involving support for both parties, hence the maintenance of political diversity among whites. The first equation establishes conditions for white Democratic support to be at equilibrium; the second equation establishes conditions for an equilibrium in white Republican support. Both equations produce straight lines in two dimensions, where one dimension is measured by the metric of white Democratic support (*WD*) and the other is measured in terms of white Republican support (*WR*). Unless the two equilibrium lines are perfectly parallel, they produce an intersection, and that intersection signifies a point at which white support for *both* parties is at equilibrium.

We do not know, however, where such an equilibrium will occur. If the intersection occurs outside the area where both white Republican support

Table 8.2. Equilibria conditions

A. General Conditions

After substitution, the definition for equilibrium in Table 8.1 generates the following general conditions

$$0 = [(m/P_w)(P_w - WD - WR) + (n/P_w)(uWR) - p]WD$$
$$0 = [(r/P_w)(P_w - WD - WR) + (s/P_w)(pWD) - u]WR$$

where

m = Democratic mobilization appeal among whites

r = Republican mobilization appeal among whites

n = Democratic conversion appeal among white Republican defectors

s = Republican conversion appeal among white Democratic defectors

p = Democratic defection rate among whites

u = Republican defection rate among whites

B. Conditions for a Politically Heterogeneous (Nonzero) Equilibrium

An important means of satisfying the conditions shown in Part A is to set the bracketed quantities equal to zero. This yields two equations which generate straight lines in a (WD, WR) plane. Any point on the first line produces an equilibrium in white Democratic support, and any point on the second line produces an equilibrium in white Republican support. A politically heterogeneous equilibrium among whites will only exist if these two lines intersect in the first quadrant — in the area of the plane where both WR and WD are positive.

$$WR = \frac{(m - p)P_w}{m - nu} - \frac{mWD}{m - nu} \quad \text{(white Democratic equilibrium)}$$

$$WR = \frac{(r - u)P_w}{r} + \frac{(sp - r)WD}{r} \quad \text{(white Republican equilibrium)}$$

and white Democratic support are positively valued, then the equilibrium is unattainable and no fourth, substantively meaningful, nonzero equilibrium is present for the electoral system. Consider the several examples portrayed graphically in Figure 8.1. In Parts A, B, and C intersections occur in a meaningful area of the plane where WR and WD are both positively valued. Thus, for these hypothetical electoral systems, meaningful equilibria are present which signify heterogeneous political preferences — situations in which political diversity is maintained among whites because both parties receive support. Now examine Parts D and E: intersections could be produced by extending the lines, but the resulting equilibria would lie beyond meaningful bounds — greater than one or less than zero in at least one of the system states. Thus, for these hypothetical systems, no fourth equilibrium exists, and the potential for a politically heterogeneous equilibrium is absent.

It is crucial to recognize that the presence of an equilibrium does not

Figure 8.1. Possible intersections between equilibrium lines.

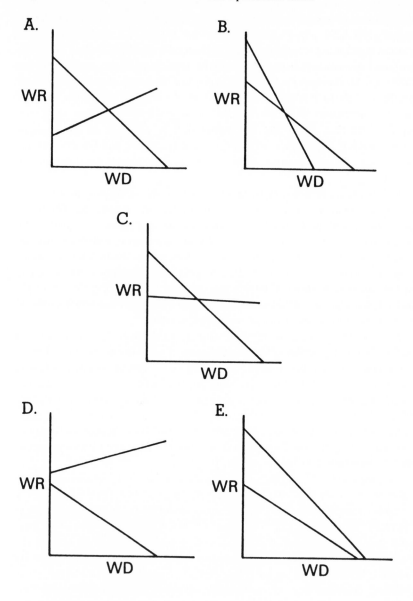

WR=White Republican Proportion
WD=White Democratic Proportion

guarantee that the equilibrium will be stable. Some equilibria are inherently unstable, and even small displacements produce a divergent process. Thus it is important to establish criteria for determining motion in the two-dimensional (WR, WD) plane (Smith 1968). As Figure 8.2 shows, horizontal motion is attracted toward the white Democratic equilibrium line ($\dot{WD} = 0$), and vertical motion is attracted toward the white Republican equilibrium line ($\dot{WR} = 0$). Motion can occur at any angle, but the angle of motion is the net product of these horizontal and vertical attractions, where the strength of each attraction is a direct function of distance from the respective equilibrium line. Thus the horizontal pull is stronger as the distance from the white Democratic equilibrium line increases, and the vertical pull is stronger as the distance from the white Republican equilibrium line increases.

Before proceeding it may be helpful to consider the manner in which our model accounts for births, deaths, and population movements. We are, in part, incorporating deaths within the defection rate from each party. One reason that parties lose supporters is that some previous supporters die. We also assume implicitly, a constant flow of births and deaths from and to the pool of citizens who are not mobilized politically. An important source of mobilization is the pool of new voters who are just entering the electorate. Indeed, the analyses in earlier chapters intentionally include newly come-of-age voters in the calculation of mobilization rates.

How would births and deaths affect the equilibrium analysis of Chapters 8 and 9? The only possible effects would occur if birth and death rates affected the social structure parameters by altering either the racial composition of the underlying population or the proportion of either race that is engaged politically. These social structure parameters could also change as the result of population movements to and from a particular area. Indeed, as we argue earlier, this latter factor was responsible for large scale changes in the social structure of cities like Chicago, and these social changes ultimately generated far-reaching consequences for city politics.

As a substantive issue, the political consequences either of birth and death rates or of population movements might be profound. In the analyses in Chapters 8 and 9, we explicitly hold social structure constant, just as we hold constant the strategic choices of parties and politicians. Subject to these assumptions, we can assess the dynamic properties of particular social and political settings. If either the structure or the strategies change, then the dynamic properties must be reassessed. In substantive terms, the set of political strategies that seemed to work very well for Chicago's Democratic politicians during the 1950s quit working during the 1970s and 1980s. The reason, quite clearly, was the transformation of the underlying social structure.

Figure 8.2. Motion in the two-dimensional plane.

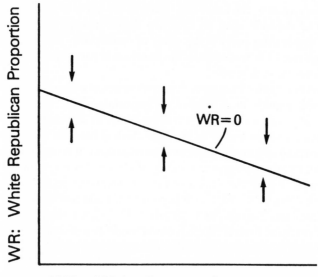

WD: White Democratic Proportion

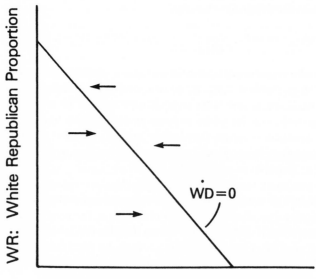

WD: White Democratic Proportion

The Dynamics of Class-based Politics

We argue that class politics tends to be predatory politics, where the lower-class party is the prey and the upper-class party is the predator. In such a predatory system, the lower-class party is the party of mobilization, and its survival depends upon an effective appeal among nonvoters. In contrast, the upper-class party is the party of conversion, and it depends upon (1) a high rate of defection from the lower-class party and (2) its own ability to convert these defectors.

The analysis in Chapter 7 suggests that postwar politics has deviated from this class-based pattern in a number of important ways, the dynamic consequences of which we explore in the remainder of this chapter. Class-based, predatory politics serves as the hypothetical baseline model from which to understand several other electoral relationships. It is our contention that this model roughly portrays the reality of electoral politics during the New Deal period, before the advent of race in American politics. Others might agree or disagree with us on this point (cf. Ladd and Hadley 1978; Clubb, Flanigan, and Zingale 1980; Shively 1971–72), but the issue is not crucial to the analysis. Even if the class based model has never served as an accurate portrayal of American electoral politics, it still serves as a useful vantage point from which to evaluate postwar American politics.

In Chapter 7 it was established that a predatory electoral relationship between the parties is present among whites when:

(white Democratic mobilization rate) > (white Democratic conversion rate)
× (white Republican defection rate)
and when:
(white Republican mobilization rate) < (white Republican conversion rate)
× (white Democratic defection rate).

The presence of a predatory relationship may also be determined on the basis of the equations in Table 8.2[B]. If the relationship is predatory, the white Democratic equilibrium line must slope downward as a function of white Republican growth, and the white Republican equilibrium line must slope upward as a function of white Democratic growth. In other words, more Republicans means a lower Democratic equilibrium, but more Democrats means a higher Republican equilibrium.

Two such predatory relationships are represented in Figure 8.3, though only one produces an equilibrium with diverse political preferences among whites. A predatory relationship only produces a nonzero equilibrium (diverse preferences) if the inequality shown in Table 8.3 is satisfied. Thus, political predation does not necessarily produce an equilibrium in which support survives for both parties—an equilibrium that sustains political diversity within a race.

Figure 8.3. Stable and unstable predation.

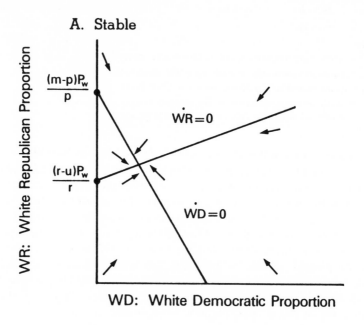

A. Stable

WR: White Republican Proportion

$\frac{(m-p)P_w}{p}$

$\dot{WR}=0$

$\frac{(r-u)P_w}{r}$

$\dot{WD}=0$

WD: White Democratic Proportion

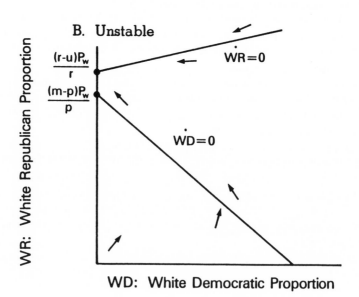

B. Unstable

WR: White Republican Proportion

$\frac{(r-u)P_w}{r}$

$\frac{(m-p)P_w}{p}$

$\dot{WR}=0$

$\dot{WD}=0$

WD: White Democratic Proportion

Table 8.3 Political heterogeneity in a predatory system

Predation only produces a politically heterogeneous equilibrium if

$$\frac{m - p}{m - nu} > \frac{r - u}{r}$$

where

m = white mobilization appeal of Democratic party
p = nonracial defection rate among white Democrats
r = white mobilization appeal of Republican party
n = white conversion appeal of Democratic party
u = nonracial defection rate among white Republicans

In general, a weak Democratic party with a reduced mobilization appeal (lower m) and a high defection rate (higher p) might foreclose the possibility of such an equilibrium. Further, an aggressive Republican party that expands its appeal by pursuing nonvoters (higher r) without suffering from higher defection rates (higher u) also undermines such a potential. Thus, political predation does not guarantee political diversity within a race, but a politically heterogeneous equilibrium is more likely to be produced to the extent that the predator is able to pursue a mobilization strategy successfully without excessive rates of defection and to the extent that the predator does not develop its own mobilization appeal. The vulnerability of predatory relationships is that the prey might be extinguished. In the politics of class-based electoral systems this is less likely to occur if the prey is able to maintain its monopoly as the party of mobilization.

The dynamic nature of predatory relationships is determined by examining the trajectories in Figure 8.3. Part A demonstrates a stable equilibrium in which motion is attracted toward the equilibrium. Indeed predatory relationships produce nonzero equilibria that are inherently stable. Thus, the inequality in Table 8.3 is not only the condition for a nonzero predatory equilibrium, but also the condition for a stable predatory relationship in which the political system is able to recover after some political disturbance moves it away from equilibrium.

In contrast, Part B of Figure 8.3 makes clear that, lacking an equilibrium, the relationship between the parties is inherently unstable. When the inequality in Table 8.3 is not satisfied—that is, when a predatory equilibrium is not present—the prey disappears. What are the consequences of instability? One party disappears and another party probably attempts to take its place; or one party dissolves and is reformulated with a modified appeal and platform (Sundquist 1983).

It is important to note that class politics is predatory politics and tends to be very stable so long as an equilibrium is present. That is, class politics tends to be very stable unless the upper-class party (the predator) is too healthy or the lower-class party (the prey) is too weak. In the following discussion we consider ways in which this might occur—ways in which a stable predatory relationship might be disturbed. Part A of Figure 8.3 serves as the baseline, from which we alter conditions and examine their consequences.

The Effects of Race Upon Class Politics

We have already considered this class-based predatory relationship in the absence of race, and now it is time to reintroduce considerations of race into the relationship. Racial animosity within the Democratic coalition is most likely to alter the electoral relationship in three ways: (1) by increasing the conversion appeal of the Republicans among white Democratic defectors, (2) by increasing the defection rate among white Democrats, and (3) by increasing the mobilization appeal of the Republicans among white nonvoters. There are other possibilities as well—for example, by reducing the mobilization appeal of Democrats—but the three stated above are most important.

What are the consequences of increased effectiveness in the conversion appeal of the predator? In Figure 8.4 we depict the consequence of altering Republican conversion appeal among Democratic defectors. The basic geometry is maintained—indeed, the equilibrium line for the white Democrats does not change, but the point of intersection does change. As the conversion rate increases, the steepness of the Republican equilibrium line increases, and the point of intersection becomes more favorable to the Republicans and less favorable to the Democrats. The basic geometry stays the same, however, and thus the stablity of the resulting equilibrium is maintained.

The effect of an increased Democratic defection rate is evident in Figure 8.5. In this instance, the equilibrium lines are affected for both parties. Increased defection rates produce parallel equilibrium lines for the Democrats that are, of course, shifted in the direction of lower Democratic support levels. Increased Democratic defection rates also produce steeper Republican equilibrium lines. Notice, however, that increased rates of Democratic defection do not necessarily produce an equilibrium that is more beneficial to the Republicans. As the white Democratic equilibrium line continues to shift toward the lower left corner, the system equilibrium will inevitably produce lower levels of support both for the Democrats and for the Republicans. In a predatory relationship, the well-being of the Republicans depends upon the well-being of the Democrats, and thus an increased Democratic defection rate has the potential to erode the position of the Republicans.

Once again the basic nature of the electoral relationships remains unchanged (compare Figures 8.4 and 8.5). In both instances, first by increasing

Figure 8.4. Effect of Republican conversion appeal among white Democratic defectors.

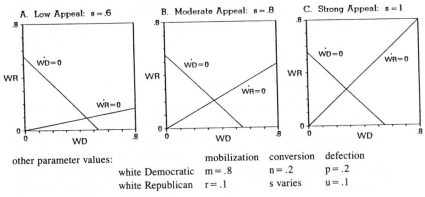

other parameter values:

	mobilization	conversion	defection
white Democratic	m = .8	n = .2	p = .2
white Republican	r = .1	s varies	u = .1

Figure 8.5. Effect of white Democratic defection rate.

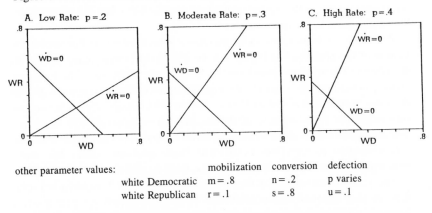

other parameter values:

	mobilization	conversion	defection
white Democratic	m = .8	n = .2	p varies
white Republican	r = .1	s = .8	u = .1

the Republican conversion appeal and then by increasing the Democratic defection rate, the relationship between the parties becomes more predatory—that is, the slope of the white Republican equilibrium line becomes steeper. Predatory equilibria are inherently stable, and thus in both instances the stability of the electoral system is likely to be maintained.

Under fairly extreme circumstances it is possible for higher Democratic defection rates to be destabilizing. As the defection rate continues to increase, the intercept for the white Democratic equilibrium line continues to decrease. Finally, when the white Democratic defection rate (p) is greater than the Democratic mobilization appeal among whites (m), the intercept for the white Democratic equilibrium line becomes negative. At that point the equilibrium line no longer passes through the substantively meaningful area of the plane where *WD* and *WR* are both positive. More important, as the defection rate increases, the condition shown in Table 8.3 is less likely to be satisfied, and thus a politically heterogeneous equilibrium is less likely to be present. In short, extremely high defection rates for the Democratic party, relative to its mobilization appeal, foreclose the possibility of an equilibrium, and as a result they can be destabilizing within the context of predatory politics.

Finally, consider the effect of increased mobilization effectiveness on the part of the Republicans. As Figure 8.6 shows, increasing mobilization effectiveness on the part of the Republicans transforms the nature of electoral politics in fundamental ways. The baseline predatory relationship in Part A is replaced by a competitive electoral relationship in Part B in which both equilibrium lines are negatively sloped: increased Democratic support levels produce decreases rather than increases in the Republican equilibrium. The stability of the equilibrium is maintained, however. A further increase in Republican mobilization effectiveness results in the absence of a nonzero equilibrium in Part C. As the trajectories show, the prey disappears in such circumstances (see also Figure 8.3[B]).

Several conclusions can be drawn. First, an increased rate of Republican conversion among white Democratic defectors only serves to make the political system more predatory. While such an increased conversion appeal bodes well for the Republican party and poorly for the Democratic party, it is not destabilizing. An equilibrium is maintained for the political system which, because it is rooted in predation, is fundamentally stable.

Second, an increased rate of Democratic defection also makes the political system more predatory, but it carries with it the potential to undermine system stability. As the rate of Democratic party defection among whites increases, the potential increases for the disappearance of a system equilibrium. In such a situation, the Democrats would disappear.

Third, an even more fundamental transformation of the political system occurs as a result of increased mobilization on the part of the Republican party. As the Republicans increase their mobilization appeal among white nonvoters, the political system is restructured from a predatory logic to a competitive logic. While it is possible to produce a stable competitive equilibrium, continued increases in Republican mobilization are likely to undermine this potential.

The Destabilizing Consequences of Competition

How does racial competition within the Democratic party affect the relationship between the parties among whites? At the very least, racial competition produces a higher rate of white defection from the Democratic party and a higher rate of conversion by the Republicans. In Chapter 7 we

Figure 8.6. Effect of Republican mobilization appeal among whites.

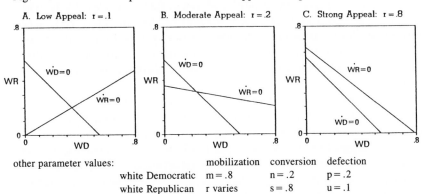

other parameter values:		mobilization	conversion	defection
	white Democratic	m = .8	n = .2	p = .2
	white Republican	r varies	s = .8	u = .1

suggest that racial competition has also created a political opportunity for the Republican party to increase its mobilization appeal among white nonvoters who are disaffected from the Democratic party.

Increased mobilization effectiveness on the part of the Republican party has consequences that are much more profound than either increased Republican conversion effectiveness or increased Democratic party defection rates. Especially in view of the relatively low rates of Democratic party mobilization among whites, even slight increases in Republican mobilization effectiveness fundamentally transform the nature of the electoral relationship between the parties. In particular, the electoral logic shifts from predation to competition, and with this shift comes a higher potential for instability.

Class-based predatory politics involves distinctive electoral strategies by each of the parties: the lower-class party pursues new recruits among the nonvoters, while the upper-class party pursues new recruits among the defectors from the lower-class party. In contrast, competitive politics is characterized by the similar strategies of the parties: both parties pursue new recruits from the same sources. This sort of electoral system, which is exactly opposite the predatory politics of a class-based system, is likely to undermine system stability. Four possible competitive dynamics are shown in Figure 8.7, but only one of these—shown in Part A—yields a stable equilibrium in which political diversity is maintained within the racial group.

Now consider two evenly matched parties with convergent electoral strategies—with equivalent conversion and mobilization appeals as well as equivalent defection rates. In such a situation, the conditions for stable competition reduce to the inequality shown in Table 8.4. This condition will always hold, because by definition for a competitive system both parties' mobilization appeals (x) must exceed the product of their conversion appeals

Figure 8.7. Four competitive dynamics.

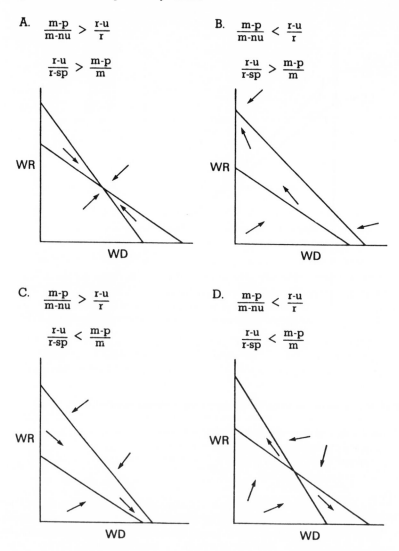

(y) and the opposite parties' defection rates (z). However, as the system becomes increasingly competitive, as x becomes increasingly larger than the product of y and z, the condition comes asymptotically closer to the point of *not* holding. In an extremely competitive system, where the parties are evenly matched and where the strategic emphasis is upon mobilization rather

Figure 8.8. The two equilibrium lines become more nearly coincidental as:

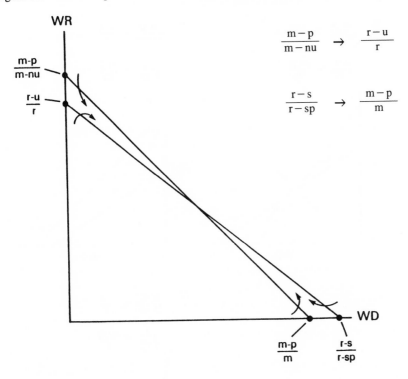

Table 8.4. Convergent electoral strategies and political competition

Political convergence is defined mathematically as
  equivalent mobilization appeal: $m = r = x$
  equivalent mobilization appeal: $n = s = y$
  equivalent defection rate: $p = u = z$
where
  m, r = white mobilization appeals of Democrats and Repubicans, respectively
  n, s = white conversion appeals of Democrats and Republicans, respectively
  p, u = nonracial defection rates among whites for Democrats and Republicans, respectively
This in turn means that the conditions for a stable equilibrium reduce to
$$\frac{x - z}{x - yz} > \frac{x - z}{x}$$

than conversion, the equilibrium lines for the parties come very close to being coincidental (see Figure 8.8).

This geometry has two important consequences. First, it means that even slight changes in the strategic successes and failures of the parties are likely to generate instability—to produce a situation in which the equilibrium lines fail to intersect. As long as the parties are evenly matched, this poses no problem and a stable equilibrium is guaranteed. Unlike a predatory equilibrium, however, this evenly matched competitive equilibrium is very delicately constructed and highly likely to come undone (Smith 1974).

Second, even when such an equilibrium exists, motion toward equilibrium is likely to be very sluggish. A political event that profits one party at the expense of the other produces a temporarily high level of support for one party and a low level of support for the other. In a fast responding system, the equilibrium will be rapidly recovered; but in a slow responding system, such as the one we have described, it may take a very long time to recover (Cortes, Przeworski, and Sprague 1974; Huckfeldt 1983b). Consider Figure 8.8 again; Once the trajectory enters the region between the two equilibrium lines, the attraction toward the equilibrium point becomes extremely weak, and the movement correspondingly slow. Even though the electoral system has a stable equilibrium, the dynamic of the system is only weakly structured by that equilibrium. If the system is frequently shocked by political events, as we would expect a competitive system to be, then the practical significance of the competitive equilibrium is greatly reduced.

To what do we owe the instability of competitive politics? In predatory politics the presence of two healthy opponents leads to a stable equilibrium. In competitive politics, even if the opponents are healthy, the presence of a stable equilibrium is genuinely problematic. The demise of class politics in America, and with it the demise of a predatory dynamic, has produced an electoral system whose very structure fosters a higher level of instability. At least on the surface, both parties seem to be very healthy: both have committed cores of supporters (strong identifiers) that have stayed relatively constant in terms of proportional sizes for more than forty years. From a somewhat different perspective, however, the importance of hard-core supporters within the parties becomes readily apparent. Without these reliable supporters, the electoral system would more clearly reflect the unstable dynamic we have described.

The Transformed Logic of American Politics

This analysis, in combination with the analysis presented in Chapter 7, helps to clarify the Democratic party's problem. The Democrats no longer have a monopoly upon the ability to mobilize support among white nonvoters. Indeed, there is strong evidence to suggest that the Republican party is becoming the party of mobilization among whites. This simple fact is not only important in terms of its short-term consequences for levels of electoral support but also because it alters the structure of American electoral politics.

We might think of postwar electoral history as occurring in two phases, with a third phase looming on the horizon. During the first phase, from roughly 1948 until 1960, the relationship between the parties was competitive. The Democratic and Republican parties had comparable levels of success at mobilizing nonvoters, and their defection and conversion rates were comparable as well. In view of their closely matched levels of success, the period is best understood in terms of the competitive logic depicted in Figure 8.7 and the inherently unstable dynamics of closely matched competitive parties.

Why did support for one of the parties not disappear during this period? In Chapter 6 we argue that some proportion of each party's support in each racial group is secluded from the dynamic; it forms a hard core of support that is much less likely to defect. These groups of hard-core supporters impose boundaries upon the dynamic and thereby maintain some minimum level of party support. In other words, a party can be sheltered from the consequences of an unstable dynamic by its hard-core supporters.

A second phase began after the watershed events of 1964, starting in 1968 and extending at least through 1980 and perhaps through the present. The chief difference between this period and the earlier period is the beginning of large-scale defections from the Democratic party. These increased levels of defection, and correspondingly higher rates of Republican conversion, pushed the system back toward a predatory logic, but this new predatory system involved a weakened prey. Unlike a class-based predatory system, the Republicans also enjoyed, overall, a slight edge in terms of mobilizing nonvoters. Thus the dynamic logic is very close to that of unstable predation (Figure 8.3[B]), where the prey disappears from the system because an equilibrium is not present. Once again, however, the process may not lead to its logical culmination because of the hard-core supporters who lie beyond the reach of the dynamic.

The logic of unstable predation also describes, in reversed partisan terms, the structure of electoral politics among blacks, but for blacks the situation is more extreme. The Democrats hold a significant mobilization advantage over the Republicans, but the relationship between the parties is still predatory because the Democrats are also able to take advantage of a very high defection rate among black Republicans. In short, during this second phase, predatory politics was present among both blacks and whites, and in both instances the prey was in danger of extinction. Thus the system generally moved toward the production of homogeneous political preferences within racial groups.

The 1984 national election may have introduced a third phase in the demise of the Democratic party, where the Republican party not only takes advantage of Democratic defections but where its mobilization appeal far surpasses that of the Democrats. In states like North Carolina during the 1984 election, the Democratic party was undeniably and dramatically eclipsed as the party of mobilization among whites. "Get out the vote" campaigns were once the sole domain of Democratic party strategists, but now it is often in the best interests of the Democrats to maximize turnout among blacks, and to minimize turnout among whites. If the Republican party has permanently increased its mobilization appeal among whites, then the relationship between the parties is one of competition (see Figure 8.7[C]), and one of the competitors—the Democratic party—is in danger of losing its basis of support within the white population.

In summary, the politics of race has altered the logic of electoral politics. The strong appeal of the Democratic party toward the black vote has produced a situation in which the party of black mobilization is also able to prey upon a greatly weakened black residual within the Republican party. The result, for all practical purposes, has been the political homogenization of black Americans. The strong black presence within the Democratic party has, in turn, often led to a significant exodus from the party on the part of white Democrats. This exodus has generated (1) a renewed predatory dynamic to the party system, but with a prey that is in danger of extinction, and (2) an opportunity for the Republican party to not only convert Democratic defectors but also to become the party of mobilization among nonvoting whites. In many locales and in many elections, the end result has been political homogenization among blacks *and* whites.

Two questions naturally arise. How long can hard core supporters sustain the Democratic party within the white population? It is doubtful that such support will allow the Democrats to survive indefinitely. The size of this core group is likely to decay over time, as the inability of the party to win national elections becomes increasingly apparent. More important, while hard-core Democrats have been able to keep their party from expiring, it is clear that they cannot restore it to competitiveness in national elections. Is it possible to sustain political heterogeneity within races? Perhaps, but only if at least one of the parties can succeed in creating a stable biracial coalition. And this is a problem that must be addressed by focusing upon internal party dynamics.

Appendix to Chapter 8

This appendix provides technical detail regarding the determination of system dynamics for the analysis in Chapter 8. It also serves as a basis for the analysis presented in Chapter 9. Readers interested in additional discussions might consult Huckfeldt, Kohfeld, and Likens (1982), Smith (1968, 1974), Gilpin (1975), Rosenzweig and MacArthur (1963), and May (1974).

If we assume that racial hostility is absent, the model for whites can be conveniently rewritten in the following form.

$$\dot{WD} = R_1 WD \tag{8.1}$$
$$\dot{WR} = R_2 WD \tag{8.2}$$
$$R_1 = \pm A - B(WD) \pm C(WR) \tag{8.3}$$
$$R_2 = \pm D - E(WR) \pm F(WD) \tag{8.4}$$

where:

R_1, R_2 = rate operators

A, B, C, D, E, F = functions of constant model parameters where $+c$ denotes values greater than zero and $-c$ denotes values less than zero.

The model form guarantees that the signs on B and E are negative, but the signs on A, C, D, and F are problematic and determined by the magnitude of model parameters

To recapitulate, the various equilibria are located by setting Equations 8.1 and 8.2 to zero and finding solutions that satisfy these conditions. They are

E1: $WD = 0$, $WR = 0$

E2: $WD = 0$, $R_2 = 0$

E3: $R_1 = 0$, $WR = 0$

E4: $R_1 = 0$, $R_2 = 0$

The fourth equilibrium is of particular substantive interest because it is the only equilibrium that might involve nonzero values for both system states.

An analysis of this fourth equilibrium is best pursued graphically, by exploring the geometries corresponding to Equations 8.3 and 8.4. Four different geometries are possible, generated by the following circumstances: (1) $+C$ and $+F$, (2) $+C$ and $-F$, (3) $-C$ and $+F$, (4) $-C$ and $-F$. Only two of these are substantively interesting: the third, in which the Democratic party is the prey and the Republican party is the predator; and the fourth, in which the parties are competitive. The directions of the signs on A and D do not affect the discussion that follows and thus are assumed to be positive for notational convenience.

Competition ($-C$ and $-F$)

When R_1 and R_2 are both equal to zero, and when Democrats and Republicans are engaged in a competitive relationship, Equations 8.3 and 8.4 can be rewritten as

$$R_1 = A - B(WD) - C(WR), \text{ and when } R_1 = 0,$$
$$WR = A/C - (B/C)WD \tag{8.5}$$
$$R_2 = D - E(WR) - F(WD), \text{ and when } R_2 = 0,$$
$$WR = D/E - (F/E)WD \tag{8.6}$$

Any point of intersection in the first quadrant generates a system equilibrium. Absent such an intersection, there is no substantively meaningful fourth equilibrium. Regardless whether a fourth, nonzero equilibrium is present, a crucial determination involves motion in the first quadrant given these equilibrium lines, or isoclines.

Not only do R_1 and R_2 affect equilibria, they also determine the direction of motion in the phase plane. When R_1 is negative, the level of white Democratic support declines, and when it is positive the level of white Democratic support increases. Similarly, positive values for R_2 produce increases in white Republican support, and negative values produce decreases.

First consider Equation 8.3: when this equation is equal to zero, $\dot{WD} = 0$ and white Democrats are at equilibrium. Using this as a baseline, what happens if there is an increase in either the level of white Democratic support or in the level of white Republican support? Quite simply, the rate (R_1) goes from zero to negative and the level of white Democratic support correspondingly declines. Similarly, as white Democratic support or white Republican support decreases from the zero baseline, R_1 becomes positive and the level of white Democratic support increases.

How is this translated into motion in the phase plane? In Part A of Figure 8.9, horizontal motion is attracted toward the white Democratic isocline. Any point that is above and to the right of the isocline generates a decrease in the level of white Democratic support, and any point that is below and to the left of the isocline generates an increase in the level of white Democratic support. The same logic applies to Equation 8.4. In Part B of Figure 8.9, vertical motion is attracted toward the white Republican isocline. Points above and to the right of the isocline generate a decrease in the level of white Republican support, and points below and to the left generate an increase in the level of white Republican support.

Any point in the plane—any paired level of Democratic and Republican support among whites—is subject both to a horizontal and to a vertical attraction. The strength of each attraction is a direct function of the distance

Figure 8.9. Horizontal and vertical attraction in the (WD,WR) plane.

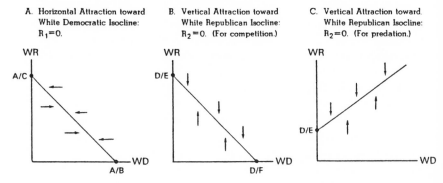

A. Horizontal Attraction toward White Democratic Isocline: $R_1 = 0$.

B. Vertical Attraction toward White Republican Isocline: $R_2 = 0$. (For competition.)

C. Vertical Attraction toward White Republican Isocline: $R_2 = 0$. (For predation.)

from the respective isocline. If a point is removed from both isoclines, its instantaneous motion will be in a generally diagonal direction. If a point lies at an intersection, it will not move at all. If a point lies on one isocline but not on another, its instantaneous motion will be parallel to one of the axes. This one-directional motion will only last for an instant, however, as the two-dimensional attraction is renewed as soon as the trajectory departs from the isocline. Thus, determining motion in the phase plane requires a form of vector algebra, where vertical and horizontal attractions are combined to produce a resulting trajectory.

Predation $(-C$ and $+F)$

The same principles apply for determining phase plane motion in a predatory relationship. When R_1 and R_2 are both set to zero, with a Republican predator and a Democratic prey, Equations 8.3 and 8.4 can be rewritten as:

$$R_1 = A - B(WD) - C(WR), \text{ and when } R_1 = 0,$$
$$WR = A/C - (B/C)WD \tag{8.7}$$
$$R_2 = D - E(WR) + F(WD), \text{ and when } R_2 = 0,$$
$$WR = D/E + (F/E)WD \tag{8.8}$$

As in the competitive relationship, the isocline for white Democrats is downsloping: the equilibrium level for white Democratic support decreases as the level of white Republican support increases. And, once again, it serves as a horizontal attractor.

A different geometry is produced because the isocline for white Republicans is upsloping: the equilibrium for white Republicans is positively affected by an increase in white Democratic support. Using $R_2 = 0$ as a baseline, examination of Equation 8.8 shows that increases in white Republican support push the rate (R_2) from zero to negative, and decreases push it from zero to positive. In contrast, increases in white Democratic support push the rate from zero to positive, and decreases in white Democratic support push it from zero to negative.

The associated vertical motion in the plane is illustrated in Part C of Figure 8.9. Points that are below and to the right of the isocline produce increases in white Republican support, and points that are above and to the left of the isocline produce decreases in white Republican support. Thus, as before, the isocline is a vertical attractor, and the combination of vertical and horizontal attractions produces two-dimensional motion in the phase plane.

Predatory and competitive geometries produce qualitatively different trajectories in time. Figure 8.10 shows two geometries — one competitive and the other predatory — that both produce convergent trajectories. The competitive trajectory produces a path that progresses monotonically toward equilibrium. In contrast, as the predatory trajectory nears equilibrium, it produces a counterclockwise spiral. If each system state is plotted against time, this counterclockwise approach appears as damped sinusoidal oscillation.

Figure 8.10. Competitive and predatory trajectories.

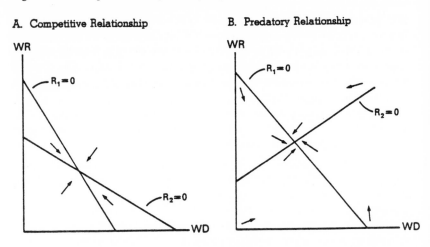

A. Competitive Relationship

B. Predatory Relationship

Global Versus Local Stability

In Chapters 8 and 9 we repeatedly — and somewhat loosely — use the concept of stability. In the technical language of dynamic systems, stability refers to a system in which perturbations disappear, so that disturbances from equilibrium are self-extinguishing and the system returns to equilibrium after a disturbance. In linear systems, a stable system is *globally* stable. This means that the return to equilibrium occurs regardless of the magnitude and direction of the disturbance. In other words, a process returns to equilibrium from any point in an *n*-dimensional system hyperspace. Thus initial conditions do not affect stability.

A nonlinear system, such as the one we have constructed, is far different in terms of its dynamic properties. In particular, for the system defined here, global stability is lacking. Rather, at most a stable, nonzero equilibrium is only *locally* stable. This means that the return to equilibrium depends upon the magnitude and direction of the disturbance, because the process will only return to equilibrium from some subset of the hyperspace. Any point outside of the restricted subspace generates divergence from equilibrium.

Therefore, whenever we discuss stability in the text, it should more technically be labeled local stability — stability in the neighborhood of the equilibrium. How large is the neighborhood? In every instance, it consists of the first, positively valued quadrant. Whenever we assert that a nonzero equilibrium is stable, this means that it is stable within the confines of the first quadrant.

How much of a restriction is this? The model is defined in continuous time to maintain trajectories in the first, positively valued quadrant. This is a theoretically valuable property of the model, because the positively valued quadrant is the only quadrant that provides a substantively plausible interpretation—that is, it is difficult to provide a meaningful interpretation for negative support levels. Thus, the equilibrium that is stable in the neighborhood of the first quadrant will always be stable because trajectories never leave the first quadrant. For this particular model and this particular analysis, the distinction between local and global stability is not crucial, and thus we speak simply of stability.

The only exception would occur if support for one or both parties was extinguished as the result of some perturbation. Lacking a subsequent perturbation that moves the trajectory off this zero equilibrium, the process will not return to the nonzero equilibrium even though it is locally stable. A substantive example might help to illustrate this situation. If two parties are locked in a stable competitive relationship, but support for one of the competitors is extinguished as the result of some scandal, then the stable competitive relationship is a thing of the past unless some series of events, beyond the scope of the normal relationship, is able to recreate a basis of support for the party.

Discrete Versus Continuous Time

The process we are modeling can be alternatively conceived as occurring in discrete or continuous time (Huckfeldt, Kohfeld, and Likens 1982; Tuma and Hannan 1984). Our modeling strategy has been to conceive the process in the abstract as occurring in continuous time, using differential equations, even though at various points we discuss the model in terms of a discrete time metric. In the previous two chapters we consider the rate operators for mobilization, conversion, and defection as they occurred between presidential elections in the post–World War II period. In Chapter 9 we conduct a series of simulations, and even though the time metric is unspecified, computer simulations depend explicitly upon a time metric that is discrete.

This is not the place to elaborate the consequences of discrete versus continuous time modeling strategies; other sources can be used to explore the differences between the two (Kohfeld and Salert 1982). It is sufficient for our purposes here to note that difference equation representations (in discrete time) are, in general, less stable than their differential equation cousins (in continuous time). Thus, while we develop stability conditions for the continuous time representations, the conditions will not always hold for a particular difference equation translation.

9 The Prospects for Racial Heterogeneity within Political Parties

The source of racial polarization in American politics lies in the inability of the Democratic party to maintain a stable biracial coalition. Postwar electoral history is clear on this point: blacks and lower-class whites are not easily accommodated within the same coalition. As a result, race has served to disrupt the ability of the Democrats to form a lower-class coalition, and the result has been increasing levels of political homogeneity within races. The origin of the problem lies in internal party dynamics—in the inability of coalition partners to cooperate in the same political effort.

In this chapter we examine a set of issues related to the electoral fortunes of a biracial party in a racially polarized society. At least since 1948 the Democratic party has pursued an electoral strategy that depends fundamentally upon its ability to attract the votes of both whites and blacks. Is such a strategy doomed to failure? Under what conditions is the strategy likely to succeed? Are these conditions likely to be attained? The Democratic party has issued strong appeals both to blacks and to working-class and lower-middle-class whites. We view the success of this strategy as problematic and consider the factors that might limit its success.

The model of party dynamics put forward in Chapter 6 is employed to consider whether a political party might achieve a biracial coalition that is at a stable equilibrium, or whether a biracial coalition necessarily degenerates and unravels. Does racial hostility inevitably drive one of the races out of the party? Two key issues must be addressed before proceeding with the analysis: the nature of a coalitional equilibrium and the conditions for stability and instability in coalitions through time.

Coalitions, Equilibria, and Stability

A party coalition is defined to be at equilibrium when the proportions of eligibles who both (1) support the party and (2) belong to a particular race remain constant through time. Thus, the Democratic coalition is at equilibrium if the proportions of eligibles who are black and Democratic and white and Democratic remain constant across elections — if the losses and gains within each race are offsetting. Just as no party system stays at equilibrium, so also no party coalition stays at equilbrium. Short-term forces that are constantly disrupting electoral politics ensure that party coalitions are constantly changing, but the concept of a coalitional equilibrium is useful because it indicates the possiblility of an accommodation between competing factions of the same coalition.

Not all equilibria provide such an accommodation, however. Some equilibria involve racial homogeneity within parties — they are only obtained when one of the competing partners disappears from the coalition. Furthermore, some equilibria involve the participation of both races in the coalition, but the equilibria are inherently unstable. Having once been disturbed, an unstable equilibrium cannot be recovered. In substantive terms, even minor political disturbances cause the coalition to unravel.

In short, the presence of a biracial equilibrium for a party's coalition is problematic: it may well be the case that no equilibrium exists and that there is no way to balance the interests of blacks and whites within the party. Alternatively, even if an equilibrium is present, or at least imaginable, the stability of the equilibrium is still problematic. The composition of a coalition at equilibrium might be extremely tenuous, so that the smallest disruption away from that delicate balance might lead to a complete unraveling of the party's basis of support. Thus, while an equilibrium may be present, holding the coalition together by maintaining that equilibrium may be nearly impossible. Even minor conflicts and disturbances within the party may lead to racial homogenization and perhaps to the party's ultimate demise at the polls. In the world of democratic politics, disturbances are the rule rather than the exception, and thus an unstable coalition becomes, de facto, no equilibrium at all.

Every party would like to redefine its coalitional equilibrium in a manner that is advantageous to its own electoral prospects. In keeping with this goal, political parties frequently adopt strategies that are aimed at permanently enlarging the size of their coalitions. These strategies do not always bear fruit, and in some instances they produce disastrous consequences. William Jennings Bryan undoubtedly expected to convert righteous indignation over the captains of industry and the cross of gold to Democratic party dominance, but the Populist strategy of the 1890s led instead to the eclipse of the party as a national force. Similarly, it is conceivable that the effort of the Democratic party to solidify its majority status by a strong appeal to black voters may have fundamentally undermined its position in American politics by creating a coalition that cannot be sustained through time.

Biracial Equilibria Within a Party

The model of party dynamics can shed light on the conditions that must be present for a biracial coalition to achieve a stable equilibrium—the set of circumstances under which blacks and whites can reside in the same coalition. Most of this discussion focuses upon the Democratic party's difficulties, but the same principles apply to the potential for creating a middle-class coalition of blacks and whites in the Republican party.

Table 9.1. Conditions for a Democratic equilibrium

A. Defections Must Be Offset by Mobilization and Conversion

$$\dot{BD}_t = 0 = M_{BD_t}(P_B - BD_t - BR_t) + C_{BD_t}(D_{BR_t}BR_t) - D_{BD_t}(BD_t)$$
(for black Democrats)

$$\dot{WD}_t = 0 = M_{WD_t}(P_W - WD_t - WR_t) + C_{WD_t}(D_{WR_t}WR_t) - D_{WD_t}(WD_t)$$
(for white Democrats)

where

M_{BD_t}, M_{WD_t} = Democratic mobilization rates among black nonvoters and white nonvoters, respectively

C_{BD_t}, C_{WD_t} = Democratic conversion rates among black Republican defectors and white Republican defectors, respectively

D_{BD_t}, D_{WD_t} = defection rates among black Democrats and white Democrats, respectively

B. Specification of Mobilization, Conversion, and Defection Rates

$$0 = [(a/P_B)(P_B - BD_t - BR_t) + (b/P_B)(gBR_t + hWR_t(1 - g)BR_t) - c - dWD_t(1 - c)]BD_t$$

$$0 = [(m/P_W)(P_W - WD_t - WR_t) + (n/P_W)(uWR_t + wBR_t(1 - u)WR_t) - p - qBD_t(1 - p)]WD_t$$

where

a = Democratic mobilization appeal among black nonvoters

m = Democratic mobilization appeal among white nonvoters

b = Democratic conversion appeal among black Republican defectors

n = Democratic conversion appeal among white Republican defectors

c = nonracial defection rate among black Democrats

g = nonracial defection rate among black Republicans

p = nonracial defection rate among white Democrats

u = nonracial defection rate among white Republicans

d = racial disaffection effect among black Democrats

h = racial disaffection effect among black Republicans

q = racial disaffection effect among white Democrats

w = racial disaffection effect among white Republicans

For the Democratic party's coalition to be at equilibrium, net changes in black and white support must both be zero. Losses due to defections must be offset by gains due to mobilization and conversion, for both white and black Democrats (Table 9.1[A]; see also Figure 6.2). To establish the conditions that yield such an equilibrium in Democratic support, it is necessary to define conversion, defection, and mobilization rates according to the discussion of Chapter 6. This is done in Part B of Table 9.1, where the general conditions for equilibrium are stated as two equations.

The value of the equations is that they provide necessary information for the determination of the several potential equilibria (Table 9.2; see also Huckfeldt, Kohfeld, and Likens 1982). First, the conditions are satisfied when both white Democratic support and black Democratic support are set to zero (Smith 1974). Second, the conditions are satisfied by setting white Democratic support to zero and solving for a nonzero value of black Democratic support. Third, the conditions are satisfied by setting black Democratic support to zero and solving for a nonzero value of white Democratic support. Thus, as in the analysis in Chapter 8, three equilibria can be defined where at least one of the support levels is set at zero. In the present context, this means that each equilibrium fails to incorporate racial heterogeneity within the coalition — they all signify the failure of a biracial coalition.

Table 9.2. Possible equilibria in Democratic support

First equilibrium
    white support $= 0$
    black support $= 0$
Second equilibrium
    white support $= 0$
    black support $= [(a - c)P_B \ - (a - bg)BR_t \ + bh(1 - g)WR_tBR_t]/a$
Third equilibrium
    white support $= [(m - p)P_W - (m - nu)WR_t + nw(1 - u)BR_tWR_t]/m$
    black support $= 0$
Conditions for possible fourth equilibrium

$$WD_t = \frac{(a - c)P_B \ + (-a + bg + bhWR_t - gbhWR_t)BR_t \ - aBD_t}{d(1 - c)P_B}$$

$$WD_t = \frac{(m - p)P_W + (-m + nu + nwBR_t - nuwBR_t)WR_t - q(1 - p)BD_t}{m}$$

Fourth and finally, it is possible that a *nonzero* equilibrium might be present where a biracial party coalition is achieved. The conditions shown in Table 9.1[B] can be satisfied if the expressions within squared brackets are set to zero. Upon algebraic rearrangement, this yields a fourth potential equilibrium in Democratic support, which is represented by the fourth set of conditions in Table 9.2. This final equilibrium, which holds out the potential (but not the certainty) of a biracial coalition, can be analyzed by focusing upon the relationship between white Democrats and black Democrats and by treating levels of Republican support as parameters affecting that relationship. This allows us to consider the relationship in a two-dimensional plane rather than a four-dimensional space.

Once again, this final equilibrium is important because it establishes, under the assumptions of our theoretical argument, the potential for a biracial coalition among Democrats. The first condition is a straight line in a two-dimensional (WD,BD) plane, and any point on the line produces an equilibrium in black Democratic support. The second condition is also a straight line in the two-dimensional (WD,BD) plane, and any point on this line produces an equilibrium in white Democratic support. Thus, an intersection in the first, positively valued quadrant of the plane produces a coalitional equilibrium in which the Democrats secure support from both blacks and whites.

As in Chapter 8, there is no guarantee that an intersection will occur in the first quadrant, and thus there is no guarantee that a biracial equilibrium in party support can be attained (see Figure 8.1). Unlike the analysis in Chapter 8, however, in this instance we do know the general nature of the geometry produced by these straight lines. So long as the nonracial defection rates for black and white Democrats (c and p) are less than one—a substantive necessity given the definition of the model—then both lines will always be negatively sloped. This means that as black Democratic support increases, the equilibrium level of white Democratic support decreases; and as white Democratic support increases, the equilibrium level of black Democratic support decreases (Smith 1968).

Given the specification of the model, the relationship between blacks and whites in the Democratic party is necessarily competitive, a fact that has important consequences for our analysis. In particular, it means that the existence and stability of nonzero equilibria are problematic. As we shall see, however, several factors make the attainment of a stable biracial coalition more probable.

The Dynamics of Biracial Coalitions

According to our model, the relationship between coalition partners in a biracial coalition is competitive, and the analysis in Chapter 8 shows that the stability of competitive relationships tends to be fragile. Indeed, it is quite possible to disrupt the stability of these delicately constructed biracial coalitions, though such coalitions are not inherently unstable. It is possible to sustain such a coalition through time, but the longevity and vitality of such a coalition are not accidental. Rather, the success of a biracial coalition depends upon the strategic capacities of party leaders and upon the strategic capacities of each group in the coalition.

The presence of a biracial equilibrium within a party, and the stability of that equilibrium, depend upon the final set of conditions reported in Table 9.2. Alternative sets of parameter values produce one of four fundamentally different geometries in the (*WD,BD*) plane (see Figure 9.1). Only two of the geometries produce a substantively meaningful equilibrium, and only one of these is stable—Part A of Figure 9.1. The questions that must be addressed are: What are the conditions that lead to the stable equilibrium depicted in Figure 9.1[A]? How might a stable biracial coalition be attained?

The conditions that lead to a stable biracial coalition are stated algebraically in Table 9.3. A first conclusion that can be drawn from these conditions is that a stable biracial coalition *can* be obtained, even in the face of racial competition within the party. The inequalities can be satisfied, and thus it is important to give attention to the circumstances that lead to this biracial accommodation.

Figure 9.1. Competitive dynamics in the Democratic party.

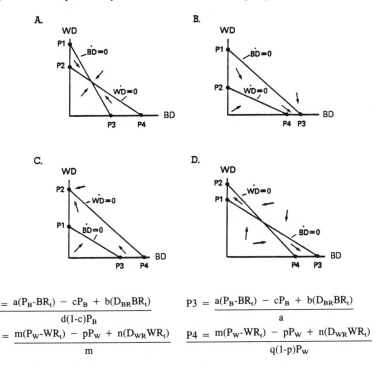

$$P1 = \frac{a(P_B\text{-}BR_t) - cP_B + b(D_{BR}BR_t)}{d(1\text{-}c)P_B}$$

$$P2 = \frac{m(P_W\text{-}WR_t) - pP_W + n(D_{WR}WR_t)}{m}$$

$$P3 = \frac{a(P_B\text{-}BR_t) - cP_B + b(D_{BR}BR_t)}{a}$$

$$P4 = \frac{m(P_W\text{-}WR_t) - pP_W + n(D_{WR}WR_t)}{q(1\text{-}p)P_W}$$

Table 9.3. Stability conditions for a biracial Democratic equilibrium

$$\frac{a(P_B - BR_t) - cP_B + b(D_{BR_t}BR_t)}{d(1 - c)P_B} > \frac{m(P_W - WR_t) - pP_W + n(D_{WR_t}WR_t)}{m}$$

$$\frac{m(P_W - WR_t) - pP_W + n(D_{WR_t}WR_t)}{q(1 - p)P_W} > \frac{a(P_B - BR_t) - cP_B + b(D_{BR_t}BR_t)}{a}$$

The political consequences of race are considered best by focusing upon the two different partisan logics developed earlier—the predatory logic of class-based politics and the competitive logic that has tended to supplant it. Rather than proceeding formally and algebraically on the basis of the stability conditions reported in Table 9.3, the analysis proceeds on the basis of several scenarios simulated by the model. This analytic strategy has two chief advantages: it avoids the mathematical complexity of Table 9.3 at the same time that it allows us to consider the entire system in all its theoretical complexity. While our focus of concern is upon the possibility of a biracial coalition, we consider this possibility subject to several different relationships between political parties.

Race in a Predatory, Class-based System

As a first step, consider a class-based predatory system with two political parties that both make racially indiscriminate appeals to the electorate and that both suffer from racially unstructured defection rates. In terms of the model, the parameters for such a party are the same among both blacks and whites. Further assume that racially competitive impulses are equally distributed across parties and races and that a large majority (90 percent) of the population is white, with a significant black minority (10 percent). The parameters for this scenario are shown in Table 9.4, where the Democratic party is the party of mobilization among both blacks and whites, and the Republican party is the party of conversion. In keeping with our earlier discussion of class-based politics, the Democratic party, as the party of mobilization, suffers from a higher defection rate than the Republican party.

Table 9.4. Racially neutral baseline model for class-based predatory politics

	Mobilization	Conversion	Nonracial defection	Racial competition
Black Democrats	$a = .8$	$b = .1$	$c = .25$	$d = .3$
Black Republicans	$e = .1$	$f = .8$	$g = .1$	$h = .3$
White Democrats	$m = .8$	$n = .1$	$p = .25$	$q = .3$
White Republicans	$r = .1$	$s = .8$	$u = .1$	$w = .3$

P_B = proportion of eligible population that is black and politically engaged = .08
P_W = proportion of eligible population that is white and politically engaged = .72

Our analytic strategy is to use this as a racially neutral baseline model of class-based politics and to consider the effect of several factors (in the form of parameter adjustments) upon it. For each simulation, we set initial party support levels equal within each race at 30 percent of the politically engaged population. Furthermore, we assume that 80 percent of each racial group in the population is politically engaged. Thus, 24 percent of eligible blacks and 24 percent of eligible whites initially support each party. In the scenarios that follow, we focus attention upon the proportions of white eligibles and black eligibles who support the Republican and Democratic parties. (A listing of the simulation is included in an appendix to this chapter.) For each scenario, we display time paths for 100 time periods (or iterations) beyond the initial conditions, as well as showing the approximate equilibrium implied by the process. The equilibrium is calculated in two different ways. First, it is displayed in the body of the figure as the proportion of each racial group supporting each party. Second, in order to determine which party achieves a winning coalition, it is reported in the title of the figure as the proportion of all supporters (of either party) who support the Democratic party.

The political consequences of the baseline model are shown in Figure 9.2. In this racially balanced strategic scenario, the parties end up being equally matched in terms of white support, but the Democrats enjoy a clear advantage in terms of black support. In one sense this outcome is quite surprising: racially neutral political strategies do not necessarily produce racially neutral outcomes. We make no explicit assumption regarding the class composition of white versus black populations, yet the party strategies yield quite different results among the white majority and the black minority.

In the context of a racially unbalanced population, even racially neutral political strategies yield outcomes with important racial implications. The consequences of political strategies are not only derivative from the strategies themselves; rather they are a product of the intersection between strategic alternatives and an underlying social structure. This simple observation is profoundly important to our analysis. It means, for example, that the national strategy of the Democratic party may yield far different outcomes in Alabama, south Chicago, and Minnesota. The level of racial polarization in politics is not simply a function of either social structure or political strategy; it is instead the result of a particular political strategy within a particular structural context.

Black Appeals. What are the consequences of a Democratic strategy that seeks to solidify the party's electoral advantage by vigorously pursuing the black vote? To consider this question we must alter the baseline model by increasing the effectiveness of the Democratic mobilization and conversion appeals among blacks and by decreasing the Democratic defection rate among blacks.

Figure 9.2. Class-based predatory baseline of Table 9.4. Democratic proportion of party supporters at equilibrium is .53.

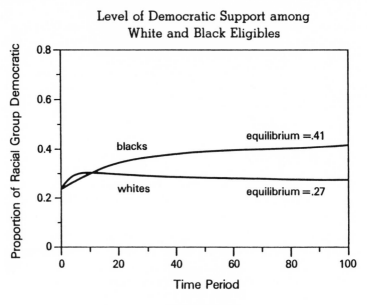

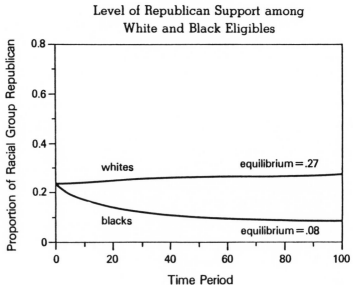

Figure 9.3. Predatory politics: black appeals. Democratic proportion of party supporters at equilibrium is .54.

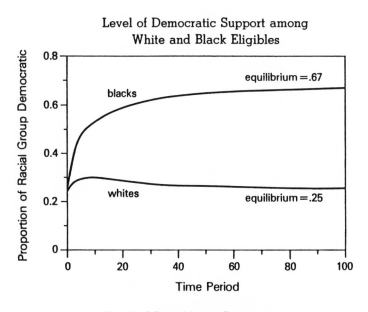

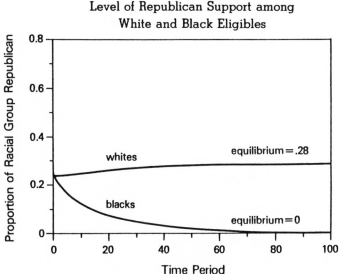

Parameter adjustments to the Table 9.4 baseline:
a = 1 b = .3 c = .1 (black Democrat)

As Figure 9.3 shows, the level of black support for the Democratic party increases in comparison to Figure 9.2, and the level of black support for the Republican party decreases. While the levels of white support for the Republican and Democratic parties are only marginally affected in favor of the Republicans, it is important to remember that 90 percent of all eligibles are white. As a net result, the strategy of vigorously pursuing the black vote pays only meager dividends for the Democrats—their total level of support climbs from 53 percent of all supporters in Figure 9.2 to 54 percent in Figure 9.3. Perhaps more important, however, the Democrats are able to maintain a biracial coalition regardless of their racially unbalanced political strategy. A vigorous appeal to blacks does not result in the alienation of white supporters.

Racial Specialization by the Parties. Figure 9.4 extends the scenario of Figure 9.3 by lessening the appeal of the Republican party among blacks. The conversion appeal of the Republican party among black Democratic defectors is decreased, and the defection rate among black Republicans is increased. We again assume that the Democratic party appeal is more effective among blacks than among whites and that the Democratic defection rate is higher among whites than among blacks. Finally, in this scenario we assume that white Democrats are more racially antagonistic than the rest of the population, that is, being a white supporter of the lower-class party creates a status ambiguity resulting in a higher level of racial antagonism. In summary, within the context of class-based predatory politics, we assume that the Democrats have an unbalanced appeal in favor of blacks, that the Republicans have an unbalanced appeal in favor of whites, and that the level of racial hostility is higher among white Democrats. What is the result?

First, the Democrats rapidly improve their advantage among blacks, but this advantage is offset once again by a lower level of support among whites. Second, even though this scenario rapidly produces political uniformity among blacks, it maintains political diversity among whites. That is, it produces a situation in which blacks are overwhelmingly Democratic, at the same time that the Democratic party is able to maintain a stable coalition including both whites and blacks.

Racial Specialization and a Balanced Population. Still other circumstances might place the Democrats at a further disadvantage in terms of maintaining support within the white population. Figure 9.5 repeats the scenario of Figure 9.4, but with a balanced social structure—50 percent black and 50 percent white. In comparison to previous scenarios, here the Democrats realize a more severe loss in terms of their proportional level of white support, even though their overall competitive position relative to the Republicans improves. The Democratic party is able to maintain a stable biracial coalition, but the level of racial polarization increases. Thus, under

Figure 9.4. Predatory politics: racial specialization by the parties. Democratic proportion of party supporters at equilibrium is .54.

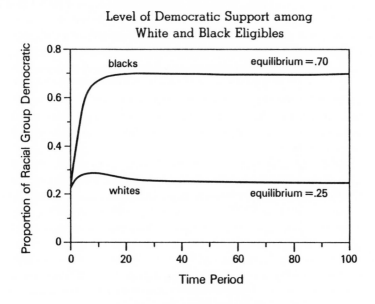

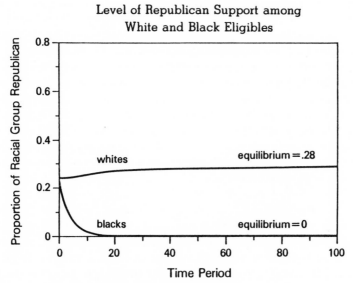

Parameter adjustments to the Table 9.4 baseline:
a = 1, b = .3, c = .1, d = .1 (black Democrat)
f = .1, g = .25, h = .1 (black Republican)
n = .1 (white Democrat)
w = .1 (white Republican)

Figure 9.5. Predatory politics: racial specialization and a balanced population. Democratic proportion of party supporters at equilibrium is .74.

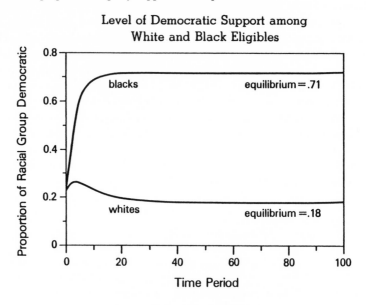

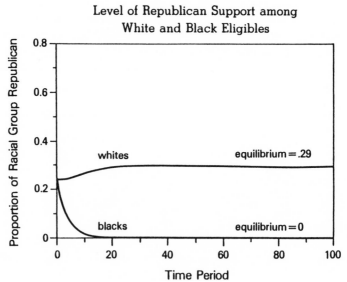

Parameter adjustments to the Table 9.4 baseline: $P_B = P_W = .4$
$a = 1$, $b = .3$, $c = .1$, $d = .1$ (black Democrat)
   $f = .1$, $g = .25$, $h = .1$ (black Republican)
   $n = .1$ (white Democrat)
      $w = .1$ (white Republican)

conditions of racially specialized appeals by the parties, a balanced social structure serves to increase rather than decrease levels of racial polarization (Kleppner 1985).

In summary, the maintenance of a stable, biracial coalition does not require that political heterogeneity be maintained within both races. This is an important result. Even under the extreme conditions considered here—a Democratic appeal oriented toward blacks, a Republican appeal oriented toward whites, and a higher level of racial antagonism among white Democrats—the Democratic party is able to maintain itself as the party of blacks and at the same time maintain a large and stable basis of support within the white population. This result is, however, subject to a class-based political environment, where the Democratic party is the party of mobilization and the Republican party is the party of conversion. Does this result also hold in a competitive environment with convergent strategies on the part of political parties?

Race in a Competitive, Politically Convergent System

A second baseline model, specified in Table 9.5, reflects our earlier discussion of political convergence and competitive politics (see Chapter 8). All parameters are set to equivalent values across parties and races—each party has the same appeal to each race. Both parties pursue a mobilization strategy rather than a conversion strategy among both blacks and whites, and both parties suffer from significant defection rates. The end product is a closely matched competitive system with highly convergent political strategies that reflect the classless nature of each party's constituency and appeal.

Table 9.5. Racially neutral baseline model for non-class-based competitive politics

	Mobilization	Conversion	Nonracial defection	Racial competition
Black Democrats	$a = .8$	$b = .1$	$c = .25$	$d = .3$
Black Republicans	$e = .8$	$f = .1$	$g = .25$	$h = .3$
White Democrats	$m = .8$	$n = .1$	$p = .25$	$q = .3$
White Republicans	$r = .8$	$s = .1$	$u = .25$	$w = .3$

P_B = proportion of eligible population that is black and politically engaged = .08
P_W = proportion of eligible population that is white and politically engaged = .72

As before, our analytic strategy is to use this as a racially neutral baseline, but in this instance the baseline is for classless, competitive politics. The population contains a large (90 percent) white majority with a small (10 percent) black minority, and initial conditions are established as before, with racial antagonisms held at a constant level across the four racial-political groups. In the scenarios that follow, we consider the political consequences of the racially neutral baseline and the effect of parameter adjustments upon these consequences.

First, as Figure 9.6 shows, the baseline model produces an outcome in which blacks are equally likely to support the Democratic and Republican parties, and thus half of all black supporters are Democrats and half are Republicans. Whites are also equally likely to support each of the parties, and thus half of all white supporters are Democratic and half are Republican. At the same time, however, the model generates overall levels of participation that are structured by race. Whites are somewhat more likely to be party supporters—blacks are less likely to support either party due to the combined effects of minority status and racial competition.

Black Appeals. A vigorous Democratic appeal to blacks is reconsidered in Figure 9.7, subject to a racially competitive political environment. The effectiveness of Democratic mobilization and conversion appeals is increased among blacks (as in Figure 9.3), and the black Democratic defection rate is decreased. The consequences are much more pronounced in the current instance of competitive politics than they were in the case of predatory politics. The Democrats realize a slight increase in black support, but they experience a serious erosion in white support. In this environment, the political cost of pursuing black votes is to experience a steady, persistent attenuation in white support that leads slowly but inevitably to the failure of biracial politics. A vigorous appeal to blacks leads ultimately to an equilibrium in which politics is racially polarized.

Racial Specialization by the Parties. In the scenario of Figure 9.8, which builds upon Figure 9.7, the black appeal of the Republican party is reduced. We also assume that whites are more racially antagonistic, that Democrats are more affective in appealing to blacks than to whites, and that Democrats realize a higher defection rate among whites than among blacks. This parallels Figure 9.4, but the political context has now changed from a class-based to a non-class-based system. The end result is the failure of a biracial coalition and racial polarization in politics. Whites become overwhelmingly Republican, and blacks become overwhelmingly Democratic. The main difference between this scenario and the scenario depicted in Figure 9.7 is that the time required for the biracial coalition to unravel is somewhat reduced—racial polarization is produced more rapidly.

Racial Specialization and a Balanced Population. The problem becomes even more acute when the scenario of Figure 9.8 is repeated in Figure 9.9, but with a balanced social structure—50 percent white and 50

Figure 9.6. Competitive baseline of Table 9.5. Democratic proportion of party supporters at equilibrium is .5.

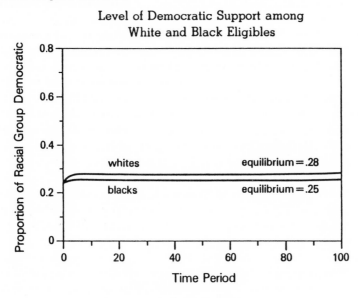

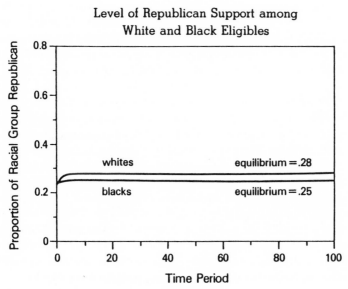

Figure 9.7. Competitive politics: black appeals. Democratic proportion of party supporters at equilibrium is .15.

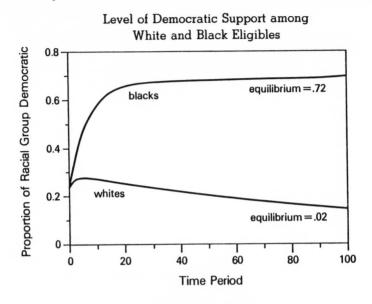

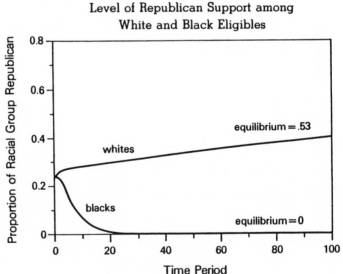

Parameter adjustments to the Table 9.5 baseline:
a = .1, b = .3, c = .1   (black Democrat)

Figure 9.8. Competitive politics: racial specialization by the parties. Democratic proportion of party supporters at equilibrium is .15.

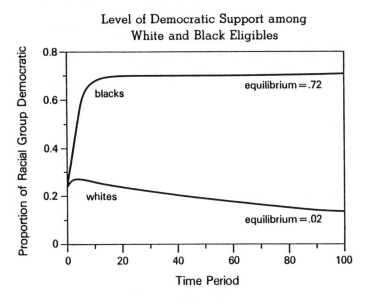

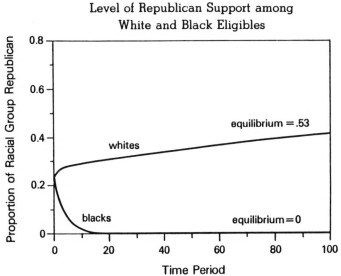

Parameter adjustments to the Table 9.5 baseline:
a = 1, b = .3, c = .1, d = .1 (black Democrat)
f = .1, g = .25, h = .1 (black Republican)
n = .1 (white Democrat)
w = .1 (white Republican)

Figure 9.9. Competitive politics: racial specialization and a balanced population. Democratic proportion of party supporters at equilibrium is .56.

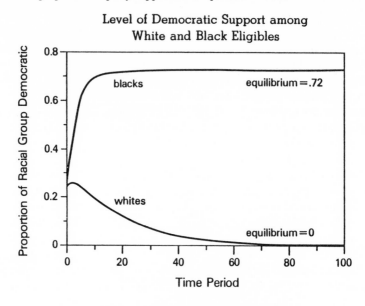

Level of Democratic Support among White and Black Eligibles

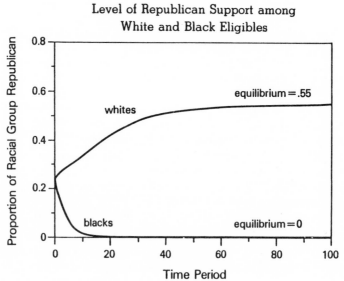

Level of Republican Support among White and Black Eligibles

Parameter adjustments to the Table 9.5 baseline: $P_B = P_W = .4$
$a = 1$, $b = .3$, $c = .1$, $d = .1$ (black Democrat)
    $f = .1$, $g = .25$, $h = .1$ (black Republican)
    $n = .1$ (white Democrat)
          $w = .1$ (white Republican)

percent black. In this instance the racial polarization of politics is produced much more rapidly. In very short order, whites become overwhelmingly Republican, and blacks become overwhelmingly Democratic. Quite obviously, the Democrats fail to maintain their biracial coalition.

In summary, this analysis shows that the Democrats are less vulnerable to the unraveling effects of race under conditions of class-based, predatory politics than they are under conditions of competitive politics. The same parameter adjustments that undermine the stability of the Democrats' biracial coalition under competitive politics produce only marginal consequences under predatory politics. The time required to produce the unraveling of a biracial coalition is problematic, but the long-term prognosis is clear: a class-based political system is better able to sustain a biracial coalition in the face of racial competition.

The sluggish recovery toward equilibrium produced by several of these scenarios is worth further attention. These time paths are highly abstract renderings of underlying political processes, absent the chaotic buffetings of day-to-day politics. The important point is that, even absent the continual disturbances of real-life politics, competitive political systems may be loosely tied to their equilibria (see Chapter 8). Thus, even if a stable coalitional equilibrium is present, it may have little practical significance. Quite simply, the equilibrium may be so weak as an attractor that it fails to structure the political process.

Democratic Vulnerability to Countermobilization

We have produced two extremely different political environments and have shown that the Democrats' biracial coalition is more vulnerable in one environment than in the other. But how do biracial coalitions fare in political environments that lie between these two? Recall the scenario depicted in Figure 9.4. Under the general conditions of class-based predatory politics, the Democrats have an appeal that is more effective among blacks, and the Republicans have an appeal that is more effective among whites. Furthermore, white Democrats are more racially antagonistic than other groups. The result is that the Democrats secure the homogeneous support of blacks and are still able to maintain a stable biracial coalition. How does the outcome of this scenario change as the Republicans begin to mobilize whites more effectively?

Our strategy is to use Figure 9.4 as a baseline and consider the effect of an increased white mobilization appeal by the Republican party. Even moderate shifts in the Republican electoral appeal generate disastrous consequences for the Democratic party. In Part A of Figure 9.10, a slight increase in the Republican mobilization appeal among whites, even when accompanied by a slight decrease in Republican conversion appeal, produces a serious erosion

Figure 9.10(A). Democratic vulnerability to countermobilization: a slight increase in the Republican mobilization appeal among whites. Democratic proportion of party supporters at equilibrium is .36.

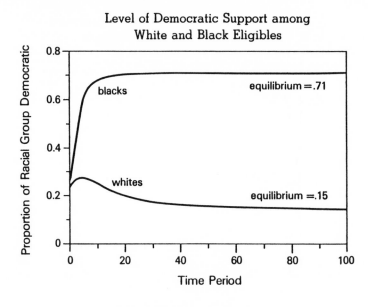

Level of Democratic Support among White and Black Eligibles

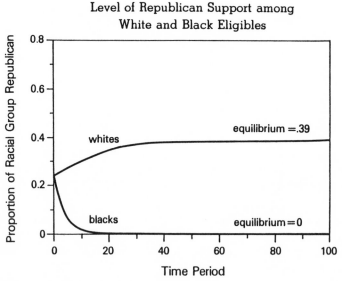

Level of Republican Support among White and Black Eligibles

Parameter adjustments to the Table 9.4 baseline:
a = 1, b = .3, c = .1, d = .1 (black Democrat)
         f = .1, g = .25, h = .1 (black Republican)
              n = .1   (white Democrat)
r = .2, s = .7,   w = .1 (white Republican)

Figure 9.10(B). Democratic vulnerability to countermobilization: a moderate increase in the republican mobilization appeal among whites. Democratic proportion of party supporters at equilibrium is .11.

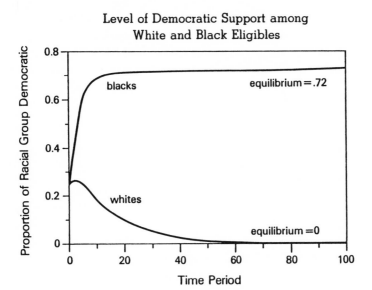

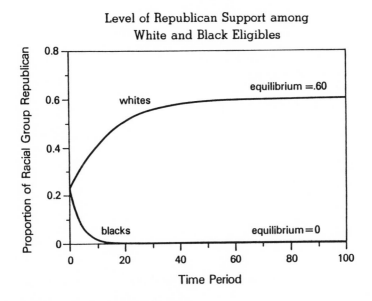

Parameter adjustments to the Table 9.4 baseline:

a=1, b=.3, c= .1, d=.1   (black Democrat)
        f=.1, g=.25, h=.1   (black Republican)
            n=.1   (white Democrat)
r=.4, s=.5,   w=.1   (white Republican)

in white Democratic support. In Part B, a moderate increase in Republican mobilization appeal among whites, even when accompanied by a moderate decrease in conversion appeal, undermines the Democrat's biracial coalition and generates racially polarized politics. In summary, it would appear that the Democrats are especially vulnerable to the countermobilization of disgruntled whites by the Republican party. Under certain circumstances the Democrats are able to maintain a biracial coalition, even when blacks are overwhelmingly Democratic and white Democrats are racially hostile. This ability is easily undermined, however, by the Republican party's counter-mobilization of whites.

Conclusion: What Should be Done?

Racially polarized politics is not the necessary or inevitable consequence of a racially polarized society. This fact is, perhaps, the most important point to be derived from this chapter. Regardless of racially based competition between coalition partners, it is possible to construct political coalitions that are racially heterogeneous. These coalitions are not acciden-tal, however, and they require politically astute behavior on the part of both party leaders and black leaders (Reed 1986). The two most important ques-tions to ask are: What should the Democrats do? What should blacks do?

The Democrats might be able to sustain a successful biracial coalition at the same time that they secure the homogeneous support of blacks, but this outcome is rendered more likely if they are also able to reinvigorate class politics. Indeed, there are striking examples in American politics of politi-cians whose success can be traced to this ability. The Long legacy in Louisiana politics — initiated by the "Kingfish" and carried on by his young-er brother Earl — was in part based upon the ability to secure strong support among blacks, while also attracting a solid core of white support. This ac-complishment derived from an ability to keep the focus of politics upon matters of class and away from matters of race (Williams 1969; Liebling 1960).

The examples of politicians who are able to accomplish this feat is, however, paralleled by numerous examples of politicians who have failed. Furthermore, the opposition has frequently engaged in countermobilization efforts to take advantage of white disillusionment with a party that represents black interests. The analysis in this chapter suggests that a conservative neopopulist appeal is uniquely positioned to exploit racial competition within the Democratic party.

Assuming that the Democratic party is unable or unwilling to maintain the class basis of politics, then the maintenance of a biracial coalition depends upon racial balance between the parties. In an environment marked by classless politics and racial competition, political homogeneity within a race makes it impossible to sustain a biracial coalition. Thus, the best hope for the sustenance of a biracial coalition is for *both* parties to incorporate supporters from *both* races.

The success of such a strategy depends, ultimately, upon the ability and willingness of the Republican party to develop a middle-class black constituency. Thus Democrats are, in a sense, at the mercy of Republican strategists. At the very least, however, the Democratic party should recognize that (1) a clear, class-based divergence of interests has developed within the black population, and (2) it may not be in the long-term interests of the Democratic party to represent all those interests. The Democrats may very well benefit by increased partisan diversity among blacks, even though such diversity would come at their own short-term expense.

More important than the strategic choices facing Democrats are the strategic choices facing blacks. An important lesson to be gained from this chapter is the advantage of a bipartisan political strategy on the part of blacks. It has long been recognized that blacks are politically disadvantaged to the extent that the Democratic party can take their votes for granted, but this problem is largely overcome by variations in black voter turnout. Democratic politicians cannot afford to ignore the black vote because it may not materialize.

Our own recommendation regarding the advantage of bipartisanship goes further: it is important that a significant portion of the black community colonize the Republican party. This will lead to several advantages for the black community. First, and most important, it will allow them to vote for winners more often in national politics. So long as blacks are overwhelmingly Democratic, there are strong reasons to believe that the Democratic party will have trouble winning presidential elections due to the simple fact that too many whites will not support such a coalition.

Second, a bipartisan strategy would be beneficial to blacks because it would serve to encourage advocates of black interests in both parties. To the extent that both major parties depend upon black votes, they would both be forced to become parties of civil rights. There is already some evidence to suggest that such a bipartisan strategy is beginning to develop and pay dividends: for example, strong black support for Thomas Kean helped to secure his re-election as the Republican governor of New Jersey, and blacks in New Jersey are now able to enjoy the benefits of a genuinely bipartisan strategy.

Finally, bipartisanship would serve as a healthy recognition of the diversity that is increasingly present among blacks. The development of such diversity is not a sign of weakness but rather one of strength, as significant numbers of group members move into positions of status, affluence, and prestige within the larger society (Dahl 1961:chap. 4; Wolfinger 1965). As the group matures, it becomes increasingly difficult to pursue a unified agenda, and thus bipartisanship becomes important. This is not to say that blacks will be, or should be, disunited on central issues affecting blacks as a group (Huckfeldt 1983a). Rather, we argue that the diversity as well as the commonality existing among blacks require political expression. And the partisan expression of diversity may lead to significant gains for blacks, for the Democratic party, and ultimately for the political system as a whole.

These two strategic alternatives—class-based bipartisanship among blacks and a class-based appeal on the part of the Democratic party—are mutually reinforcing. To the extent that blacks are bipartisan, it will become easier for the Democratic party to succeed with a class-based strategy, and to the extent that the Democratic party pursues a class-based strategy, it will become more attractive for middle-class blacks to become Republican. Such a strategic course has an inherent danger: a political system that might ignore black interests and thus erode hard-won political gains by blacks. It is not clear, however, that the danger to black interests would be heightened over the current state of affairs in American politics—a party that strongly advocates black interests but cannot elect a president. As long as blacks are the captives of the Democratic party, and as long as the Democratic party is the captive of blacks, neither the Democratic party nor blacks are likely to succeed in American electoral politics.

Appendix to Chapter 9

See following illustration for a list of the simulation program.

```
10 A=.8:B=.1:C=.25:D=.3:BP=.1:BL=.8:PB=BP*BL
20 E=.1:F=.8:G=.1:H=.3
30 M=.8:N=.1:P=.25:Q=.3:WP=.9:WL=.8:PW=WP*WL
40 R=.1:S=.8:U=.1:W=.3
42 LPRINT " "
43 LPRINT "fig92"
44 LPRINT " "
50 LPRINT"black democratic parameters are:"
60 LPRINT"     a="A"b="B"c="C"d="D"pb="PB
70 LPRINT"black republican parameters are:"
80 LPRINT"     e="E"f="F"g="G"h="H
90 LPRINT"white democratic parameters are:"
100 LPRINT"     m="M"n="N"p="P"q="Q"pw="PW
110 LPRINT"white republican parameters are:"
120 LPRINT"     r="R"s="S"u="U"w="W
190 BD0=.3*PB:BR0=.3*PB:WD0=.3*PW:WR0=.3*PW
200 FOR I=1 TO 100
205 BDR=BD0/PB:BRR=BR0/PB:WDR=WD0/PW:WRR=WR0/PW
210 BD1=BD0+A*BDR*(PB-BD0-BR0)+B*BDR*(G*BR0+H*WR0*(1-G)*BR0)-C*BD0-D*WD0*(1-C)*BD0
220 BR1=BR0+E*BRR*(PB-BD0-BR0)+F*BRR*(C*BD0+D*WD0*(1-C)*BD0)-G*BR0-H*WR0*(1-G)*BR0
230 WD1=WD0+M*WDR*(PW-WD0-WR0)+N*WDR*(U*WR0+W*BR0*(1-U)*WR0)-P*WD0-Q*BD0*(1-P)*WD0
240 WR1=WR0+R*WRR*(PW-WD0-WR0)+S*WRR*(P*WD0+Q*BD0*(1-P)*WD0)-U*WR0-W*BR0*(1-U)*WR0
300 BD0=BD1:BR0=BR1:WD0=WD1:WR0=WR1
310 NEXT I
311 DBP=BD1/BP:RBP=BR1/BP:WDP=WD1/WP:WRP=WR1/WP
320 LPRINT "bd100=blkdem/elig="BD1"  prop of eligible blacks="DBP
330 LPRINT "br100=blkrep/elig="BR1"  prop of eligible blacks="RBP
340 LPRINT "wd100=whtdem/elig="WD1"  prop of eligible whites="WDP
350 LPRINT "wr100=whtrep/elig="WR1"  prop of eligible whites="WRP
351 PRINT "bd100=blkdem/elig="BD1"  prop of eligible blacks="DBP
352 PRINT "br100=blkrep/elig="BR1"  prop of eligible blacks="RBP
353 PRINT "wd100=whtdem/elig="WD1"  prop of eligible whites="WDP
354 PRINT "wr100=whtrep/elig="WR1"  prop of eligible whites="WRP
359 LPRINT CHR$(12)
360 LIST 10-45
700 END
```

10 Race, Class, and the Future of American Politics

> Conflicts and controversies can arise out of a great variety of relationships in the social structure, but only a few of these tend to polarize the politics of any given system. There is a hierarchy of cleavage bases in each system and these orders of political primacy not only vary among polities, but also tend to undergo changes over time.
>
> Lipset and Rokkan (1967: 6)

Race occupies a position of primary importance among the competing bases of cleavage in American politics. This is not to say that other bases of conflict and controversy are unimportant, or even that they do not take precedence over race at particular times in particular settings. Neither does it mean that most Americans are racists, nor that the primacy of race is the result of widespread virulent racism. Rather, race is important because of its potential to unravel another fundamentally important basis of coalition formation, the politics of class. A significant portion of the lower-class population in America is black, and thus a successful lower-class political movement must win the support of lower-class blacks and whites. The history of American politics shows that such a coalition continues to be an extraordinarily difficult achievement.

Race is invoked in one of two ways: either as the result of a numerical threat by blacks to the political standing of whites or due to the political manipulation of race by politicians. The first of these causes has been illustrated most clearly in the American South, where numerically threatened white populations have continually attempted to maintain their dominance. This effort has taken various forms — the political disenfranchisement of blacks, the maintenance of at-large elections that foreclose black representation, southern run-off primaries that keep blacks from being nominated as the result of split white votes. We have attempted to show that racially structured politics is in no sense unique to the South and that the level of political polarization between races is also subject to the numerical threat posed by blacks to lower-status white voters. We think the evidence is quite clear on this point—lower-class whites are less likely to vote Democratic when blacks make up a larger part of the Democratic electorate.

Race is also invoked by the direct efforts of politicians, some of whom are honorable spokespersons of particular viewpoints, while others are more sinister in their goals and ideals. When a gubernatorial candidate in a southern state tries to focus public concern on the flying of the Confederate flag over the state capital in his effort to drive a wedge into the Democrats' "unnatural" coalition, the sinister nature of the appeal seems fairly clear. In contrast, while they are legitimate expressions of democratic politics, the candidacies of Jesse Jackson and Harold Washington could not help but increase the salience of race as a dividing line between Democrats and Republicans.

In this final chapter we undertake two tasks. First we address some natural criticisms of our argument. Have we exaggerated the importance of race? Have we exaggerated the (latent) importance of class? Second, we explore several alternative futures for the Democratic party, and thus for electoral politics in America. Can the Democratic party survive with a class based coalition? Can it succeed on the basis of a grand coalition of liberals, blacks, and lower class whites? What are the advantages of class based politics?

The Importance of Race

Are we exaggerating the importance of race? There are, of course, other issues and sources of conflict in American politics: abortion, foreign affairs, nuclear proliferation, arms control, energy, the environment, government spending on social welfare programs, budget deficits, trade deficits, women's rights, urban policy. Why should race be so important relative to this long list of important and controversial issues?

As a set of issues, it is often difficult even to locate the lines of conflict over race, because few people are willing to admit that they are opposed to equal rights, due process, and equal protection across racial boundaries. While all the other issues and debates have proponents and opponents, the lines of conflict over race are less clearly articulated. Yet, without saying that these other issues are unimportant, we argue that race is frequently dominant. In particular, race tends to drive out class as the fundamental organizing principle in American politics. Why?

Race looms large with respect to the other issues and concerns of American politics because our society is organized around race. It is certainly no exaggeration to say that race is the primary social cleavage within the population. Thus the political salience of race is so high because it galvanizes and mobilizes the electorate along social boundaries that are deep and thoroughgoing in the social life of the nation. As we argue earlier, there are very few cross cutting cleavages with respect to race—whites and blacks continue to live in separate social worlds.

What is the evidence for this argument? Perhaps the most impressive empirical footprint leading to our conclusion is the degree of political polarization that exists between racial groups. One of the authors taught at the University of Notre Dame during the early 1980s, and his students would ride the electric train to the Chicago Loop for weekend excursions. On the weekend before the 1983 mayoral election, the one in which Harold Washington was elected Chicago's first black mayor, several students reported a bizarre and frightening experience. As they walked down State Street, they repeatedly saw whites wearing plain white buttons—a clear message regarding the racial significance of the upcoming election.

The students were unanimous in expressing shock at such behavior, but some of them were from Chicago, and they were genuinely alarmed regarding the election of Harold Washington. It is important to understand that these students were not racists. Quite the opposite: they were compassionate, liberal-minded, socially concerned citizens. The important point is that the polarizing effects of race touch not only racists. When 90 percent of voting blacks vote one way and 90 percent of voting whites vote the opposite way, we are witnessing a phenomenon that is not restricted to racists and Nazis. Indeed, even liberal-minded, compassionate young people are capable of being swept along by the hysteria surrounding such an election.

Should Chicago in 1983 be seen as the exception rather than the rule? Perhaps, but there are more than enough of these exceptions to present a pattern of persistent (if not consistent) racial polarization—South Carolina in 1986, Mississippi in 1984, North Carolina in 1984, Chicago in 1987, and so on. Thus, even if these examples are in some sense exceptional, they are too numerous to disregard as being wholly idiosyncratic.

The extent to which whites are willing to support the Democratic party is directly related to the reliance of the party on black voters. As the Democratic coalition becomes blacker, whites become less willing to participate. This unwillingness is especially apparent among lower-class white voters, and thus we see a major factor underlying the decline of class in American politics: race is the wedge that disrupts lower-class coalitions. This pattern is demonstrated using two different and independent sources of information that differ in both substantively and methodologically important ways. We see it over time in the postwar urban South, and we see it in the cross-section for the 1984 election across states.

We do not argue that political polarization between races is an inescapable or inevitable outcome. The best evidence for the potential of a biracial coalition comes from the South, where many white Democratic politicians have learned the art of attracting blacks and lower-class whites to the same coalition. Liberal northerners tend to undervalue this accomplishment, even though the history of presidential elections since 1964 can be written in terms of the national party's failure to accomplish the same feat.

How can we defend the argument that race tends to overshadow other issues and lines of cleavage? We have no regression coefficients to offer and there is no easy empirical test for such an argument. One way to proceed is to use a counterfactual argument. Imagine the United States without blacks. What would such a society be like? First, it would be infinitely poorer and more impoverished on a cultural basis. Perhaps the chief cultural advantage of the United States over European nations is the social diversity that has been provided, in large part, by the black presence. It is no exaggeration to say that the infusion of black culture into the United States is one of the country's richest cultural legacies.

While an all-white society would in no way be desirable, its political implications would be profound. Who can doubt that there would be a more potent lower-class political movement? Remember that most poor people in this country are white. Thus, absent blacks, we would still face the glaring inequities that arise due to the maldistribution of social resources. This is nothing new. Michael Harrington (1962) made it clear more than twenty-five years ago when he published *The Other America,* but we still tend to think of poverty as a black problem. Absent blacks, we would be unable to perpetuate this myth, and a chief impediment to the pursuit of a lower-class political agenda would be removed.

Finally, while the importance of the racial cleavage between blacks and whites looms large throughout the country, in some areas it is one among several important lines of ethnic and racial division. In cities like Houston, Los Angeles, and New York, the political significance of race must increasingly be seen within the larger context of several groups—blacks, Hispanics, Asians, and non-Hispanic whites. Our analysis has focused upon the more theoretically tractable problem of two politically competing groups—blacks and whites. How does the inclusion of multiple groups alter our analysis?

Two possibilities stand out. First, if each group enters the competitive fray of politics as a separate participant, then politics becomes Balkanized and increasingly complex. In this context we are employing a dual meaning for the concept of complexity. Certainly, the presence of multiple, competing groups increases complexity in the common usage of the term; that is, politics becomes difficult to follow and hard to unscramble. More important, multiple competing groups increase complexity in the ecological sense of the term (May 1974). (According to ecologists, an ecosystem is complex to the extent that increasing numbers of species interact within the same ecosystem. In terms of our mathematical model, this complexity would manifest itself as two additional equations for each additional group.)

What are the consequences of ecological complexity? A theoretically derived conclusion of mathematical ecology is that complexity undermines stability. Carried over into the world of politics, this suggests that an increase in the number of competing groups decreases the likelihood that a racially and ethnically heterogeneous coalition would be able to sustain itself through time. In short, the politically disintegrative effects of race that we have identified would only become more severe in the presence of multiple competing racial and ethnic groups. One might hope that, as the number of ethnic and racial divisions increase, the importance of any single division would decrease, but such a prognosis is much closer to being simply a hope rather than an analytically based expectation.

A second possibility is that several racial-ethnic groups might, for purposes of practical politics, fuse into a single political group. Thus, for example, we might see non-Hispanic whites competing with a political fusion of blacks, Hispanics, and Asians. To the extent that such a group is truly a fusion rather than a temporary coalition, the original analysis holds. Racial-ethnic competition would continue to threaten the ability of parties to maintain a stable basis of support that includes supporters from both racial-ethnic groups. The practical consequences for particular elections would depend, of course, on numbers—the sizes of the respective groups. But as before, racial and ethnic competition would continue to threaten the viability of a class-based coalition.

The Importance of Class

Have we exaggerated the historical importance of class in American politics and thus given too much credit to race as a factor that disrupts class politics? In other words, if class politics has never really thrived on American soil, how can it be eclipsed by race?

At least since Sombart (1976) questioned the reasons underlying the absence of a socialist party in America, political analysts have developed a series of explanations to account for the difficulty experienced by the left in the United States. We offer no monocausal answer to Sombart's question. A variety of explanations are clearly in order: the durability of the liberal tradition in American politics, the generally high level of material prosperity, the presence of the frontier, ethnic and cultural pluralism among the lower classes, the openness of American social structure both in terms of social mobility and also in terms of continuing immigration from outside the country (for an extended discussion see Schlozmann and Verba 1979).

Without necessarily dismissing any of these explanations, it is important to focus once again upon the way in which race "has always overwhelmed class" in the politics of the nation (Degler 1972:102). The first opportunity for a nationally based lower-class movement failed in the South when populist leaders were unable to accommodate lower-class blacks and whites in the same political coalition during the period following Reconstruction. Writing in 1940, Ralph Bunche argued that,

> Though we speak of the solid South, the region has not in any sense been solid in the past, nor is it today, except in its traditional adherence to the doctrine of white supremacy on the one hand and to the political derivative of that doctrine—a blind allegiance to the one-party system—on the other. There have always been severe class distinctions in the South. Negroes and poor whites have always occupied the two bottom rungs of the ladder, and the white landlords, industrialists, and bankers—the Bourbons—have always been at the top. . . . Between these upper and lower classes in the South there has been a traditional and deep-seated hostility. Only the clever manipulation of the threat of black dominance has kept the underprivileged white masses and the privileged upper classes of the South from coming to a parting of the political ways. (Bunche 1976:10)

The threat posed by the black population to white political hegemony inevitably led to the disenfranchisement of blacks. Thus was the South transformed into a region of one-party politics, lacking a partisan vehicle for the expression of class conflict at the state level. Moreover, the one-party status of the Democrats in the South meant that the Democratic party served as an inadequate *national* vehicle for lower-class aspirations. The durable core of the national Democratic party came from the South in the early part of the twentieth century, and southern Democrats were conservative Democrats. In short, the one-party South served to blunt the potential for class politics both in the South and in the nation. Class was overwhelmed by region, but region served as a euphemism for race. Race held class at bay, not only in the South but also in the nation as a whole.

Within this political context, the significance of the New Deal was that it reintroduced class into American electoral politics. We recognize that a revisionist school of political analysis questions the class basis of the New Deal coalition, but we do not pretend that class was the only important cleavage in the New Deal period—region, ethnicity, religion, and race were important as well. The importance of the New Deal was not that it erased the importance of factors other than class but rather that its logic and motive force were essentially class-based. Working-class Republicans and middle-class Democrats became the exceptions rather than the rules.

In his foreword to a new translation of Sombart (1976), Harrington draws attention to a distinction between socialism and social democracy. While we have never had socialism in American politics, we have experienced a measure of social democracy. One element within the Democratic party was a labor party organized to seek state intervention in the workings of capitalism on behalf of workers. Social democracy in this sense has realized enormous successes, particularly through the intervention of Franklin Roosevelt's Democratic party on behalf of workers and the rights of unions. These actions served to guarantee the success of industrial labor unions, and thus it is no exaggeration to say that the CIO was among the progeny of the New Deal.

While this class-based Democratic party was enormously successful, its success was also extremely vulnerable. The Democratic party of the 1930s relied on a white electorate. As the black population first moved north and then won the vote, the Democratic party faced an old problem. Once again, combining lower-class blacks and whites within the same coalition became the crucial challenge of American politics. The re-emergence of race in the political life of the nation following World War II meant that the New Deal's reinvigoration of class was fundamentally endangered.

Perhaps the biggest difference between the role of race in an earlier era and the role of race in the more recent period is that the locus of racial conflict is no longer restricted to the South. Williamson (1986:285) argues that sometime in the 1970s, white northerners quit denouncing white southerners as racists. "In the twentieth century, it seems clear that the white South and the white North, in spite of their real cultural differences, have reached a practical congruence in their behavior in regard to black people. In all regions, when black people in large numbers have become relatively assertive in their pursuit of a fair share of the good things in life, white people have proved themselves ready for violence."

In summary, we argue that race has persistently obstructed the development of class politics across more than one hundred years of American political history. During the late nineteenth and early twentieth centuries, race served to impede the development of a unified lower-class coalition, both in the South and in the nation. Class emerged as an important basis of electoral conflict during the 1930s, but the re-emergence of race in the post–World War II period and the enfranchisement of blacks during the 1950s and 1960s meant that the divisive consequences of race came into play once again.

Race is not the only factor that has impeded the development of class-based politics in the United States, but it is perhaps the most important. The history of American class relations is intimately tied up with the history of American race relations. In this book we are concerned primarily with race and American electoral politics in the post–World War II period, but it is important to realize that we are only examining the most recent evidence of a relationship that extends far back in time.

Democratic Futures

In an earlier chapter we argue that the Democratic party has three potential constituencies: blacks, the old left, and the new left. The old left is composed primarily of lower-class whites who adhere to an earlier established social welfare agenda. They support labor unions, national health insurance, social security, and other measures aimed at providing various forms of social equity to the people of the country. The new left is composed primarily of upper-middle-class whites who support one or more of the post-material agendas in American politics: women's liberation, the environment, the antinuclear movement, and so on. As we have argued, the black agenda overlaps with portions of both the old-left and the new-left agendas, but it is distinct from them as well.

The challenge of the Democratic party is to put together an appeal that attracts enough voters to win elections. That challenge is made more difficult because the formula for success differs across the country. In Los Angeles and Berkeley and Philiadelphia, as well as in many other cities, a black–new-left coalition has been able to win elections. The victories of Tom Bradley and of many other black mayors provide the best examples of this strategy's success. In these cities, black voters in combination with white new-left voters are able to win elections.

The problem of the Democratic party is that this strategy is doomed to failure in other areas of the country. Blacks in combination with new-left whites are not sufficiently numerous to win elections in states such as Mississippi or Alabama or South Carolina. Indeed, for some purposes, such a coalition may not generate sufficient support for statewide electoral success anywhere in the nation. If blacks and new-left whites could not elect Tom Bradley as governor of California, where else would such a coalition be able to succeed in electing a black governor? or a black president?

These difficulties become even more acute at the national level. We have hesitated to refer to the new left as being liberal, because on many social welfare issues it is so conservative. In the common vocabulary of American politics, however, the new left is "liberal," and the liberal–black Democratic coalition has shown itself to be incapable of winning national presidential elections. Indeed, the problem is even worse than this — the liberal label has become a political stigma across large portions of the country.

How should the Democratic party respond to this problem? One solution is to reinvigorate the class basis of the party. It is important to realize that such a strategy would require a clear shift in emphasis for much of the party. Particularly for the new-left constituency, such an adjustment might prove to be very difficult. Much of the new left is not particularly sympathetic to the problems of lower classes in American politics, and many in the lower classes are not particularly sympathetic to the new-left agenda.

Could the party win elections with the support of lower-class blacks and whites? The answer to this question depends upon the definition for "lower class." If the lower class is restricted to welfare recipients, or even if it is restricted to the industrial working class, the answer is probably not. There are not enough welfare recipients, and the armies of industrial workers continue to shrink in size. If, however, lower class is defined to include members of the working- and lower-middle-classes, then the chances of success improve dramatically. The political challenge would be to articulate persuasively the politically shared interests among these groups, for both blacks and whites.

The Achilles heel of such a coalition continues to be the wedge of race. Is it possible to overcome the difficulties inherent in a coalition that seeks the participation of lower-class blacks and whites? The answer to this question must be yes, because Democratic politicians in the South are able to win elections with the help of just such a coalition. Our own analysis suggests that a lower-class coalition is more likely to succeed if blacks pursue a bipartisan strategy—that is, the unraveling consequences of race are more likely to be overcome if blacks populate both parties. It is possible to maintain a biracial Democratic coaliton even if all blacks are Democrats, but it becomes more difficult.

Perhaps ironically, the greatest difficulty in achieving such a biracial, lower-class coalition does not occur in the South but rather in the urban North. The current circumstances in northern cities such as Chicago make the attainment of a lower-class biracial coalition inconceivable at the local level. The danger for the Democratic party is that the racial fissure in local areas such as Chicago will lead to the wholesale exit of lower-class whites from the Democratic party. The exit is made easier for these whites to the extent that the national Democratic party has sacrificed its character as the party of lower-class Americans.

The Democrats' best hope is to maintain these conflicts within the party as local intramural conflicts and to keep them from leading to locally inspired realignments along racial lines. Such a feat is not easily accomplished. National Democratic politicians are inexorably drawn into these local conflicts. In the 1983 Chicago mayoral election, national political figures, including Walter Mondale, faced the difficult task of choosing sides between the incumbent Jane Byrne and the black challenger, the late Harold Washington.

The only political alternative to a lower-class Democratic coalition is for the party to continue its attempt at maintaining a grand coalition of blacks, the new left, and the old left. Not surprisingly, such a strategy has continually failed at the national level. In some locales, blacks and lower-class whites win elections; in other locales, blacks and upper-middle-class white "liberals" win elections. But in national politics, this grand coalition has too many internal contradictions to succeed, and thus the Democratic party is faced with some difficult strategic choices.

The Advantages of Class Politics

Carried to extremes, politics structured along class lines involves inherent dangers, but we need not worry about these extremes in the current context of American politics. Given the history of the republic, it is difficult to imagine that class politics would reach such dangerous proportions. According to Eulau (1961:13), an extremely class-based partisan structure presents dangers for democratic processes, but at the same time, ". . . the theoretical opposite—complete dissociation—is likely to condemn the party system to an issueless, which means, valueless, struggle between the 'ins' and the 'outs.' As, however, values are differentially distributed by virtue of the existence of a class structure, the parties cannot be altogether indifferent to and independent of class relations when the political process involves the allocation of values."

So long as a society is class-structured, democratic politics must also be structured by class if it is to have legitimate meaning and content. The danger of a class-free democratic politics is that democracy becomes irrelevant to the distribution of material well-being within a society. Thus, the postwar decline of class politics must be seen as an indicator of diminished health and vitality within democratic politics, just as the concurrent decline in participation levels is also seen as a sign of decreased vitality.

It is important to recognize that the decline of class in American politics is not only bad for Democrats, it is bad for both parties. If democratic politics is to possess legitimacy, both ends of the class distribution must be represented in the political process. To the extent that politics is unstructured by class, neither side is represented. In practical terms, the rise of conservative neopopulism within the Republican party means that the party does a less-adequate job of representing its traditional constituencies.

Unlike class, race is not an appropriate basis for the organization of democratic politics because, in a democracy, both parties must be concerned with the egalitarian treatment of blacks and whites. Indeed a crucial rule of the game in any democracy is that all racial, ethnic, and religious groups be treated equally within the political system. Thus, race can only be legitimately treated as a bipartisan issue—both the Democratic and Republican parties must be parties of civil rights. This is not to say that blacks and whites should support the same parties at the same proportional levels. To the extent that blacks are proportionally less advantaged than whites, we would expect them to support the party of the disadvantaged at a proportionally higher level. Such a state of affairs is far removed from the present situation in national politics, where one party has increasingly become the party of blacks and the other party has increasingly become the party of whites. This racial structuring of politics is fundamentally at odds with democratic politics, and it bodes poorly for the future of democracy in America.

Bibliography

Abramson, Paul R., John H. Aldrich, and David W. Rohde
1986   *Change and Continuity in the 1984 Elections.* Washington, D.C.: CQ Press.
Alford, Robert R.
1963   *Party and Society: The Anglo-American Democracies.* Chicago: Rand McNally.
Andersen, Kristi
1979   *The Creation of a Democratic Majority, 1928–1936.* Chicago: University of Chicago Press.
Asher, Herbert
1984   *Presidential Elections and American Politics: Voters, Candidates, and Campaigns since 1952.* 3d ed. Homewood, Ill.: Dorsey Press.
Bailey, Fred A.
1985   "Class and Tennessee's Confederate Generation." *Journal of Southern History* 51 (February): 31–60.
Baily, Martin Neil
1986   "What Has Happened to Productivity Growth?" *Science,* October 24, pp. 443–51.
Banfield, Edward, and James Q. Wilson
1963   *City Politics.* New York: Vintage Books.
Bartley, Numan V., and Hugh D. Graham
1975   *Southern Politics and the Second Reconstruction.* Baltimore: Johns Hopkins University Press.
1978   *Southern Elections: County and Precinct Data, 1950–1972.* Baton Rouge: Louisiana State University Press.
Bartos, Otomar J.
1967   *Simple Models of Group Behavior.* New York: Columbia University Press.

Beck, Paul Allen
1976   "A Socialization Theory of Partisan Realignment." In Richard G. Niemi and Herbert F. Weisberg, eds., *Controversies in American Voting Behavior*. San Francisco: W.H. Freeman, pp. 396–411.
1985   "Micropolitics in Macro Perspective: The Political History of Walter Dean Burnham." Paper prepared for the Tenth Annual Meeting of the Social Science History Association, Chicago, November 21–24.
Berelson, Bernard R., Paul F. Lazarsfeld, and William N. McPhee
1954   *Voting: A Study of Opinion Formation in a Presidential Election*. Chicago: University of Chicago Press.
Berger, Bennett M.
1960   *Working-Class Suburb: A Study of Autoworkers in Suburbia*. Berkeley: University of California Press.
Black, Earl, and Merle Black
1987   *Politics and Society in the South*. Cambridge: Harvard University Press.
Boynton, G. R.
1963   "Southern Republican Voting in the 1960 Election." Ph.D. diss., University of North Carolina at Chapel Hill.
Brace, Kimball, Bernard Grofman, and Lisa Handley
1987   "Does Redistricting Aimed to Help Blacks Necessarily Help Republicans?" *Journal of Politics* 49 (February): 169–85.
Brown, Courtney
1987   "The Mass Dynamics of U.S. Presidential Competitions from 1928 to 1936." Ms., Emory University, Atlanta.
Browning, Rufus P., and Dale Rogers Marshall, eds.
1986   "Black and Hispanic Power in City Politics: A Forum." *PS* 19 (Summer): 573–640.
Browning, Rufus P., Dale Rogers Marshall, and David H. Tabb
1984   *Protest Is Not Enough: The Struggle of Blacks and Hispanics for Equality in Urban Politics*. Berkeley: University of California Press.
Bunche, Ralph J.
1973   *The Political Status of the Negro in the Age of FDR*, ed. Dewey W. Grantham. Chicago: University of Chicago Press. (Originally written in 1940.)
Burnham, Walter Dean
1967   "Party Systems and the Political Process." In William N. Chambers and Walter Dean Burnham, eds., *The American Party Systems: Stages of Development*. New York: Oxford University Press, pp. 277–307.
1970   *Critical Elections and the Mainsprings of American Politics*. New York: W.W. Norton.
1982   *The Current Crisis in American Politics*. New York: Oxford University Press.
Carmines, Edward G., Steven H. Renten, and James A. Stimson
1984   "Events and Alignments: The Party Image Link." In Richard G. Niemi and Herbert F. Weisberg, eds., *Controversies in Voting Behavior*. 2d ed. Washington, D.C.: CQ Press, pp. 545–60.

Carmines, Edward G., and James A. Stimson
1981   "Issue Evolution, Population Replacement, and Normal Partisan Change."
        American Political Science Review 75 (March): 107–18.
1989   *Issue Evolution: Race and the Transformation of American Politics.*
        Princeton, New Jersey: Princeton University Press.
Caro, Robert A.
1983   *The Years of Lyndon Johnson,* vol. 1: *The Path to Power.* New York:
        Vintage Books.
Chafe, William H.
1968   "The Negro and Populism: A Kansas Case Study." *Journal of Southern
        History* 34 (August): 401–19.
Chambers, William N.
1963   *Political Parties in a New Nation: The American Experience, 1776–1809.*
        New York: Oxford University Press.
1967   "Party Development and the American Mainstream." In William N.
        Chambers and Walter Dean Burnham, eds. *The American Party Systems.*
        New York: Oxford University Press, pp. 3–32.
Clubb, Jerome M., William H. Flanigan, and Nancy H. Zingale
1980   *Partisan Realignment: Voters, Parties, and Government in American
        History.* Beverly Hills, Calif.: Sage Publications.
Cnudde, Charles F.
1971   *Democracy in the American South.* Chicago: Markham.
Congressional Quarterly Service
1967   *Revolution in Civil Rights.* 3d ed. Washington, D.C.: Congressional
        Quarterly Service.
1970   *Civil Rights: Progress Report.* Washington, D.C.: Congressional Quar-
        terly Service.
Converse, Philip E.
1966   "The Concept of a Normal Vote." In Angus Campbell, Philip E.
        Converse, Warren E. Miller, and Donald E. Stokes, *Elections and the
        Political Order.* New York: John Wiley and Sons, pp. 9–39.
Converse, Philip E., Aage R. Clausen, and Warren E. Miller
1965   "Electoral Myth and Reality: The 1964 Election." *American Political
        Science Review* 59 (June): 321–34.
Cortes, Ferdinand, Adam Przeworski, and John Sprague
1974   *Systems Analysis for Social Scientists.* New York: John Wiley and Sons.
Cosman, Bernard
1966   *The Case of the Goldwater Delegates: Deep South Leadership.* Univer-
        sity, Ala.: Bureau of Public Administration.
Dahl, Robert A.
1961   *Who Governs? Democracy and Power in an American City.* New Haven:
        Yale University Press.
Davison, Donald Lambert
1985   "The Political Consequences of the Voting Rights Act of 1965." Ph.D.
        diss., Washington University, St. Louis.

Degler, Carl N.
1972   "Racism in the United States: An Essay Review." *Journal of Southern History* 38 (February): 101–8.
Donovan, John C.
1973   *The Politics of Poverty.* 2d ed. Indianapolis: Pegasus.
Downs, Anthony
1957   *An Economic Theory of Democracy.* New York: Harper and Row.
Eulau, Heinz
1962   *Class and Party in the Eisenhower Years.* New York: Free Press of Glencoe.
Gaither, Gerald H.
1977   *Blacks and the Populist Revolt: Ballots and Bigotry in the "New South."* University, Ala.: University of Alabama Press.
Gilpin, Michael E.
1975   *Group Selection in Predator-Prey Communities.* Princeton: Princeton University Press.
Ginzberg, Eli
1979   *Good Jobs, Bad Jobs, No Jobs.* Cambridge: Harvard University Press.
Goldthorpe, John H., David Lockwood, Frank Bechofer, and Jennifer Platt
1968   *The Affluent Worker: Political Attitudes and Behavior.* Cambridge: Cambridge University Press.
Granovetter, Mark
1978   "Threshold Models of Collective Behavior." *American Journal of Sociology* 83 (May): 1420–43.
Grofman, Bernard, Michael Migalski, and Nicholas Noviello
1985   "The Totality of Circumstances Test in the 1982 Amendments to the Voting Rights Act: A Social Science Perspective." *Law and Policy* 7 (April): 199–223.
1986   "Effects of Multimember Districts on Black Representation in State Legislatures." *The Review of Black Political Economy* 14 (Spring): 65–78.
Harrington, Michael
1962   *The Other America.* New York: Macmillan.
Heard, Alexander
1952   *A Two Party South?* Chapel Hill: University of North Carolina Press.
Hirschman, Albert
1970   *Exit, Voice, and Loyalty: Responses to Decline in Firms, Organizations, and States.* Cambridge: Harvard University Press.
Holmes, Michael S.
1972   "The New Deal and Georgia's Black Youth." *Journal of Southern History* 38 (August): 443–60.
Huckfeldt, Robert
1983a   "The Social Contexts of Ethnic Politics: Ethnic Loyalties, Political Loyalties, and Social Support." *American Politics Quarterly* 99 (January): 91–123.
1983b   "The Social Context of Political Change: Durability, Volatility, and Social Influence." *American Political Science Review* 77 (December): 929–44.

1986 *Politics in Context: Assimilation and Conflict in Urban Neighborhoods.* New York: Agathon Press.

Huckfeldt, Robert, C. W. Kohfeld, and Thomas W. Likens
1982 *Dynamic Modeling: An Introduction.* Beverly Hills, Calif.: Sage Publications.

Huckfeldt, Robert, and John Sprague
1987 "Networks in Context: The Social Flow of Political Information." *American Political Science Review* 81 (December): 1197–1216.

1988 "Choice, Social Structure, and Political Information: The Informational Coercion of Minorities." *American Journal of Political Science* 32 (May): 467–82.

Inglehart, Ronald
1971 "The Silent Revolution in Europe: Intergenerational Change in Post-Industrial Societies." *American Political Science Review* 65 (December): 991–1017.

1977 *The Silent Revolution: Changing Values and Political Styles among Western Publics.* Princeton: Princeton University Press.

1981 "Post-Materialism in an Environment of Insecurity." *American Political Science Review* 75 (December): 880–900.

1985 "The Changing Structure of Political Cleavages in Western Society." In Russell J. Dalton, Scott C. Flanagan, and Paul Allen Beck, eds., *Electoral Change in Advanced Industrial Democracies: Realignment or Dealignment?* Princeton: Princeton University Press, pp. 25–69.

Judd, R. Dennis
1984 *The Politics of American Cities: Private Power and Public Policy.* 2d ed. Boston: Little, Brown.

Katznelson, Ira
1981 *City Trenches: Urban Politics and the Patterning of Class in the United States.* New York: Pantheon.

Kemeny, John G., and J. Laurie Snell
1960 *Finite Markov Chains.* Princeton, N.J.: Van Nostrand.

Key, V. O.
1949 *Southern Politics: In State and Nation.* New York: Alfred A. Knopf.
1955 "A Theory of Critical Elections." *Journal of Politics* 17 (Feb.): 3–18.
1959 "Secular Realignment and the Party System." *Journal of Politics* 21 (May): 198–210.
1966 *The Responsible Electorate.* Cambridge: Harvard University Press.

Kleppner, Paul
1985 *Chicago Divided: The Making of a Black Mayor.* DeKalb: Northern Illinois University Press.

Kohfeld, C. W., and Barbara Salert
1982 "Discrete and Continuous Representations of Dynamic Models." *Political Methodology* 8 (No. 1): 1–32.

Ladd, Everett Carll
1982 *Where Have All the Voters Gone? The Fracturing of America's Political Parties.* 2d ed. New York: W. W. Norton.

Ladd, Everett Carll, and Charles D. Hadley
1978   *Transformations of the American Party System.* 2d ed. New York: W. W. Norton.
Lamis, Alexander P.
1984   *The Two-Party South.* New York: Oxford University Press.
Lazarsfeld, Paul F., Bernard Berelson, and Hazel Gaudet
1968   *The People's Choice.* 3d ed. New York: Columbia University Press.
Lewinson, Paul
1932   *Race, Class, and Party: A History of Negro Suffrage and White Politics in the South.* New York: Oxford University Press
Liebling, A. J.
1960   *The Earl of Louisiana.* Baton Rouge: Louisiana State University Press.
Lipset, Seymour Martin
1981   *Political Man: The Social Bases of Politics.* rev. ed. Baltimore: Johns Hopkins University Press.
1986   "Beyond 1984: The Anomalies of American Politics." *PS* 19 (Spring): 222–36.
Lipset, Seymour Martin, and Stein Rokkan
1967   "Cleavage Structures, Party Systems, and Voter Alignments: An Introduction." In Seymour Martin Lipset and Stein Rokkan, eds., *Party Systems and Voter Alignments: Cross National Perspectives.* New York: Free Press, pp. 1–64.
Lubell, Samuel
1956   *The Future of American Politics.* New York: Anchor Books.
Matthews, Donald R., and James W. Prothro
1963   "Social and Economic Factors and Negro Voter Registration in the South." *American Political Science Review* 57 (March): 24–44.
Matthews, John Michael
1974   "The Georgia 'Race Strike' of 1909." *Journal of Southern History* 40 (November): 611–30.
May, Robert M.
1974   *Stability and Complexity in Model Ecosystems.* Princeton: Princeton University Press.
Miller, Arthur, Warren E. Miller, Alden E. Raine, and Thad H. Brown
1976   "A Majority Party in Disarray: Policy Polarization in the 1972 Election." *American Political Science Review* 70 (Sept.): 753–78.
Miller, Merle
1980   *Lyndon: An Oral Biography.* New York: G. P. Putnam's Sons.
Miller, Warren E.
1956   "One Party Politics and the Voter." *American Political Science Review* 50 (September): 707–25.
Mollenkopf, John H.
1983   *The Contested City.* Princeton: Princeton University Press.
1986   "New York: The Great Anomaly." *PS* 29 (Summer): 591–97.
Munõz, Carlos, Jr., and Charles Henry
1986   "Rainbow Coalitions in Four Big Cities: San Antonio, Denver, Chicago, and Philadelphia." *PS* 29 (Summer): 598–609.

Murray, Richard, and Arnold Vedlitz
1978   "Racial Voting Patterns in the South: An Analysis of Major Elections from 1960 to 1977 in Five Cities." *Annals of the American Academy of Political and Social Science* 439 (September): 29–39.

Newfield, Jack, and Jeff Greenfield
1972   *A Populist Manifesto: The Making of a New Majority.* New York: Praeger.

Niebuhr, Reinhold
1932   *Moral Man and Immoral Society.* New York: Charles Scribner's Sons.

Niemi, Richard G., and Herbert F. Weisberg
1976   "Is the Party Balance Shifting?" In Richard G. Niemi and Herbert F. Weisberg, eds., *Controversies in American Voting Behavior.* San Francisco: W. H. Freeman, pp. 358–69.

Peltason, J. W.
1971   *Fifty-Eight Lonely Men: Southern Federal Judges and School Desegregation.* Urbana: University of Illinois Press (First published in 1961.)

Petrocik, John R.
1981   *Party Coalitions: Realignments and the Decline of the New Deal Party System.* Chicago: University of Chicago Press.
1987   "Realignment: New Party Coalitions and the Nationalization of the South." *Journal of Politics* 49 (May): 347–75.

Phillips, Kevin P.
1969   *The Emerging Republican Majority.* New Rochelle, N.Y.: Arlington House.
1982   *Post-Conservative America: People, Politics, and Ideology in a Time of Crisis.* New York: Random House.

Piven, Frances Fox, and Richard A. Cloward
1982   *The New Class War: Reagan's Attack on the Welfare State and Its Consequences.* New York: Pantheon.

Prude, James C.
1972   "William Gibbs McAdoo and the Democratic National Convention of 1924." *Journal of Southern History* 38 (November): 621–28.

Przeworski, Adam, and John Sprague
1987   *Paper Stones.* Chicago: University of Chicago Press.

Putnam, Robert D.
1966   "Political Attitudes and the Local Community." *American Political Science Review* 60 (September): 640–54.

Reed, Adolph L., Jr.
1986   *The Jesse Jackson Phenomenon: The Crisis of Purpose in Afro-American Politics.* New Haven: Yale University Press.

Rosenzweig, M. L., and R. H. MacArthur
1963   "Graphical Representation and Stability Conditions of Predator-Prey Interactions." *American Naturalist* 97 (July–August): 209–23.

Scammon, Richard M., and Ben J. Wattenberg
1970   *The Real Majority.* New York: Coward, McCann, and Geoghegan.

Schattschneider, E. E.
1942   *Party Government.* New York: Farrar and Rinehart.
1960   *The Semisovereign People.* New York: Holt, Rinehart and Winston.

Schelling, Thomas C.
1978   *Micromotives and Macrobehavior.* New York: W. W. Norton.
Schlozman, Kay Lehman, and Sidney Verba
1979   *Injury to Insult: Unemployment, Class, and Political Response.* Cambridge: Harvard University Press.
Sears, David O., and John B. McConahy
1973   *The Politics of Violence: The New Urban Blacks and the Watts Riot.* Boston: Houghton Mifflin.
Shively, W. Phillips
1971–72   "A Reinterpretation of the New Deal Realignment." *Public Opinion Quarterly* 35 (Winter): 621–24.
Smith, J. Maynard
1968   *Mathematical Ideas in Biology.* Cambridge: Cambridge University Press.
1974   *Models in Ecology.* Cambridge: Cambridge University Press.
Sombart, Werner
1976   *Why Is There No Socialism in the United States?* trans. Patricia M. Hocking and C. T. Husbands. White Plains, N.Y.: International Arts and Sciences Press. (First published in 1906.)
Sonenshein, Raphe
1986   "Biracial Coalition Politics in Los Angeles." *PS* 29 (Summer): 582–90.
Sprague, John
1982   "Is There a Micro Theory Consistent with Contextual Analysis?" In Elinor Ostrom, ed., *Strategies of Political Inquiry.* Beverly Hills, Calif.: Sage Publications, pp. 99–121.
Stevenson, Adlai E.
1953   *Major Campaign Speeches of Adlai E. Stevenson.* New York: Random House.
Sundquist, James L.
1983   *Dynamics of the Party System: Alignment and Realignment of Political Parties in the United States.* rev. ed. Washington, D.C.: Brookings Institute.
Thurow, Lester C.
1987   "A Surge in Inequality." *Scientific American* 256 (May): 30–37.
Tuma, Nancy Brandon, and Michael T. Hannan
1984   *Social Dynamics: Models and Methods.* Orlando, Fla.: Academic Press.
Verba, Sidney, Bashiruddin Ahmed, and Anil Bhatt
1971   *Caste, Race, and Politics: A Comparative Study of India and the United States.* Beverly Hills, Calif.: Sage Publications.
Verba, Sidney, and Norman H. Nie
1972   *Participation in America: Political Democracy and Social Equality.* New York: Harper and Row.
Wattenberg, Martin P.
1984   *The Decline of American Political Parties, 1952–1980.* Cambridge: Harvard University Press.
Williams, T. Harry
1969   *Huey Long.* New York: Alfred A. Knopf.

Williamson, Joel
1986   *A Rage for Order: Black-White Relations in the American South since Emancipation.* New York: Oxford University Press.
Wilson, William Julius
1978   *The Declining Significance of Race: Blacks and Changing American Institutions.* Chicago: University of Chicago Press.
Wolfinger, Raymond
1965   "The Development and Persistence of Ethnic Voting." *American Political Science Review* 59 (December): 896–908.
Woodward, C. Vann
1966   *The Strange Career of Jim Crow.* 2d rev. ed. New York: Oxford University Press.
Wright, Gerald C., Jr.
1976   "Community Structure and Voting in the South." *Public Opinion Quarterly* 40 (Summer): 200–15.
1977a   "Contextual Models of Electoral Behavior: The Southern Wallace Vote." *American Political Science Review* 71 (June): 497–508.
1977b   "Racism and Welfare Policy in America." *Social Science Quarterly* 57 (March): 718–30.

Index

Names

Subjects

Note on Authors

Robert Huckfeldt is a member of the faculty of Political Science at Indiana University in Bloomington. His interests lie in the political consequences of social structure, in political dynamics, and more generally in American urban and electoral politics.

Carol Weitzel Kohfeld is a member of the faculty of Political Science and a Fellow in the Center for Metropolitan Studies at the University of Missouri in St. Louis. Her interests lie in political dynamics, public policy processes, especially urban crime systems, urban party systems, and urban politics.